The Public Career
of
Sir Thomas More

The Public Career
of
Sir Thomas More

J.A. GUY

NEW HAVEN AND LONDON

YALE UNIVERSITY PRESS

Library of Congress Cataloging in Publication Data

Guy, John Alexander.
  The public career of Sir Thomas More.

  Includes index.
  1. More, Thomas, Sir, Saint, 1478–1535. 2. Great
Britain – History – Henry VIII, 1509–1547. 3. Statesmen
– Great Britain – Biography. 4. Christian saints –
England – Biography. I. Title.
DA334.M8G87   1980   942.05′2′0924 [B]   80–16259
ISBN 0–300–02546–7

Typeset by Inforum Ltd, Portsmouth
Printed in England by
Redwood Burn Ltd., Trowbridge and Esher

FOR G.R. ELTON

CONTENTS

PREFACE

Among a plethora of works on Sir Thomas More, this is one book never previously written. It is a comprehensive account of his public career from first beginnings in the City of London to his resignation as Henry VIII's most famous lord chancellor in May 1532. As such, it is arranged in three parts, comprising More's moment of decision and earliest years in the King's Council, his legal contribution as lord chancellor, and his active role in the factional politics of the initial years of the Henrician Reformation. Why has the book not been written before? The answer is simply that More's official papers, unlike Wolsey's and Cromwell's, did not enter the government's archives at the time of his disgrace, and have not survived elsewhere. In preparation for this book, the entire gamut of public records, some not formerly available to scholars, had to be searched as a means to reconstruct the bones of what had been obliterated by specific archival loss. This considerable task, not least the examination of the Chancery Proceedings, was undertaken during my service for four years as an Assistant Keeper of Public Records. I recall without nostalgia that both Chancery bills and warrants for the great seal, the latter class proving unexpectedly vital for interpreting More's hitherto obscure relationship with Wolsey, were searched through the night on several occasions in 1976 and 1978. As More himself complained to Peter Gillis in 1516, 'Quando ergo scribimus?' – 'when, then, can we find time to write?'. 'Nor have I spoken a word about sleep', continued More, 'nor even of food. . . I get for myself only the time I filch from sleep and food'.

In fact, More finished *Utopia* regardless, and this book is at last finished too. But in another sense, I now feel it is barely begun. My original aim was to discover More's career and assess his achievement, and that is complete. However, the political world of Henry VIII turned out to be a jungle of ancient traditions, modern conjectures and undated documents, with very little undisputed historical certainty. Clinging closely to More, I have attempted to cut a path through this jungle, but it is a route I intend to retrace at a future date. In particular, the career of Christopher St German, More's polemical (and now political) opponent, must be properly worked out and included in the Reformation story.

In writing a book, an author accumulates heavy debts both to fellow-workers and institutions. This study is no exception, and owes more than I can say to G.R. Elton, who taught me all I know about Tudor History and first stirred my interest in Thomas More. This book is an unworthy gift to him. Sincere thanks are also due to T.G. Barnes, J.J. Scarisbrick, A.J. Slavin, and the late Richard S. Sylvester. It is my lasting regret that Dick Sylvester was unable to see the end product of a project in which he had taken such enthusiastic interest. I am also most grateful to Dr David Starkey and Dr Graham Nicholson for permission to use their unpublished dissertations, and to Mr D.E.C. Yale for the gift of a microfilm and advice on legal matters. Needless to say, none of these persons is responsible for any errors or misinterpretations which remain. To the University of Bristol, the University of California at Berkeley, and the Public Record Office, I express thanks for material support and good company. Lectures associated with the book's genesis were given at University College Dublin, Georgetown University Washington D.C., the Institute of Historical Research, the University of Wisconsin at Madison, and the University of Liverpool. I gladly thank both those who invited me and who offered criticism. Other institutions to which I am indebted are the Henry E. Huntington Library, San Marino, California, and the Folger Library. The British Academy kindly paid for xeroxes of works by St German. Although actually intended for my future work, these proved too important not to preview here and I am very grateful to the authorities for their help.

Quotations from documents in the Public Record Office and Henry E. Huntington Library appear by respective permissions of the Controller of H.M. Stationery Office and the Director.

Clifton, Bristol   J.A.G.
August 1979

ABBREVIATIONS

Allen	*Opus Epistolarum Des. Erasmi Roterodami.* Ed. P.S. Allen *et al.* 12 vols. Oxford, 1906–58.
B.L.	British Library
Ellesmere MS.	Henry E. Huntington Library, San Marino, California. Ellesmere Manuscript.
Harpsfield	N. Harpsfield, *The Life and Death of Sir Thomas Moore, knight.* Ed. E.V. Hitchcock and R.W. Chambers. Early English Text Society, London, 1932.
Lansdowne	B.L. Lansdowne Manuscript
LP	*Letters and Papers, Foreign and Domestic, of the Reign of Henry VIII.* Ed. J.S. Brewer *et al.* 21 vols. and *Addenda.* London, 1862–1932.
P.R.O.	Public Record Office
St. Pap.	*State Papers during the Reign of Henry VIII.* Record Commission, London, 1830–52.
Rogers	*The Correspondence of Sir Thomas More.* Ed. E.F. Rogers. Princeton, 1947.
Roper	*The Lyfe of Sir Thomas Moore, knighte, written by William Roper, Esquire, which married Margaret, daughter of the sayed Thomas Moore.* Ed. E.V. Hitchcock. Early English Text Society, London, 1935.

Manuscripts preserved at the P.R.O. are quoted by the call number there in use. The descriptions of the classes referred to are as follows:

C 1	Chancery, Early Chancery Proceedings
C 47	Chancery, Files, Miscellanea
C 54	Chancery, Close Rolls
C 65	Chancery, Parliament Rolls
C 66	Chancery, Patent Rolls
C 78	Chancery, Decree Rolls
C 82	Chancery, Warrants for the Great Seal, Series II
C 142	Chancery, Inquisitions Post Mortem, Series II
C193	Chancery, Miscellaneous Books
C 244	Chancery, Files, Corpus Cum Causa
C 263	Chancery, Files, Legal Miscellanea (Injunctions)

CP 40   Common Pleas, Plea Rolls
DL 5   Duchy of Lancaster, Entry Books of Orders and
               Decrees
DL 6   Duchy of Lancaster, Draft Decrees
DL 28   Duchy of Lancaster, Various Accounts
E 36   Exchequer, Treasury of the Receipt, Miscellane-
               ous Books
E 404   Exchequer of Receipt, Warrants and Issues
E 407   Exchequer of Receipt, Miscellanea
HCA 3   High Court of Admiralty, Acts
KB 9   King's Bench, Ancient Indictments
KB 27   King's Bench, Coram Rege Rolls
KB 29   King's Bench, Controlment Rolls
KB 145   King's Bench, Files, Recorda
OBS   Public Record Office, Obsolete Lists and Indexes
PSO 2   Warrants for the Privy Seal, Series II
REQ 1   Court of Requests, Miscellaneous Books
REQ 2   Court of Requests, Proceedings
REQ 3   Court of Requests, Miscellanea
SC 6   Special Collections, Ministers' Accounts
SC 12   Special Collections, Rentals and Surveys
SP 1   State Papers, Henry VIII, General Series
SP 2   State Papers, Henry VIII, Folio Volumes
SP 6   State Papers, Henry VIII, Theological Tracts
STAC 2   Star Chamber Proceedings, Henry VIII
STAC 10   Star Chamber Proceedings, Miscellaneous

Figures after references to *LP, Calendar of State Papers, Spanish, Calendar of State Papers, Venetian,* and Rogers' edition of More's Correspondence are to numbers of documents; in all other cases they are to pages. Where the original of a document calendared in *LP* has been used, the reference to the manuscript is given, followed by the reference to *LP*. Printed entries in the *Calendar of State Papers, Spanish* were supplemented by reference to the editors' drafts and transcripts of originals held in the departmental archives of the Public Record Office. In quotations, abbreviations have been extended, and modern spelling and punctuation adopted, with the result that capitals have occasionally been put where there is none in the original. In giving dates, the Old Style has been retained, but the year is assumed to have begun on 1 January.

PART ONE

MORE AND THE COUNCIL

1

THE KING'S SERVANT

SIR THOMAS MORE was meant to be a lawyer. After two years at
Oxford University (c. 1492–4), the brilliant youth of seventeen was
recalled to London and sent to New Inn to study English law.[1] It
was a move which owed everything to parental ambition. John
More was anxious that his eldest son should achieve both place and
profit in his own profession. Himself the eldest of a baker's six
orphans, John was a self-made man — jovial but assuredly rigid.
Admitted to Lincoln's Inn in 1475, he had steadily built up the
London law practice which was to restore the family fortunes.[2]
Equally successful within his Inn, he had served as a double reader
by 1495; and while promotion was rather late in coming, high rank
did not finally elude him. Created a sergeant-at-law aged fifty-two
(in 1503), he was subsequently elevated to the bench of Common
Pleas (1518) and King's Bench (1520).[3]

Thomas later described his father as 'affable, sweet-tempered,
upright, gentle, compassionate, just and impartial'.[4] Nevertheless,
John More's choice of his son's career caused a temporary split
between them. Although Thomas dutifully entered Lincoln's Inn in
1496, being called to the bar five or six years later, he did so with
uncertain commitment.[5] He was strongly attracted instead to a life
of contemplation and letters, something John More viewed with
unmitigated horror. For three years indeed, Thomas rebelled
against his father's plans for his future. He lectured to law students
at Furnivall's Inn, but lived meanwhile as a Carthusian monk
'without vow' at the London Charterhouse.[6] He studied Greek in
the circle of William Grocyn, Thomas Linacre and William Lily,
meeting Erasmus for the first time in 1499. He immersed himself
alongside London's leading humanists in classical scholarship,

1 R. O'Sullivan, 'St Thomas More and Lincoln's Inn', in *Essential Articles for the
Study of Thomas More*, ed. R. S. Sylvester and G. P. Marc'hadour (Hamden,
Connecticut, 1977), 161–8; M. Hastings, 'The Ancestry of Sir Thomas More',
in *Essential Articles*, 92–103. In this book, the view is accepted that More was
born on 6 February 1477.
2 Hastings, *art. cit.*
3 *The Reports of Sir John Spelman*, ed. J. H. Baker, vol. ii (Selden Society,
London, 1978), 394.
4 Epitaph, Harpsfield, 279–81.
5 O'Sullivan, *art. cit.*
6 Roper, 6.

Pauline Christianity and neo-Platonism, scientifically applying his new learning to the Bible and the Early Church Fathers.[7] At Grocyn's invitation, More lectured on St Augustine's *City of God* at the Church of St Lawrence Jewry. John More, we may presume, was not among the 'learned men of London' who flocked to attend.[8] When the senior, perhaps the greatest English humanist, John Colet, returned from Oxford to London as dean of St Paul's, Thomas More at once became his disciple.[9]

The family breach widened about 1503. John More withdrew his son's allowance. He almost disowned his son, wrote Erasmus, 'because he seemed to be neglecting his father's chosen studies.'[10] But Thomas continued to test his vocation, and alluded to his spiritual trials in a letter to Colet:

> By following your footsteps I had escaped almost from the very gates of hell, and now, driven by some force and necessity, I am falling back again into gruesome darkness. I am like Eurydice, except that she was lost because Orpheus looked back at her, but I am sinking because you do not look back at me.[11]

Perhaps it was Colet who persuaded More that he was unsuited to a monastic life? At any rate, the matter was settled by January 1505. More had decided by then to marry Jane Colt, eldest daughter of Sir John Colt, who lived within easy riding distance of John More's country house at North Mimms.[12] As Erasmus knew, Thomas had subjected himself to a rigorous course of watching, fasting and devotional exercises, but 'could not shake off his wish to marry. He thus decided to be a chaste husband rather than a licentious priest'.[13]

The immediate result of More's marriage was his acceptance of a legal career. Soon he began to enjoy the professional advance for which his father had hoped.[14] He was appointed pensioner (i.e. financial secretary) of Lincoln's Inn in 1507, in which role he seized the goods of Thomas Thwaites, lately deceased, for unpaid dues and amercements. He was then chosen as butler, an office his father had once held. In 1510 he was elected marshal of the Inn, and named autumn reader for 1511. Excused service as treasurer, he was a year

7 J. K. McConica, *English Humanists and Reformation Politics* (Oxford, 1965), 46–51.

8 Harpsfield, 13–14.

9 McConica, 46.

10 Allen, vol. iv. 17.

11 *St Thomas More: Selected Letters*, ed. E. F. Rogers (New Haven, 1961), 4.

12 E. E. Reynolds, *The Life and Death of St Thomas More* (New York, 1978), 53.

13 Allen, vol. iv: 18.

14 This account closely follows R. O'Sullivan, *art. cit.*

later made one of the Inn's four governors. We may thus assume
that he was one of the 'whole bench' who in October 1512 put
Roger Hawkins out of office as butler for 'keeping of women in his
chamber'. He may also have joined those who, in July 1513, ordered
that 'no gentleman of Ireland shall be admitted to this Company
without the assent of a bencher'. On the Feast of All Saints 1514,
More was nominated Lent reader for 1515 — the highest honour
that an Inn of Court could confer on a barrister. More's privilege
was to address the assembled society in Hall over a period of days or
weeks, expounding some statute or legal doctrine which interested
him. His reading is alas not extant in print or manuscript.

More's career as a judge began in September 1510, following his
appointment as an undersheriff of London.[15] As invariably happened, the place must have come his way partly through influence.
Thomas Graunger, More's maternal grandfather, had been sheriff
from 1503–4,[16] and John More had obvious contacts among the
City notables. More may also have forged his own connections by
this time. He was a member of the Mercers' Company, alongside
his father, and may already have been retained as counsel by the
Merchants of the Staple.[17] However, influential friends were not
enough; More's selection as undersheriff — a minor but useful
public office — has to be viewed primarily as a measure of his
ability. While we cannot fully verify More's early legal success in
the absence of better sources, the signs are that his talent was
conspicuous. Roper was told that, after becoming undersheriff,
More 'by his office and his learning together' was earning £400 a
year — a considerable salary for a thirty-three year old lawyer.
Rumour had it that there was 'in none of the Prince's courts of the
law of this realm any matter of importance in controversy, wherein
he [More] was not with the one part of counsel'.[18]

As an undersheriff of London, More was a permanent legal
official who advised the sheriffs and sat as judge in the Sheriff's
Court.[19] This court was ancient and respected, its existence being
implied as early as Henry I's reign. Its archives no longer survive,

15 Harpsfield, 312.

16 *Stow's Survey of London*, ed. H. B. Wheatley (London, 1956), 467.

17 W. Nelson, 'Thomas More, Grammarian and Orator', in *Essential Articles*,
150–60.

18 Roper, 9.

19 For the work of an undersheriff of London, see *Calendar of Early Mayor's Court
Rolls*, ed. A. H. Thomas (Cambridge, 1924); *Calendar of Select Pleas and
Memoranda of the City of London, 1381–1412*, ed. A. H. Thomas (Cambridge,
1932); *Liber Albus: The White Book of the City of London*, ed. H. T. Riley
(London, 1861), 274–5.

but a steady stream of its cases were removed by writ into Chancery and may thus be gleaned from the Chancery files. These fragments show that the court dealt with almost all matters except the recognized pleas of the Crown. Ordinary assaults and violence, minor wrongdoing, debt, account, covenant, defamation, and disputes over bonds and obligations were its staple diet.[20] It met at Guildhall, generally on Thursday mornings, and the profits of its jurisdiction went to the sheriffs, who thereby recouped themselves for their outlay of £300, paid to the Exchequer for their joint shrievalties of London and Middlesex. More apparently enjoyed his new duties, showing a dislike only of unduly persistent suitors and proving popular with the majority of Londoners. Erasmus supposed that 'no judge ever disposed of more cases, or showed greater integrity'.[21] As to the tangible advantages, an undersheriff had the right to represent the City in the central courts at Westminster as assistant counsel under the recorder, London's chief law officer. It was there that More's profit lay; indeed since he remained in post until July 1518, the month following his belated grant of a councillor's annuity, it would appear that fees from court appearances on the City's behalf made up a fair proportion of his £400 income at that time.[22] It can hardly have been the weekly sessions of the Sheriff's Court alone which kept More in civic harness for a year after his admission to the King's Council.

No aspect of Thomas More has troubled his biographers quite as much as his entry into the Council of Henry VIII in 1517. Why did he take this step? He had the previous year published *Utopia*, the Latin novel which was his tribute to Erasmus's *Praise of Folly* and which brought him fame as England's premier humanist after Colet. Why, then, did he reject the advice of Erasmus and opt for a political career? Between them More and Erasmus have left behind a strong impression that Thomas entered royal service with great reluctance and under immense pressure.[23] Erasmus later assured both Ulrich von Hutten and Brixius that More had to be 'dragged' into Henry's Court, since 'no-one tried more energetically to obtain court appointment than he strove to avoid it'.[24] More was disinclined to Court life and to intimacy with princes, 'because he always

20 C 244/166–73.
21 Allen, vol. iv. 20.
22 More resigned as undersheriff on 23 July 1518. Cf. Harpsfield, 313.
23 The myth of More's reluctance was debunked by G.R. Elton, 'Thomas More, Councillor', in *Studies in Tudor and Stuart Politics and Government* (Cambridge, 1974), vol. i. 129–33.
24 Allen, vol. iv. 20, 294.

had a special hatred of tyranny and a great fancy for equality'. But his unwillingness to serve simply increased the king's solicitations — so the story goes. Henry could take no rest until More had agreed to become his personal adviser. The king's determination to fill his household with brilliant men made More's selection inevitable.[25]

Erasmus, however, protests too much. The evidence of the record, as opposed to what More wanted his friend to believe, suggests that, far from being the reluctant intellectual who manfully endured adversity, More instead had steadily worked towards the goal of royal service. Over a period of years, Thomas had made it his business to do various jobs for the government, probably at his father's introduction. He joined his father on a Middlesex special commission in July 1509, and as a commissioner of sewers for the Thames district between Greenwich and Lambeth in February 1514.[26] He assisted the staff of Chancery as a part-time examiner and arbitrator.[27] He was then sent in May 1515 on the embassy to Flanders which produced *Utopia*, the mission's purpose being to renegotiate commercial treaties of 1495 and 1506.[28] After that, More was asked by Wolsey and the Council to investigate the Evil May Day riots of 1517, a serious political disturbance which had rocked momentarily the stability of London.[29] More's inquiry was indeed a crucial assignment, performed with sensitivity and sound judgment. He then agreed to go on a second embassy to Calais — the commission was dated 26 August 1517 — by which time he had been sworn as Henry VIII's councillor.[30]

The argument is strong that More's call to counsel was the climax of a progression by which he gained the attention of Henry and Wolsey. Why else would he undertake unremunerative and time-consuming tasks for the state? How else could Ammonio observe in February 1516 that More 'haunted' the Court after his return from Flanders, adding that no one bid Wolsey good morrow 'earlier than he'?[31] It is, of course, possible that More's freedom of action was always notional rather than real, since a prime fact of his life was his legal dexterity. The suspicion is that royal recruitment of outstan-

25 Allen, vol. iv. 15, 20.
26 *LP* i. 132 (26), 2684 (8).
27 C 244/163/101B. Chancery Miscellanea, various unsorted commissions left over from latest rearrangement of Chancery Files at P.R.O.
28 Rogers, no. 10.
29 Reynolds, *Life and Death of St Thomas More*, 120–3.
30 Rogers, no. 42.
31 *The Correspondence of Erasmus, Letters 298 to 445*, ed. R. A. B. Mynors and D. F. S. Thomson (Toronto and Buffalo, 1976), 239.

ding lawyers was by command rather than invitation under Henry VII and VIII. As the councillor's oath put it, their 'cunning and discretion' demanded that they should serve the Crown in preference to private parties and corporations.[32] More was ultimately not created a sergeant-at-law and judge after his father's pattern, offices for which he was qualified as a double reader, although that is explicable simply in terms of predominant humanist and literary attractions which marked him out as a future royal secretary, diplomat and public orator. Nevertheless, the question of free choice is quite distinct from that of More's alleged reluctance to serve. More was not unwilling to become a state servant, because he himself prompted Henry into granting him a councillor's fee. Admitted to the Council in mid-1517, More was unable at that point to obtain a grant of a councillor's usual salary of £100 a year. After nine months had elapsed, still nothing had been done, and More took the initiative himself in June 1518, submitting a petition for both salary and arrears to Henry, which the king's signature turned into a warrant for the great seal.[33] More's original petition has survived, and its existence cannot be satisfactorily reconciled with Erasmus's story of an eager king who would not rest until he had forced a fee upon More in order to bind him to his service. Everything goes to suggest, rather, that More, after his return from Calais, was forgotten about until he himself drew Henry's attention to the matter. Manifestly, Erasmus was misled in some way as to More's true motivation: a mysterious episode which smacks of apprehensiveness on Thomas's part for the consequences of breaking his friend's rule that intellectuals should not commit themselves to princes. Erasmus was strict on the point, himself only serving Charles V with his 'liberty reserved by the vote of the Council'.[34] Erasmus believed that scholars must always be free to criticize, shunning the association with corrupt policy that public service invariably demands. He wrote to Pace in June 1521 that More was so successful at Court, 'that I am sorry for him'.[35]

The indication is that More's entry into the Council was an act of positive, not negative motivation. Royal service was a natural avenue to advancement, the only one that offered unlimited scope. But other considerations were directly relevant. In the first place, many humanists of More's circle were already Henry VIII's sworn

<hr>

32 C 193/1, fo. 87v.
33 C 82/463. Elton, *Studies*, vol. i. 131–2.
34 *The Complete Works of St Thomas More*, vol. iv, *Utopia*, ed. E. Surtz and J. H. Hexter (New Haven, 1965), xxxiv.
35 Allen, vol. iv. 506.

councillors, among them John Colet, John Young, Richard Pace, John Clerk, Cuthbert Tunstall, lord Mountjoy (patron of scholars) and lord Berners (translator of Froissart).[36] Their views about princely courts must have served to dilute those of Erasmus. Notably, too, More's entry in 1517 had been preceded by his father's in May 1516.[37] Secondly, More's decision was influenced by immediate personal needs. Unlike Erasmus, he had a family to support, for Jane Colt had borne him four children before her premature death in 1511, and a fifth child had been adopted.[38] More remarried within a month of losing Jane, choosing Dame Alice Middleton, widow of a wealthy London mercer and merchant of the Staple — it was a match of convenience, as More himself confessed.[39] Yet despite Dame Alice's contribution to the household expenses, More was in severe financial difficulties by the time he returned from his Flanders embassy in October 1515. For six months he had faced the cost of an ambassador's state abroad as well as a lawyer's at home; and as he joked in a letter to Erasmus, 'I failed completely . . . to persuade my family for my sake to go without eating for a short time until my return'.[40] Despite a diplomatic allowance, More's mission had greatly increased his outgoings at a fraction of his normal income: so much so that Tunstall, when the embassy was but two months old, had needed to cajole Wolsey in favour of 'Master More', who 'as being at a low ebb, desires by your grace to be set on float again'.[41]

This interpretation of More's call to counsel gains added conviction in that it perhaps accords with his own opinion as worked out in Book One of *Utopia*. Written during 1516 to preface the previously completed Book Two, Book One is dominated by a remarkable debate between a fictional 'Thomas More' and a traveller, Raphael Hythlodaeus.[42] More seems to speak for himself in the debate, while Hythlodaeus doubles as More's humanistic other self. The subject is that of princely service, and the piece is justly dubbed More's 'Dialogue of Counsel'.[43] It began when Hythlodaeus gave More's friend Peter Gillis two reasons why a man should not put

36 Ellesmere MS. 2655, *passim*.
37 Ellesmere MS. 2655, fo. 10.
38 Reynolds, *Life and Death of St Thomas More*, 53–4, 75–6.
39 *LP Add*. i. I. 1024; Allen, vol. iv. 19.
40 *The Correspondence of Erasmus, Letters 298 to 445*, 234.
41 *LP* ii. 679.
42 *Complete Works of St Thomas More*, vol. iv. 55–103.
43 The most brilliant analysis is by J. H. Hexter, *More's Utopia: the Biography of an Idea* (Princeton, 1952), esp. 103–55.

himself in bondage to kings. The first was that kings prefer war to peace, bothering more about winning new lands than governing those they have. Secondly, councillors rarely profit by each other's advice, but tend to become sycophants who will echo the most foolish remarks of royal favourites. Against this line of argument, More erected a contrary case. Plato, he recalled, opined that commonwealths will finally be happy only if philosophers become kings or kings adopt philosophy: 'what a distant prospect of happiness there will be if philosophers will not condescend even to impart their counsel to kings?'. Hythlodaeus then replied that intellectuals had regularly offered their advice through the medium of published books; the problem was that kings always ignored them. Rather, Plato was right to forecast that real-life kings will never be guided by scholars, short of themselves turning philosophers, because they are satiated from their youth with corrupt ideas. Had not Plato, Hythlodaeus reminded More, learned the truth of this from bitter experience?[44]

More was in a tight corner; but as *Utopia*'s author, he was able to wriggle free. Agreeing with Hythlodaeus that 'academic' philosophy was indeed useless in the councils of kings, he proposed a subtler form of enlightenment.[45] This was 'practical' philosophy, a type 'which knows its stage, adapts itself to the play in hand, and performs its role neatly and appropriately'. 'Practical' philosophy was flexible enough to avoid instant antagonisms, so enabling the intellectual to operate politically under cover of tacit co-operation. It thus answered the stock objection that to advise rulers honourably led to immediate banishment or ridicule. Applied with regard to possible results alone, it was a valid response to the otherwise corrupt attitudes of courts and councils. Hythlodaeus naturally disagreed, but he did not manage to refute More's proposition.[46] However, this rebuff for the Erasmian position is a plainly contrived device: 'Thomas More' stands firm in the 'Dialogue of Counsel' because More decided that he should — significantly, this was the one occasion in *Utopia* on which he persuasively matched the opinion of his humanistic *alter ego*.[47] The passage also included a striking summons to political action by 'Thomas More':

> If you cannot pluck up wrongheaded opinions by the root, if you cannot cure according to your heart's desire vices of long stan-

44 *Complete Works of St Thomas More*, vol. iv. 87.
45 *Ibid.*, 99.
46 *Ibid.*, 101–3.
47 Hexter, *More's Utopia*, 131–2.

ding, yet you must not on that account desert the common-wealth. You must not abandon the ship in a storm because you cannot control the winds. On the other hand, you must not force upon people new and strange ideas which you realize will carry no weight with persons of opposite conviction. On the contrary, by the indirect approach you must seek and strive to the best of your power to handle matters tactfully. What you cannot turn to good you must make as little bad as you can.[48]

The intellectual's call to counsel, More argued, should be heeded on grounds of public duty and moral responsibility. Adopting an 'indirect approach', he must pursue the ideal of human happiness. He knew that the ideal was unattainable in practice, but the act of pursuit was in itself beneficial. In other words, More's 'Dialogue of Counsel' served not only to pose the classic dilemma of sixteenth-century humanists; it also created a distinct impression that, when writing the passage in 1516, More's desire to enter the King's Council was already strong. On the other hand, it left the reader unable to judge More's true opinion in the final analysis.

More's first assignment as a councillor was his visit to Calais in the autumn of 1517. As the junior envoy to Sir Richard Wingfield and William Knight, he was engaged in settling commercial dis-putes between English and French merchants there.[49] When he returned home, Cardinal Wolsey was about to complete his second full year as lord chancellor and chief minister to Henry VIII. It was under Wolsey's direction that More's career would take shape, since the great minister enjoyed almost total control of the Council during his ascendancy. He concentrated it about himself at West-minster, never allowing groups of councillors to act much outside its plenary sessions, held during the law terms in Star Chamber, and leaving the king without a formally organized Council attendant. Wolsey's policy indeed ensured that few councillors were ever in attendance on the king, and Henry made occasional complaints about this, feeling that Wolsey left him destitute. All this was part of Wolsey's power game: it meant that, unless Henry troubled to come himself to Council meetings at Westminster — which he did only five times in fourteen years — he would have to depend fully on Wolsey to formulate policy, govern the realm, and write him regular progress reports.[50] Plainly, though, Henry had to have

---

48 *Complete Works of St Thomas More*, vol. iv. 99–101.
49 Elton, *Studies*, vol. i. 140.
50 The system under Wolsey is fully described by J. A. Guy, *The Cardinal's Court: the Impact of Thomas Wolsey in Star Chamber* (Harvester, Hassocks, 1977), ch. 2.

some counsel, and Wolsey had to have his own men scattered about the Court, in case political enemies in the king's Privy Chamber started plotting against him.[51] So Wolsey did allow a small handful of trusted councillors to follow the royal Court as it travelled about the countryside, to advise the king when necessary and to attend to the complaints of poor suitors.

Within this framework, More's contribution was considerable. His most meaningful and extensive work in the Council before Wolsey's fall in 1529 was among the trusted group in regular attendance on the king, but it should not be thought that he was inactive at the centre as a result.[52] As is well known, an archival disaster in the seventeenth century has imposed stringent limitations on our appreciation of the Henrician Council, but something worthwhile can be reconstructed.[53] Of the fifty-two sessions of the Council held in Star Chamber between More's return from Calais and Wolsey's fall for which presence lists are extant, More attended thirteen.[54] This rate of attendance (25%) might not be thought great, until it becomes clear that it places More on a par with the thirty or so most active councillors who discharged the Council's executive function — men like Cuthbert Tunstall, Charles Booth, Sir William Fitzwilliam, Sir Andrew Windsor and others.[55] Only the principal officers of state, top civil servants and chief justices attended all Council meetings at Westminster irrespective of the business to be taken.[56] As to More's low overall total of attendances, the sources now lack essential data concerning the

---

51 Reorganized in 1518, the Privy Chamber comprised the king's closest companions, who occupied a formal and powerful place at Court. As such, it formed a centre of political gravity which was a potential threat to Wolsey's ascendancy. The growth and role of this institution was discovered and worked out by Dr D. R. Starkey in an excellent dissertation (unfortunately unpublished), 'The King's Privy Chamber, 1485–1547' (Ph.D., University of Cambridge, 1973).

52 Cf. Elton, *Studies*, vol. i. 133–4.

53 J. A. Guy, 'Wolsey's Star Chamber: a study in archival reconstruction', *Journal of the Society of Archivists*, v (1975), 169–80.

54 More attended on 29 October 1518; 27 and 28 October, and 21 November 1519; 30 January 1521; 6 November 1524; 26 January, 13 February, 23 June and 10 July 1525; 15 May and 30 June 1526; and 8 July 1527. Cf. Ellesmere MS. 2655, fos. 13v.–18; Ellesmere MS. 2653 (28 October 1519); STAC 2/17/406; STAC 10/4, Pt. 2; SP 1/33, fos. 165–66 (*LP* iv. 1082); SP 1/234, fos. 118–19 (*LP Add.* i. I. 430); Lansdowne 160, fo. 312; *Bibliotheca Phillippica*, Sotheby's sale of 26 June 1967, lot 581 (photocopies in the B.L. refs. RP 152 (5) and RP 236).

55 Guy, *The Cardinal's Court*, 28–9.

56 Tables are available in J. A. Guy, 'The Court of Star Chamber during Wolsey's Ascendancy' (Ph.D., University of Cambridge, 1973), appendix ii.

Council's history between 1485 and 1540. During Wolsey's ascendancy alone, we know that at least 600 plenary sessions of the Council were held in Star Chamber, but presence lists and minutes of business survive for only one in ten of these meetings.[57]

More's work at the centre turns out to have covered the full range of conciliar activity. He assisted in Star Chamber at the swearing-in of sheriffs and justices of the peace — by no means a trivial matter under Wolsey.[58] He was personally involved in several of the Council's projects to contain vice and vagabondage in London and its suburbs.[59] He took part in a high policy debate with Wolsey and the duke of Norfolk in June 1525, which resulted in the close confinement of Richard Rawlyns, bishop of St David's.[60] A year later he gave his opinion at an important policy discussion of the fiscal loss caused to the Exchequer by evasions of the king's feudal rights. At this meeting, it was agreed that all evasions should be rigorously prosecuted by the attorney-general, the beginning of a hardline attitude which came to fruition in the Statute of Uses (1536).[61] More was next deputed by the Council to spend two days in May 1527 observing the cloth trade at Blackwell Hall, 'and to report the demeanour both of Londoners and clothiers in buying and selling'.[62] He then helped the Council devise a Star Chamber order against heresy and seditious preaching. Promulgated in July 1527, the order followed by six months a raid he led on the German Steelyard in search of vernacular bibles and Lutheran writings imported by the merchants of the Hanse.[63] More was also commissioned by the Council to search for grain supplies during 1528, just one aspect of a national exercise following a disastrous harvest the previous year. Corn prices had risen to their highest level within living memory, and social unrest had resulted. More and John Packington searched all the barns and garners in nine Middlesex parishes, while checking that speculators were not forcing prices up further by rigging the market. More noted that he had enough food himself to last the year, with some barley and oats to spare for open sale, despite the fact that he was feeding a hundred people a day at his house in Chelsea.[64]

Still based at Westminster, More was a councillor much concer-

---

57 *Ibid.*
58 Ellesmere MS. 2655, fos. 13v.–18.
59 SP 1/33, fos. 165-66; SP 1/234, fos. 118–19.
60 STAC 10/4, Pt. 2.
61 Sotheby's sale of 26 June 1967, lot 581.
62 Ellesmere MS. 2652, fo. 12.
63 Lansdowne 160, fo. 312; Elton, *Studies*, vol. i. 148.
64 E 36/257, art. 6, fo. 55.

ned with administering two of Wolsey's favourite policies. The first aimed at efficient and impartial enforcement of existing English law, and More worked towards this goal during 1525 and 1526. Wolsey had then issued special commissions of *oyer et terminer* to reduce the nation to good order, naming councillors, judges and legal counsel to the commissions, and often omitting the less reliable component of nobility, local gentry and justices of the peace. He also required the commissioners to file reports direct to Star Chamber, so that while offenders were dealt with locally in accordance with standard procedure, the inquiries themselves marked a move towards a centralized prosecutional function to combat crime — a new development in Tudor justice.[65] More was one of those appointed to the commissions, his designation to the *quorum* ensuring his active participation.[66] His colleagues in the work included Sir Thomas Neville, Sir Andrew Windsor, John Daunce and John Rastell. Wolsey next aimed at popularizing conciliar justice in Star Chamber and the White Hall court,[67] an approach which soon swamped the Council with a deluge of tedious real property suits. More sat with Wolsey and other councillors, judging these cases in Star Chamber; but the bulk of the work was delegated to committees, especially after three years of futile experiments by Wolsey aimed at expediting poor men's causes.[68] From 1520 onwards, a growing backlog of Star Chamber cases was referred to committees which met several times a week in the Council's name. More sat on these in 1521 and early 1522, taking suits through each of their procedural stages. For instance, he and three other councillors tried a case of alleged abduction in Star Chamber during February 1522, eventually dismissing it as being unproved.[69] Away from the centre from late 1522 to mid-1526, More returned there shortly after a modified system of judicial delegation was introduced by Wolsey. Following the collapse of various projects aimed at conciliar reform, cases in Star Chamber came to be referred to new committees now organized on a regional basis.[70] More, Thomas Neville and Sir Henry Wyatt were appointed delegates for Middlesex in May 1526, and were obliged to judge most Star Chamber suits arising there for the remainder of Wolsey's ascendancy.

65 C 193/3, fo. 95; STAC 10/4, Pt. 2; KB 9/501–4.
66 *Ibid.*
67 Guy, *The Cardinal's Court*, 35–45.
68 *Ibid.*
69 Lansdowne 160, fo. 311.
70 Ellesmere MS. 2655, fo. 18.

More's status as a councillor was manifestly that of an executive in government. But from first entering royal service, most of his time was spent not at Westminster but as a member of the royal household on progress. He remained close to the king's person, being resident at Court as early as 29 March 1518, when he wrote a letter at Abingdon to the University of Oxford.[71] Other councillors then attendant at Court were the dukes of Buckingham and Suffolk, Sir Thomas Lovell, Sir Henry Marney and John Clerk.[72] With the exception of Clerk, these men were hardly the flower of the English Renaissance: they were either boon companions in the chase, or household officials whose duties required their physical presence. More was a world apart from them. Cultured, learned and subtle, he had much in common with Henry VIII in the king's more aesthetic moments. According to Roper, Henry would send for More to discuss astronomy, geometry and theology, as well as mere worldly trifles. He would drag More out on the roof on cloudless nights to gaze at the stars.[73] The king found More's company so pleasant, his wit so penetrating and amusing, that Thomas was obliged to mope dejectedly for days, feigning stupidity in order to bore Henry into letting him go home to supper.[74] There can be little doubt that the king's own motive in admitting More to the Council had not been the simple one of acquiring outstanding talent for the royal service — that was only part of the story. More was also to be 'Henry's pledge of Renaissance excellence, his intellectual courtier'.[75]

As expected, Wolsey and Henry soon took advantage of More's literary and linguistic (rather than his legal) gifts by his employment as a secretary, diplomat and orator. Since Henry, unlike his father, found writing 'both tedious and painful', two or more secretaries were often needed, and More acted regularly in this role as directed by Wolsey until late 1526. Starting in 1518, Wolsey used the official secretary, Richard Pace, and More without distinction to receive and despatch letters between Westminster and the royal Court.[76] From mid-1519, the flow of correspondence between Wolsey and Henry was frequently channelled through More.[77] More was taken abroad, accompanying Henry to the Field of Cloth of Gold in June

71 Rogers, no. 60.
72 *LP* ii. 4124.
73 Roper, 11.
74 Roper, 11–12.
75 Elton, *Studies*, vol. i. 147.
76 Elton, *Studies*, vol. i. 142.
77 *Ibid*.

1520. He then helped the king perfect his book against Luther, entitled *Assertio Septem Sacramentorum*, sorting-out and placing the 'principal matters therein contained'.[78] He was next with Wolsey as diplomat and orator at Calais and Bruges.[79] When they returned, More was again exchanging letters between Henry and Wolsey; probably he was also keeping a watch on Pace, whom Wolsey now suspected of conspiring against him.[80] Pace was sent away completely in December 1521, ostensibly on embassy to Rome. Richard Sampson, dean of the Chapel Royal, obtained his post, but he, too, was shipped abroad in September 1522 as English ambassador to Spain.[81] More then undertook alone the duties of royal secretary until the middle of 1526, apart from brief absences in London on the business of Council and Star Chamber, as Speaker of the House of Commons in 1523, as a member of Wolsey's *oyer et terminer* commissions, and as a member of the team which negotiated the Anglo-French treaty of August 1525.[82] In other words, More spent over three and a half years at Court as Henry's sole secretary; years of political upheaval, in which More showed astonishing finesse in the art of supporting both Henry and Wolsey, even when the two were at odds over policy. Wolsey knew that More could be trusted not to damage his political position, while More's integrity as intermediary was sufficient to keep both king and minister 'happier than either might have thought possible'.[83] It was for this reason that Wolsey had More back at Court in late 1526, and momentarily both in 1527 and 1528, when he suspected guile in Henry's new official secretary, William Knight.[84]

As Henry's secretary, More had a strategic part to play in the politics of the 1520s. This arose from the fact that, as well as managing the king's correspondence, he had custody of the king's signet seal. The signet was at this date both the authenticating seal for warrants authorizing expenditure in the household — and therefore a vital element in the bureaucratic chamber machinery of Wolsey's ascendancy — and also a key instrument, along with the

---

78 Roper, 67. *Assertio Septem Sacramentorum* was Henry's reply to Luther's *The Babylonian Captivity of the Church*, and earned him the title *Defensor Fidei* from Leo X. It was the work which More advised the king to tone down on the matter of papal authority. Rogers, no. 199.

79 Elton, *Studies*, vol. i. 140.

80 J. J. Scarisbrick, 'Thomas More: the King's Good Servant', *Thought: Fordham University Quarterly*, lii (1977), 252–4.

81 *Ibid.*

82 Elton, *Studies*, vol. i. 140–2.

83 Scarisbrick, *art. cit.*, 254.

84 Scarisbrick, *art. cit.*, 255.

privy seal, in the ordinary course of making a grant under the great seal — with all the influence this could provide over royal patronage and power.[85] Wolsey himself had the great seal, and the 1520s witnessed a campaign by which he gained effective control of the lesser seals too. As John Palsgrave knew, Wolsey 'found the means to order the signet' at his pleasure, and one of the methods by which he did this was by using Thomas More.[86] We have seen that Wolsey distrusted Richard Pace, whom he accused in October 1521 not just of editing the king's letters and misreporting Wolsey's, but also of getting grants bestowed on his friends.[87] Pace was even alleged to have profited himself. The signet's safe custody raised real problems for Wolsey, whose supremacy could be put at risk should the seal's keeper decide to ally himself with the interests of those in the king's Privy Chamber, the traditional stronghold of Wolsey's enemies.[88] The exact moment when More got responsibility for the seal in preference to the other secretaries has unfortunately been obfuscated in the archival havoc caused by fire in 1619. However, it is certain that by 15 February 1520, when he attested Sir Francis Bryan's grant of stewardship of some Berkshire and Buckinghamshire manors, More was the man closest both to the signet and the privy seals.[89] Grants of lands, offices and annuities, licences, protections, pardons and the rest were checked by him in and after 1520 to an extent unmatched by any other person.[90] Warrants attested by him from his normal base within the royal household survive for month after month, and as late as September 1528 he checked Leonard Skeffington's appointment as gunner at the Tower of London — this long after he had ceased to be Henry's regular secretary.[91]

The predominance of More's secretarial over his other duties as a councillor in the 1520s is best illustrated by reconstructing his personal itinerary. The year 1525 has been chosen as an example (see table 1), because the political instability caused by rebellions in the South-East, the Midlands and East Anglia over Wolsey's Amicable Grant ensured that no one person was then allowed unnecessary

85 J. Otway-Ruthven, *The King's Secretary and the Signet Office in the Fifteenth Century* (Cambridge, 1939), 63–75; G. R. Elton, *The Tudor Revolution in Government* (Cambridge, 1953), ch. 4.
86 *LP* iv. 5750.
87 Scarisbrick, *art. cit.*, 253.
88 As n. 51 *supra*.
89 C 82/485.
90 C 82/485–609; PSO 2/4, file 9–20 Henry VIII.
91 C 82/606.

proximity to the king for fear of intrigue. The table makes it abundantly plain that More was first and foremost Henry's secretary in 1525. His was a position of extreme trust, and his selection was at Wolsey's behest. More's integrity was a valuable source of support to the cardinal chancellor, and it is noteworthy that the other substitute royal secretaries whom Wolsey supplied when Henry's official secretaries were abroad were not allowed custody of the signet. We learn, for instance, that between 13 and 30 December 1522, when More was away from Court, the signet was handed to Wolsey himself — an irregular but telling act.[92] An equally significant barometer is the unusual basis on which More sometimes supervised the clerks in the privy seal as well as the signet office. As secretary, the privy seal office was outside his formal jurisdiction, so that his signature of warrants to the great seal prepared there suggests that he held a supervisory position akin to that later exercised by Thomas Wriothesley during the ministry of Thomas Cromwell.[94] By virtue of a medieval precedent, the staff of the privy seal office could include an outsider, and More fits this description.[95] But his work in that office, like his work for the signet, was the result of Wolsey's need there for someone he could rely on not to get caught up in plots either concocted or condoned by the Privy Chamber. Although Wolsey could not exercise daily supervision over the lesser seals, he could not allow them to slip out of his control. We must therefore conclude that More came near to becoming Wolsey's 'man at Court' in this aspect of his service, though how conscious More himself was of such a role is quite another question.[96]

Additional to More's Court duties as resident humanist, royal secretary and diplomat was a good deal of routine judicial work. In the reign of Edward IV, a vigorous tradition had developed by which the councillors who travelled with the king dealt equitably with bills of complaint brought to them by the king's subjects.[97] The large Council attendant on Henry VII had formalized this arrangement: sitting after 1495 under a president, an itinerant Council of Requests resembled a travelling version of Star Cham-

---

92 *LP* iii. 2719; C 82/525.
93 C 82/554–567; *LP* iv. 1063, 1254, 1431 (8), 1526, 1570, 1600 (3), 1601; *Calendar of State Papers Venetian, 1520–1526* (London, 1869), 1037; STAC 10/4, Pt. 2; references as n. 54 *supra*.
94 Elton, *Tudor Revolution*, 310–11.
95 *Ibid.*
96 For a suggestion that More was conscious of partnership with Wolsey, see Scarisbrick, 'Thomas More: the King's Good Servant', 256–8.
97 Ellesmere MS. 2652, fo. 2v.

Table 1

More's Itinerary in 1525[93]

January 3, 7	Royal secretary (Greenwich)
19, 22–23	Royal secretary (Ampthill)
26	Council in Star Chamber
27	Royal secretary (Ampthill)
February 13	Council in Star Chamber
March 18	Royal secretary (London)
24	Royal secretary (Greenwich)
April 8	Diplomatic duties (Greenwich)
14, 29	Royal secretary (Greenwich)
May 8, 17, 24	Royal secretary (Windsor)
June 6	Public orator (Windsor)
18	Public orator (Bridewell)
23	Council in Star Chamber
28	Royal secretary (Greenwich)
July 10	Council in Star Chamber, then royal secretary (Greenwich)
20	Royal secretary (Windsor)
21–25	*Oyer et terminer* commissioner in Berkshire
29	Diplomatic duties (Richmond)
31	Diplomatic duties (Anglo-French negotiations)
August 14	Diplomatic duties (Anglo-French negotiations)
20	Royal secretary (Hunsdon)
23	Royal secretary (Hatfield)
27	Royal secretary (Dunstable)
28–30	Diplomatic duties (Treaty of the More)
September 3, 8, 10, 11, 13	Royal secretary (Stony Stratford)
17	Royal secretary (Olney)
October	
November 1	Royal secretary (Windsor)
8, 19	Royal secretary (Reading)
December 10	Royal secretary (Greenwich)
12	Royal secretary (Windsor)
27	Royal secretary (Eltham)

ber.[98] The tradition did not wane with the Council attendant after Wolsey's rise to power. The few councillors present at Henry VIII's Court after 1515 were thus much occupied with the petitions of poor suitors. More was involved from the moment he arrived at Court, working with John Vesey (dean of the Chapel to 1519), Richard Rawlyns (almoner to 1523), John Clerk (dean from 1519), John Stokesley (almoner from 1523), and Richard Pace.[99] The suits brought to the dean of the Chapel and his associates were both boring and numerous, mostly being petty squabbles about land, animals or debt.[100] But More applied himself conscientiously to them, and the pressure was sometimes relieved from the centre by Wolsey. The cardinal's various committees in Star Chamber attracted many cases which would otherwise have come before councillors at Court, though More, being himself a committee man after 1520, soon lost the advantage so gained.[101] Wolsey also set up a permanent White Hall court in 1519 — the body later known as the court of Requests — its purpose being simultaneously to ease both the backlog in Star Chamber and inconvenience to poor suitors previously obliged to seek out the itinerant king's Court.[102] How far the White Hall court helped is now impossible to tell. More did not sit there, continuing to work either in Star Chamber or with the dean of the Chapel. However, some relief from the merciless importunities of the poor may have come to the dean's men, since the White Hall arrangements included the assignment of two councillors, Richard Wolman and Thomas Englefield, to follow the king's progress for matters of justice.[103] By hearing cases at Henry's Court, while maintaining constant liaison with Star Chamber and its offshoots, Wolman and Englefield amply discharged the old judicial function of the Council attendant. Nevertheless, total relief from conciliar justice could never be obtained by the councillors resident at Henry's Court, and More continued to judge complaints. Early in 1521, for example, he sat alone 'in Curia domini Regis' at Greenwich, ending a dispute between Nicholas Prout and Thomas Pycher of Hawkesbury in Gloucestershire.[104]

---

98 Guy, *The Cardinal's Court*, 13, 147.
99 REQ 2/2/76, 2/7/53; REQ 3/5 (*Porter* v. *Mathewe*), 3/10 (*Pante* v. *Knyght*); *LP* ii. 4055; *LP* iii. 491, 577. This involvement justified Roper's anachronistic statement (p. 11) that More was made a master of requests.
100 E.g. REQ 3/1–10, much of which is the litigation of this period.
101 Guy, *The Cardinal's Court*, 38–45.
102 *Ibid*.
103 *Ibid*.
104 REQ 1/104, fo. 58.

In view of the level and diversity of Thomas More's service as a councillor, it is perhaps surprising that he achieved so little influence over the affairs of state before 1529. Erasmus may have voiced a popular impression in thinking More to be constantly in Henry's inner counsels, with a share in the nation's secrets.[105] But More's influence was in reality slender, as he himself confessed to Fisher.[106] His impact on the formation of policy was confined to his expressions of opinion at Westminster, when attending the Council in Star Chamber. While a royal secretary, he plainly could not act independently; as Pace pointed out from sad experience, the secretary's duty was to obey the king, 'especially at such times as he would . . . be obeyed, whosoever spake to the contrary'.[107]The truth of More's position was best expressed by Wolsey's abortive plans of 1525–6 for conciliar reform. The Eltham Ordinances, published in January 1526, proposed a new, reduced Council of twenty members, whose duties were to attend and advise the king while maintaining all existing work at Westminster.[108] But by permitting the obvious absence in London of all important office-holders, this attendant Council was to be reduced in practice to a committee of ten and subcommittee of four. The four were John Clerk (then bishop of Bath), William Knight (Henry's latest secretary), Richard Sampson (by now back from Spain as dean of the Chapel), and More.[109] In other words, Wolsey meant all along to perpetuate the *status quo*, and his project can only be regarded as a final victory over Henry's wish, intermittently expressed, for a true Council of his own. More's primary role, as envisaged by Wolsey in 1526, was nonetheless spelled out in this scheme: continued residence at Court in the service of king and minister, and further attention to the complaints of poor suitors.[110] A second project, dated February 1526, to divide 'such matters as shall be treated by the King's Council' then named More to a committee of twenty-eight councillors, who were to be employed in future on full-time legal duties.[111]

These plans never left the drawing-board. However, they are of tantalizing interest, suggesting that More, despite his favoured

105 Allen, vol. iii. 286; Elton, *Studies*, vol. i. 145–8.
106 Rogers, no. 105.
107 *St. Pap.*, vol. i. 79.
108 Guy, *The Cardinal's Court*, 45–6.
109 *A Collection of Ordinances and Regulations for the Government of the Royal Household* (London, 1790), 159–60.
110 *Ibid.*
111 SP 1/59, fo. 77 (*LP* iv. App. 67); SP 1/235, fo. 37 (*LP Add.* i. I. 481).

situation in the king's entourage, would never have gained any real influence over policy while Wolsey held a monopoly of power. The point can be considered most profitably in the light of continuing debate.[112] Traditionally, More's entry into the Council has been explained as an act of faith in Wolsey's impartial justice, his attack on rural depopulation and enclosures, and his quest for a European peace. An early affinity has been thought to have existed between Wolsey and More, which was given fuller expression in the period 1517–29.[113] But this interpretation raises bigger problems than it solves. It is not just that Roper's account is against it, though that is no small matter in itself.[114] A greater difficulty is that next to nothing by way of real personal affection from More to Wolsey can be discerned from their correspondence — as opposed to the formal compliments due from royal secretary to minister.[115] Ample lists of Wolsey's favourites and intimates are also extant, but none includes More's name. Trickiest of all is the question of Wolsey's foreign policy, for the humanists in Henry VIII's Council could see as pellucidly as modern historians the sordid realities that lay under 'the tinsel of Wolsey's peace policy'.[116] The realities were that Wolsey had to satisfy a king eager to emulate the glorious campaigns in France of the Black Prince and Henry V, while maximizing ruthlessly his own ministerial ascendancy. Knowing this, could More have failed to suspect Wolsey's zeal for peace during the turbulent years 1522 to 1525? Can it be without significance that the one time More offered his own opinion to Wolsey, while serving as Henry's secretary, was during the earl of Surrey's invasion of France in 1522? More told Wolsey that, if war really was good for both king and realm, 'I pray God . . . it may prove so, and else in the stead thereof, I pray God send his Grace [the king] one honourable and profitable peace'.[117] It was well enough known, certainly to More and Wolsey, that Surrey had achieved little military advantage at vast cost, while bringing abject misery to thousands of innocent peasants. In 1525, too, More and Wolsey disagreed entirely about foreign affairs, at the time of the Anglo-French treaty

112 A different interpretation is offered here from that suggested by Scarisbrick, both in *art. cit.*, and *Henry VIII* (London, 1968). It is still too soon for definitive views about Wolsey.

113 Scarisbrick, *art. cit.*, 256–8. Professor Scarisbrick here falls into the trap of confusing our Thomas More with his Hampshire namesake, regarding an enclosure commission of May 1517.

114 Roper, 19–20.

115 Rogers, nos. 77–79, 109–10, 115–27, 136, 145, 161.

116 Hexter, *More's Utopia*, 146–55.

117 *St. Pap.*, vol. i. 111; Rogers, no. 110.

which More helped negotiate. More himself later recalled that the pacifists in Council argued forcibly for an English withdrawal from European rivalry. Wolsey, however, had rebuked them with the fable of the men who wrongly thought that they could rule their neighbours after sheltering in caves from rain, which, they believed, made all whom it wetted fools. Fools, Wolsey admonished, were not willing to be ruled by 'wise' men. The English would lose by diplomatic isolation, since the French and Imperialists would soon agree to attack them across the Channel. He would not make such a blunder. Writing in 1534, More gave his view of Wolsey's position quite plainly: men espousing folly in order to rule over fools were, he thought, themselves 'stark fools before the rain came'.[118]

The most likely interpretation of More's relationship with Wolsey is that the cardinal capitalized wholesale on More's scrupulousness, moral responsibility, aversion to intrigue, and ability to harmonize the desires of king and minister without doing violence to either. Since it is also true that Wolsey had a natural tendency to suspect Henry's secretaries, however irrationally, it is most probable that this applied to More too. Shortly after More's resignation as lord chancellor, Erasmus told Faber that Wolsey had treated More badly because 'he feared him more than he loved him'.[119] The source of this assertion is unknown, but the student of Wolsey cannot miss its meaning. Periods of friction apart, the cardinal did not dislike More, who proved so useful to him as a trusted royal servant, but he did not permit him to realize his potential as a councillor. He may indeed have feared More: not as a rival, but as one with easy access to the king who needed to be watched. Another of Wolsey's quirks was that he demanded intellectual inferiority of his colleagues in government, something More could not offer. Brilliant and ambitious (as it seemed), yet discreet and austerely religious, More was too complex for the cardinal. Wolsey was no doubt irritated, too, by More's sardonic humour; though here was another mystery, for More was most witty when least amused. Wolsey liked to size up his men, to assess their motivation and the extent of their greed, and to manipulate, promote and patronize them accordingly.[120] But More defied analysis; he

---

118 Rogers, no. 206. It is now accepted that this letter was written by More, rather than by his daughter Margaret Roper.
119 Allen, vol. x. 136.
120 The argument advanced here is supported by Harpsfield, 34–8. The supposition that friction between Wolsey and More was of slender extent and duration was first advanced by R.W. Chambers, esp. in his notes to Harpsfield, 320–1.

was an enigma. Possessing magisterial tact and nuance as a secretary and diplomat, he could also be inflexible and impervious to suggestion.[121] It would thus appear that More could only have achieved influence in this phase as a willing protégé of Wolsey, perhaps as a replacement for Thomas Ruthall who died in 1523. While his attitude to Wolsey's rule remained unenthusiastic, any hopes of high rank in the executive had to remain unfulfilled.

But despite More's lack of influence, he did achieve both office and profit. The step forward came with his knighthood and appointment as under-treasurer of the Exchequer in May 1521, less than four years after his entry into the Council.[122] The post was unusually valuable. More's annual salary was £173 6s 8d, the second highest in the Exchequer.[123] Furthermore, the duties were not exacting. It is true that Tunstall, dedicating his arithmetical treatise *De Arte Supputandi* to More in 1522, wrote that Sir Thomas was fully occupied by his new work, but this was an exaggeration as extreme as Erasmus's report that the job was 'especially distinguished and honourable'.[124] The under-treasurer was in fact a middle manager: he supervised those responsible for receiving and disbursing money, and those engaged in the Lower Exchequer's main formal activity, the production of tallies. He deputized for the treasurer of England (the duke of Norfolk) in the Lower Exchequer, checking and signing the annual declarations of the state of the Treasury.[125] His balance sheets and sub-accounts were, however, drawn up by subordinates.[126] Indeed, More's personal presence at the Exchequer was probably needed only at the 'knitting up' of each of the four legal terms, when a week's solid auditing was required to finalize the accounts, after which any surplus cash would be transferred to the Tower, the Mint or the king's coffers.[127] More's appointment was thus a mark of favour: a sign of Henry's satisfaction with his services as secretary, and an indication that Wolsey's attitude was not unfriendly in 1521.

To supplement the income derived from the under-treasurership, More received other grants and perquisites appropriate to his status and service. In November 1520 he had been given a sinecurist half-share, with George Ardeson the Genoese merchant,

---

121 *LP* iv. 4562, 4604.
122 E 407/67/3; Elton, *Studies*, vol. i. 134.
123 Elton, *Studies*, vol. i. 135.
124 Rogers, no. 111; Allen, vol. iv. 576.
125 Elton, *Studies*, vol. i. 134–5, 356–60.
126 E.g. E 407/67/3. More's first declaration (for 1521–22) begins at fo. 10v.
127 *St. Pap.*, vol. i. 146–7; G. R. Elton, *Reform and Reformation* (London, 1977), 30. Elton relies here on Starkey's dissertation (*supra* n. 51).

in the keepership of the foreign exchanges.[128] Since unlicensed foreign exchange dealing was a statutory offence, More and Ardeson, acting by deputy, enjoyed a monopoly of legal exchange broking in London.[129] Together, they probably received a clear profit of ten times their annual rent of £30 6s 8d. More then obtained in May 1522 the grant of South manor in Kent, a fragment of the estates of the executed duke of Buckingham, worth £67 per annum net under direct exploitation.[130] The following month, he was given the valuable wardship of Giles Heron, heir of Sir John Heron (a former treasurer of the Chamber). Giles was a pleasant youth who obligingly married More's daughter Cecily in 1525, just two months after entering his inheritance.[131] In January 1525 More was next granted a small Oxfordshire component of the reallocated lands of Sir Francis Lovell (attainted in Henry VII's first Parliament), property yielding an annual return of £32 10s.[132] Another lucrative windfall came in June 1526, when More got a licence to export 1,000 woollen cloths.[133] This was a typical courtier's gift, exploited by selling it to a real cloth-exporter.[134] Five months later, More was granted jointly with Tunstall the next presentation to a canonry in St Stephen's, Westminster.[135] In January 1527 he obtained the wardship of John Moreton, a lunatic.[136] Other pickings included a pension of 150 crowns (£35) from Francis I, awarded for More's work on the treaty of 1525, and an annual retainer of £21 from the earl of Northumberland.[137] Lastly, More got another wardship, that of Anne Cresacre, daughter and heir sole of Edward Cresacre of Barnborough Hall, Yorkshire. This came about in an unusual way worth recounting.

What happened was that Anne was placed in More's custody during a Star Chamber case.[138] After her father's death, the child had been seized illegally by a neighbour, Ralph Rokeby, who

128 C 66/635, m. 4 (*LP* iii. 1073).
129 E.g. 3 Hen. VII, c.7.
130 *LP* iii. 2239; SC 6/Hen. VII/1076; SC 6/Hen. VIII/5795; SC 6/Hen. VIII/5842. It was worth only £20 p.a. when leased.
131 *LP* iii. 2900; C 66/645, m. 17 (*LP* iv. 1533 [18]).
132 C 66/665, m. 18 (*LP* viii. 149 [16]); SC 12/23/51, p. 288; C 66/776, mm. 13–14 (*LP* xx. II. 266 [5]).
133 *LP* iv. 2248.
134 Elton, *Studies*, vol. i. 138.
135 *LP* iv. 2644.
136 *LP* iv. 2817.
137 Elton, *Studies*, vol. i. 138.
138 STAC 2/29/44; Ellesmere MS. 2652, fo. 13; SP 1/34, fos. 5–8 (*LP* iv. 1115); Lansdowne 639, fos. 56v.–7.

brought her to his house at Bishop's Burton. There he 'married' her to his bastard, John, both parties still being under six years old. A man of power locally, Rokeby by 'sinister and crafty labour' prevented the Crown from discovering its rights of wardship, thereby holding both Anne and her property for five years. But by 1524, Anne was old enough to resolve that 'she would rather never have husband than to have John Rokeby'.[139] Simultaneously, Sir Robert Constable of Flamborough, Rokeby's rival, saw a possible opening. Constable told the master of the wards, Sir Richard Weston, the true position, after which he forcibly abducted Anne from the Rokeby household, claiming the king's authority. Rokeby himself then complained to the Council, charging Constable with riot and abducting his son's wedded wife.[140] Constable was meanwhile soliciting Henry VIII for a grant of Anne's wardship, but wildly jumped the gun by 'affiancing' the girl to his son Thomas, and 'suffering him before marriage to know her carnally'.[141] Wolsey was furious, his anger kindled the more because these outrages had been committed within his own liberty of Beverley. Constable and Rokeby were hauled into Star Chamber.[142] As to poor Anne, Wolsey placed her in the civilized surroundings of More's household — a splendid arrangement all round. Not only rich, but attractive and delightful, the girl brightened up More's somewhat sober Chelsea establishment. Then in 1529, she followed Heron's example and married More's son John.[143]

More's regular income was between £400 and £500 a year by the beginning of 1525. He had not done at all badly at Court. However, royal service had compelled him to give up private law practice with its £400 a year; thus his overall income was at best only marginally increased.[144] Prior to 1521, More might even have been worse off than before. Although still included in Wolsey's list of qualified pleaders in 1518, he was already then registered as on leave from the law courts.[145] Yet he learned with dismay in September 1525 that he had lost his most remunerative office. Wolsey in that month engineered a reshuffle by which More was named successor to Sir Richard Wingfield as chancellor of the Duchy of Lancaster,

139 STAC 2/29/44.
140 *Ibid.*
141 Ellesmere MS. 2652, fo. 13.
142 SP 1/34, fos. 5–8. Through influence in the Privy Chamber, Constable obtained a pardon, while Rokeby seems to have escaped equally lightly. *LP* iv. 1136 (22).
143 R. W. Chambers, *Thomas More* (London, 1938), 184.
144 Cf. Elton, *Studies*, vol. i. 139.
145 C 82/474.

Wingfield having died the previous July at Toledo.[146] For an under-treasurer, this was a transfer as much as a promotion, and Wolsey was behind it. The move was just one in a series of ingenious deals by which Wolsey achieved his ambition to reduce the influence of Henry's Privy Chamber, ousting some political opponents there.[147] Sir William Compton, keeper of Henry's privy purse, supplanted More at the Exchequer; Sir Richard Weston was made treasurer of Calais; Sir William Kingston, a man more favourable to Wolsey, obtained the stewardship of South Parts, a Duchy sinecure worth an impressive £100 a year which Wingfield had combined with the chancellorship.[148] Quite the last person Wolsey considered during the haggling, though, was Thomas More, despite the fact that More's displacement was essential to the reshuffle. For what More actually got was the chancellorship of the Duchy without the stewardship or other reward thrown in to make up the salary. As chancellor of the Duchy, More was paid only £66 13s 4d salary, plus £28 board wages per annum.[149] He was entitled in addition to a share in the sealing fees of the Duchy and County Palatine, but would have been lucky if this had even equalled the £80 or so he lost by leaving the Exchequer. Manifestly, Wolsey chose in 1525 to exploit More's diffidence in matters of patronage, relying on Henry to connive. He knew well enough that More was 'not the most ready to speak and solicit his own cause', since he used those words exactly to Henry on another occasion.[150] More's 'promotion' was arranged to place him in a position markedly inferior to that of his predecessor — something everyone would have noticed. To make matters worse, a chancellor of the Duchy had onerous duties to perform unlike an under-treasurer. More assumed full responsibility for the Duchy lands and finances, to which a heavy workload as an equity judge in the Duchy court at Westminster was added.

On the other hand, the Duchy gave More far greater scope for his talents than the Lower Exchequer. His legal training and judicial

146 Elton, *Studies*, vol. i. 135–6; Harpsfield, 322.
147 Elton, *Reform and Reformation*, 99–100.
148 Wolsey's draft of the reshuffle is SP 1/37, fo. 102 (*LP* iv. 1939 [14]), entitled 'A provision for such as should be discharged out of the king's Privy Chamber'. For an illuminating account, see D. R. Starkey, 'The King's Privy Chamber, 1485–1547' (Ph.D., University of Cambridge, 1973), 149–53. For the Duchy sinecure, DL 28/6/22, fo. 6; DL 28/6/23, fo. 6.
149 Elton, *Studies*, vol. i. 136; Kingston collected the income from his stewardship of South Parts at once, DL 28/6/24, fo. 6. The duke of Suffolk (characteristically) held the stewardship of North Parts.
150 *LP* iii. 3267.

experience more than qualified him for the chancellor's duties. Aged forty-eight in 1525, it was surely time, too, that he achieved his potential as a royal servant. This he plainly began to do, working hard alongside his fellow councillors Sir Andrew Windsor, Sir Robert Drury, Sir John Husy and Richard Wolman.[151] Steady labour and attention to detail were essential in the post, not least because the lands within More's control were scattered across England and Wales, being contiguous only within the County Palatine of Lancaster.[152] More's duties involved him personally in matters of account and arrearage, land management, mineral rights, and wardship; matters of legal title and the problems of local franchises, inquests of office, and inquisitions *post mortem*; and liaison with the separate Chancery at Lancaster, the judges there, and the sheriff of Lancashire.[153] As an equity judge in the Duchy Chamber, More dealt with municipal disputes, encroachments on royal property, arguments between lords and tenants, and commons cases. He tried unquiet titles, riots, routs, unlawful assemblies and forcible entries, corrupt juries, official malfeasance, hunting offences, counterfeiting, trespass, tithes disputes, tortious enclosure, illegal distraint, and even testamentary cases on occasion.[154] This was an immense range of work, comparable to that undertaken nationally in Star Chamber.[155] Indeed, many cases in Star Chamber would be specifically transferred by Wolsey to the Duchy Chamber, when the matter in dispute had arisen in Lancashire.[156]

Something of More's profile emerges from the Duchy materials, the striking features being his drive, industry and concern for legal minutiae.[157] The records reveal that 'Master More' himself took sureties for a defendant's future appearance. He lost patience with the farmer of a mill for not making proper repairs, and called 'hastily for the bond', presumably to collect the penalty due to the king. A sergeant-at-arms appeared in court to answer a petition 'by commandment of Master Chancellor'. More then asked his clerk to remind him to speak with the sheriff of Lancashire about some men

151 DL 5/5, fos. 236, 246, 247, 252, 258, 294v., 366v., 470v., 479.
152 *Thirtieth Annual Report of the Deputy Keeper of Public Records* (London, 1869), iii–viii.
153 This is based on DL 6/1–2; DL 5/5, *passim*; St. Pap., vol. i. 176.
154 DL 5/5, fos. 299v., 300v., 305–6, 309, 314, 318, 324–6, 328, 332–8, 341–2, 344–5, 347v., 352, 357, 360–90.
155 Guy, *The Cardinal's Court*, ch. 3.
156 DL 5/5, fos. 268v., 300v., 354, 367.
157 These points were first worked out by M. Hastings, 'Sir Thomas More: Maker of English Law?', *Essential Articles*, 104–18. I have added a few examples of my own.

in prison for burning down houses.[158] He next wrote a letter to an executor, demanding arrears of the king's rent. He put hasty notes on a memorandum for a decree in an enclosure case. 'Master Chancellor himself' then examined a witness. He bound over parties to abide by his personal arbitration in a title dispute.[159] He delivered 'by his own hands into this court . . . three books of patents sealed with the Duchy seal . . . concerning the honour of Leicester', to be kept safe in a chest behind the clerk's chair in the Duchy Chamber. More then commissioned 'Master Roper . . . of Lincoln's Inn' to make an extra-legal award by compromise.[160] He and others next reasoned with a plaintiff, urging him to settle with his opponents — unsuccessfully, since the latter were discharged *sine die*. More delivered by his own hand the proofs in a particularly awkward case. He wrote on an information 'fiat privatum sigillum' with bold pen strokes. Finally, the king's poor tenants of Enfield petitioned that during his absence abroad with Wolsey, defendants against whom they were litigating had started a cross-suit. The sly ploy had worked, and injunctions were out against the poor tenants, commanding them to attend daily at Westminster when they should have been at Enfield. This would never have happened, they argued, if More had been present.[161] All the evidence thus points to the view that More was both a busy administrator in the Duchy, and an astute lawyer and judge 'who could cut through a mass of detail to the heart of the matter in hand'.[162]

The chancellorship of the Duchy gave More an invaluable period of preparation for his later office of lord chancellor of England. It should, however, be realized that he had no expectation of such promotion before 1529. Wolsey had soon regained his fullest supremacy after the rebellions of 1525, so that within a year his freedom of manoeuvre was as great as ever before. He needed only to ensure that the dukes of Norfolk and Suffolk, increasingly also the Boleyns, were associated with the public promulgation of sensitive or vulnerable policies. Even this need to consult became a source of strength in Wolsey's hands. When things went well, he always took sole credit; if anything went awry, his excuse was his devotion to Henry's will which was misled by the Council's errors.[163] Wolsey slipped back a little between May and October

158 DL 5/5, fo. 314.
159 DL 5/5, fo. 334v.
160 DL 5/5, fo. 341v.
161 Hastings, *art. cit.*, 106.
162 *Ibid.*, 118.
163 For an interesting (but sometimes quite misleading) interpretation of Wolsey

1527, when the king himself took a rare initiative in state affairs, ominously in the matter of his marriage. But he recovered Henry's confidence almost as quickly as it had been lost.[164] Charles V's ambassador might believe Wolsey to be popularly hated in 1527 and 1528, but his opinion that Henry was actually poised to dismiss his minister was either a guess or wishful thinking.[165] Nevertheless, Wolsey's ascendancy was under growing siege in Council and at Court. His position had to be worked for as never before, especially after 1528, when a hostile aristocracy led by the duke of Suffolk rallied an alliance with the relations of Anne Boleyn.[166] As Cavendish knew, the dukes of Norfolk and Suffolk had for years headed an aristocratic party in Council, which one day hoped to discredit Wolsey and succeed him in power.[167] Popular hatred of Wolsey indeed existed, but it was the aristocracy that had been stirring the pot since 1522, when John Skelton (a client of the Norfolks) had unleashed his bitter satires *Speke, Parrot* and *Why Come Ye Nat to Court?*[168] According to Skelton, the aristocracy had been ousted from its rightful place in the realm by a 'butcher's dog': a puffed-up prelate, who ruled the roost 'with bragging and with boast, born up on every side with pomp and with pride'.[169] Modesty was truly not Wolsey's greatest virtue. But that meant that his undoubted achievements at home and abroad were resented all the more by outsiders. Norfolk smarted from political isolation, being kept away by Wolsey both from Westminster and the king's Court in 1528.[170] Suffolk had also endured the cardinal's contempt long enough. As Henry's own brother-in-law, too, he believed he had an irrefutable claim himself to ministerial office.[171]

Henry VIII meanwhile became obsessed with Anne Boleyn and his wish to obtain an annulment of his marriage to Catherine of Aragon. The royal temper was soon subject to great extremes of

along these lines, see R.L. Woods's dissertation, 'The Amicable Grant: Some Aspects of Thomas Wolsey's Rule in England, 1522–1526' (University Microfilms: Ann Arbor, Michigan, 1974).

164 Scarisbrick, *Henry VIII*, 154–62, 229–30.
165 A. F. Pollard, *Wolsey* (London, 1929), 221.
166 Scarisbrick, *Henry VIII*, 228–32.
167 *Two Early Tudor Lives*, ed. R. S. Sylvester and D. P. Harding (New Haven, 1962), 38.
168 J. Skelton, *Pithy, Pleasant and Profitable Works* (Scholar reprint: London, 1970); W. O. Harris, *Skelton's Magnyfycence and the Cardinal Virtue Tradition* (Chapel Hill, 1965), 21.
169 *Pithy, Pleasant and Profitable Works*, sig. L.iv.
170 *LP* iv. 4045, 4162, 4192, 4320, 4398.
171 Suffolk had married Henry VIII's sister Mary in 1515, shortly after the demise of Louis XII of France, her first husband.

passion and frustration. Even so, Wolsey remained in control until the summer of 1529. What ruined him then was the failure of his legatine court at Blackfriars to pass sentence for Henry's divorce, a disaster promptly followed by the Peace of Cambrai, the Franco-Imperial truce which annihilated at a stroke England's foreign policy.[172] Wolsey was the first to predict the dire consequences of failure at Blackfriars.[173] Meticulous plans had been laid prior to 1 July 1529 by Suffolk, Norfolk and their political satellites, and the *coup d'état* was announced by Suffolk on 31 July.[174] At the adjournment by Cardinal Campeggio of the legatine court, the duke gave the table 'a great clap' and said, 'by the Mass, now I see that the old said saw is true, that there was never legate nor cardinal that did good in England'.[175]

Henry faltered over Wolsey's dismissal, postponing a final decision until 8 October 1529.[176] The next day (the first of the Michaelmas law term) Wolsey 'came into Westminster Hall with all his train':

> But none of the king's servants would go before, as they were wont to do. And so he sat in the Chancery, but not in the Star Chamber, for all the lords and other the king's Council were gone to Windsor to the king.[177]

Simultaneously, the *praemunire* charge which was Wolsey's destruction was filed in the court of King's Bench.[178] Eight or nine days later he resigned as lord chancellor, handing back the great seal to Norfolk and Suffolk 'in a high chamber' at York Place.[179] The seal was with Henry at Windsor on the 20th,[180] and a vigorous debate on the succession and struggle for power began in the Council.

Needless to say, Thomas More was not involved in these high politics. He is known only to have been present in Council on 19 October 1529, when Norfolk and Suffolk announced judicial sittings in Star Chamber three days a week.[181] On Saturday 23

172 Scarisbrick, *Henry VIII*, 232–3.
173 *LP* iv. 5703.
174 *LP* iv. 5210, 5581, 5749. For a full discussion of these plans, see ch. 6.
175 Edward Hall, *The Triumphant Reigne of Kyng Henry the VIII*, ed. C. Whibley (London, 1904), vol. ii. 153; Scarisbrick, *Henry VIII*, 227.
176 Scarisbrick, *Henry VIII*, 235.
177 Hall, *Henry the VIII*, vol. ii. 156.
178 Pollard, 242–3.
179 C 54/398, m. 19. There is confusion as to the date of Wolsey's deprivation. The Close Roll gives it as 17 October.
180 *Ibid.*
181 Lansdowne 1, fo. 108v.

October, the political scene moved to Greenwich, where the king 'much consulted with his Council for a meet man to be his chancellor'.[182] Suffolk had ambitions; however, these were thwarted by Norfolk, who at last was close to influence and had no wish to be overruled in Council by the king's semi-literate relations.[183] Archbishop Warham reappeared at Court, but refused (apparently) the office from which Wolsey had driven him in 1515.[184] Cuthbert Tunstall, by now bishop of London, was a fine candidate in the traditional mould.[185] But opinion turned on the choice of a layman.[186] The reaction to Wolsey was fierce, and the French ambassador rightly supposed that the clergy had lost the chancellor's office for many years.[187] In the end, it may have been Wolsey's own recommendation that was accepted. Despite his lack of 'true hearty affection, yet did he confess that Sir Thomas More was the aptest and fittest man in the realm'.[188] Erasmus and Archdeacon Harpsfield both got to hear this, and by 25 October More had indeed emerged as the compromise solution between Suffolk and Tunstall.[189] Henry VIII was enthusiastic. Not only was More uniquely qualified for the chancellor's duties, his former political obscurity was now a positive asset. No one could possibly have associated him with Wolsey's discredited clientage.[190] More's personal position was, of course, already tortuous. The chancellorship, the highest office in the realm, was the consummation of the career begun when he entered the Council in 1517. On the other hand, Thomas was a declared opponent of the king's divorce, the greatest future political issue.[191] More hesitated; he perhaps even refused, until the king angrily told him to accept.[192]

Thus at 3 p.m. on Monday 25 October 1529, Sir Thomas More entered Henry's inner chamber at Greenwich, took the great seal from the king's hands, and was created lord chancellor of England.[193] His salary was fixed at £542 15s a year, plus £200 for attending the court of Star Chamber, £64 in lieu of twelve tuns of

182 Hall, *Henry the VIII*, vol. ii. 158.
183 *Calendar of State Papers Spanish, 1529–30* (London, 1879), 211 (p. 326).
184 Pollard, 254–6.
185 *Ibid.*
186 Hall, *Henry the VIII*, vol. ii. 158.
187 *LP* iv. 6019.
188 Harpsfield, 39.
189 Allen, vol. x. 136; C 54/398, m. 19.
190 Elton, *Studies*, vol. i. 151.
191 Rogers, no. 199.
192 Harpsfield, 222.
193 C 54/398, m. 19.

wine, and £16 for wax — a total of £822 15s.[194] At 10 a.m. on the 26th, Norfolk, Suffolk and other leading councillors escorted More down the winding stairs from Star Chamber into Westminster Hall, and led him to his place as head of the court of Chancery.[195] By Henry's express command, Norfolk then made a public announcement introducing the new chancellor, declaring that England was much in debt to More 'for his good service, and how worthy he was to have the highest room in the realm'.[196] The usual bustle of the Hall — judges, lawyers, court officials and litigants about their daily business — was abruptly silenced by this, the event being a barometer of just how surprising More's promotion was.[197] More delivered a modest reply to Norfolk's speech, confessing himself 'unmeet for that room'. He next took his oath of office, after which the ceremonials were concluded by the public sealing of a few unimportant state documents.[198] The Council finally withdrew from the Hall, leaving More to begin his first day's work in Chancery.

194 C 82/622.
195 C 54/398, m. 19.
196 Roper, 39.
197 Elton, *Studies*, vol. i. 151–2.
198 C 54/398, m. 19.

PART TWO

MORE AND THE LAW

2

THE SITUATION OF 1529

BY ACCEPTING the chancellorship, Thomas More scaled the sum-
mit of ambition; aged fifty-two, he was at the climax of his public
career. The timing was auspicious, especially for the legal profession. By 1529 a large question mark hung over the traditional legal
system, and the future shape of English royal justice was in doubt.
The business of the central law courts of King's Bench and Common Pleas had fallen into a steep recession after 1440, and it
appeared that nothing save drastic reform could reverse a decline
which reached its maximum point in 1524–5.[1] Recession in the
fifteenth century was the inevitable consequence of dynastic upsets,
economic depression and demographic stagnation. However, the
trend worsened in the sixteenth century despite dynastic con-
tinuity, general economic growth and rising population. It was
clear that the failure of the common-law courts to stage a recovery
was due to a mass defection of litigants to the chancellor's courts of
Chancery and Star Chamber, a defection which was most noticea-
ble under Wolsey. The attraction was that Chancery and Star
Chamber were new and flexible courts which responded swiftly to
changing patterns of public need and so outpaced the rigidity of the
older benches. Advancing under Henry VI, Chancery took its
significant strides under Edward IV and Richard III, when Thomas
Rotherham, archbishop of York, and John Russell, bishop of Lincoln, successively disregarded the accepted limits of the chancellor's
jurisdiction in the wider interests of public justice. The result was
the shift in the chancellor's position as a member and servant of the
King's Council dealing equitably with petitions to that of being
head of an established Chancery court of equity.[2] It was to Chancery that both old and new legal business was extensively deflected
after 1475, mainly that generated by complex commercial practices,
modern methods of property settlement, recent investments in
farms, renewed exploitation of mineral resources, the expansion of
foreign trade, the growth of the towns (notably London, where the
courts were), and (latterly) inflation. The final consolidation of
Chancery in its classic late-medieval format was accomplished

1 M. Blatcher, *The Court of King's Bench 1450–1550* (London, 1978), ch. 2.
2 N. Pronay, 'The Chancellor, the Chancery and the Council at the end of the
  fifteenth century', in *British Government and Administration*, ed. H. Hearder and
  H. R. Loyn (Cardiff, 1974).

under Henry VIII by More's predecessor, Wolsey, when the court's workload increased to an average annual level of 535 suits, as against the 500 or so petitions filed each year between 1487 and 1515 under Archbishops Morton and Warham.[3]

The rise of Star Chamber, which soon attracted numerous litigants who might otherwise have pleaded in King's Bench, was Wolsey's work alone.[4] His ministerial policy had aimed first at strict and impartial enforcement of existing law upon all the king's subjects, irrespective of social status and private power; secondly, the cardinal deliberately popularized the conciliar courts of which Star Chamber was chief almost as an extension of his exuberant personality, offering speedy and efficient justice to anyone who travelled to seek it. Within sixteenth-century limitations, these were admirable and enlightened goals, and it should be better known that the stability and statesmanship which were the passwords of the Tudor age owed everything to Wolsey's drive, ingenuity and philosophic originality. But Wolsey's record was far from unblemished, and the falling business of King's Bench and Common Pleas openly testified to his neglect of the fundamental issue of law reform. By the 1560s, Star Chamber would have assumed its place as the brightest star in the firmament of the legal system, the premier fount of legal knowledge and creativity at a time when common lawyers were less insensitive to their own reformist failings. Yet in origin, the court's development arose from Wolsey's basic desire to hear complaints about crime and wrongdoing from private individuals.[5] It was axiomatic under his scheme that men with grievances who were eager to obtain justice, and who feared the corruption of local sessions and assizes by hostile vested interests, should be allowed to file bills in Star Chamber 'where the complainants shall not dread to show the truth of their grief'.[6] Such bills were sometimes received in Chancery, too, but most went to Star Chamber. Rarely do judges advertise their willingness to provide justice, but Wolsey did and the impact on Star Chamber was immediate. In the reign of Henry VII, a mere 300 or so suits had been initiated before the Council in Star Chamber (12.5 per annum).[7] During Wolsey's government, 1,685 suits (120 per annum) were filed, a workload which was the

3 F. Metzger, 'Das Englische Kanzleigericht unter Kardinal Wolsey, 1515–1529' (Erlangen Ph.D., 1976), ch. 3.

4 J. A. Guy, *The Cardinal's Court: the Impact of Thomas Wolsey in Star Chamber* (Harvester, Hassocks, 1977), ch. 2.

5 *Ibid.*, chs. 3, 5.

6 *Ibid.*, 121.

7 *Ibid.*, 15.

clear consequence of ministerial encouragement.[8] Admittedly, Wolsey had not resolved the ultimate question of Star Chamber's status *vis-à-vis* the executive function of the King's Council prior to his disgrace, but litigants and their advisers were in no doubt that a separate 'Curte of the Sterre Chambre', presided over by the lord chancellor, had emerged in practical terms by 1529.

It was inevitable that as Chancery and Star Chamber gained in business and prestige, the courts of King's Bench and Common Pleas would fail to recover lost ground. The profits of the sealing fees offer an adequate index of the fortunes of the common-law courts from 1358 to 1559, and they suggest that the combined business of King's Bench and Common Pleas was in 1515–16 at 62% of the level reached in 1439–40, in 1521–2 at 30% and in 1524–5 at 20% of that level.[9] A return to a figure of 51% in 1528–9 was an encouraging move in the other direction, but was hardly satisfactory.[10] Equally disturbing was the acquisition by Chancery and Star Chamber of recognized interests in particular areas of jurisdiction. During the fourteen years of Wolsey's chancellorship, 7,476 suits were filed in Chancery. Of these, 3,492 (46.7%) were disputes over real property and chattels real; 2,204 suits (29.5%) were purely mercantile, concerning merchant debts, equitable debt/detinue, bonds or recognisances; and 1,780 suits (23.8%) were essentially miscellaneous.[11] For the same period, 473 out of the total quota of Star Chamber suits are sufficiently complete to be placed in safe subject categories. Of the sample, 194 (41%) concerned real property or chattels real, and 279 (59%) resulted from riot or trespass, maintenance or barratry, perjury or false verdict, municipal or economic disorder, official malpractice or individual wrong-doing.[12] In other words, the striking bulk of the litigation deflected into the chancellor's courts from King's Bench and Common Pleas under Wolsey— 46% in Chancery and 41% in Star Chamber— was in the sphere of real property, the next largest single category being the commercial and mercantile litigation brought into Chancery. No wonder then that common lawyers were anxiously debating the future by the end of the 1520s, since the areas of proprietal and

8 *Ibid.*, 51.

9 Blatcher, 15–21, and appendix.

10 Business did not stage a full recovery until after 1550.

11 Metzger, 332–3. I have re-grouped Dr Metzger's categories, in order to facilitate direct comparison with More's work in Chancery (see below, ch. 3). It is not thought that this has introduced any significant error, but the specialist should refer to Metzger's own calculations.

12 Guy, *The Cardinal's Court*, 51–3.

commercial law were indubitably those of greatest professional profit. The proverb 'crime does not pay' applied as much to lawyers as offenders in the sixteenth century, and the seemingly deliberate specialization of Chancery and Star Chamber in business of advantage suggested that the older benches, for all their ancient pretensions, had become 'two inconsiderable courts in a complex of courts, most of them more flourishing and many bound by different principles'.[13]

Not unnaturally perhaps, it has long been thought that Wolsey's emphasis on Chancery and Star Chamber progressively alienated common lawyers and judges *en masse*, creating a breach between Chancery and common law which it fell to his successor, More, to heal.[14] But this tradition is highly misleading and deserves refutation.[15] The truth was that Wolsey's emphasis on Chancery and Star Chamber was only possible in the first place because he had secured the co-operation of many top common lawyers. First, the judges and lawyers were prominent in Wolsey's executive and enforcement work, the most active of them including John Fineux, Richard Broke, Robert Brudenell, Anthony Fitzherbert, Humphrey Coningsby, Lewis Pollard and John Fitzjames.[16] As king's councillors, justices of King's Bench, Common Pleas and assizes, commissioners of the peace, *oyer et terminer* and gaol delivery, their support was essential to the success of Wolsey's regime, and they gave energetic assistance irrespective of personal antagonisms.[17] Secondly, far from the common lawyers being unanimously hostile to Chancery and Star Chamber, they provided the expert services without which neither institution could function as a court. It was common-law counsel, not civil lawyers, as has been alleged, who increasingly advised clients to litigate in Chancery and Star Chamber, and who regularly, and in Star Chamber exclusively, pleaded cases there.[18] Leading common lawyers who practised in Chancery and Star Chamber during the 1520s included Robert Norwich, John Skewys, Roger Cholmeley and John Densell from Lincoln's Inn; Robert Chidley, John Packington and Baldwin Malet from Inner Temple; John Orenge, Humphrey Brown and Walter Luke from

---

13 Blatcher, 31.
14 See R. J. Schoeck, 'The Place of Sir Thomas More in Legal History and Tradition', *Moreana*, li (September 1976), 85–90.
15 A vigorous refutation is J. A. Guy, 'Thomas More as Successor to Wolsey', *Thought: Fordham University Quarterly*, lii (1977), 275–92.
16 Guy, *The Cardinal's Court*, 29, 131.
17 Guy, 'Thomas More as Successor to Wolsey', 297–81.
18 Metzger, 355–7; J. A. Guy, 'The Court of Star Chamber during Wolsey's Ascendancy' (Ph.D., University of Cambridge, 1973), 209–10.

Middle Temple; and John Hynde and Roger York from Gray's Inn.[19] The same learned counsel acted as arbitrators, mediators, umpires, referees and valuers in Wolsey's courts, and the judges and king's sergeants (invariably sworn king's councillors) were prominent in the making of his Star Chamber decrees. When Wolsey put his Chancery jurisdiction into commission in June 1529, those appointed to determine outstanding suits included the judges Anthony Fitzherbert, Thomas Englefield and Richard Lyster, and the common lawyers Baldwin Malet, Humphrey Wingfield, William Coningsby, John Baldwyn, Christopher Jenney and others.[20] In other words, the Tudor legal landscape was marked not by conflicting theory between common law and civil law, as so many lawyers and historians have erroneously thought, but by shifting areas of jurisdiction. This has nothing to do with a supposed reception of Roman law, but is the simple reality that the courts of Chancery and Star Chamber could meet the everyday needs of litigants better than the courts of King's Bench and Common Pleas in the sixteenth century. Little danger existed of the reception of substantive Roman law into the English royal courts, as opposed to the quasi-Roman procedures which were the basis of Chancery's speed and flexibility, and at no point did Wolsey aim to transform the courts over which he presided into civil law courts. This point is amply proved by his prompt dismissal in January 1523 of John Stokesley from the bench of the White Hall court for pronouncing decrees not 'allowable' to common lawyers.[21] Nevertheless, the shift of jurisdictional emphasis had progressed by 1529 almost to the point of creating a new, 'rival' forum for litigation in England; a forum based on Chancery and Star Chamber rather than common law, but within which common lawyers actively participated as professionals, and in which the chancellor's decisions were founded on existing principles of common law, however flexibly strict law was in practice interpreted.

What happened after More's elevation to the chancellorship was that the choice of a common lawyer to succeed Wolsey stimulated lively controversy as to future official policy between competing factions in the legal profession itself. Opinion was plainly divided at the Inns of Court. Wolsey's disgrace cast a shadow over his whole contribution to government, in particular his emphasis on Chancery and Star Chamber. What would his successor do? What ought

19 See the lists in *ibid*.
20 *LP* iv. 5666.
21 Guy, *The Cardinal's Court*, 45.

he to do? Some lawyers interpreted More's appointment as a triumph for reaction: seeing the first common-law lord chancellor for 150 years, they assumed that Wolsey's policy was due for rapid reverse. Others shared their prejudices, but remained sceptical as to the future. More had, after all, been tutored for twelve years in Wolsey's nursery; he was also the author of *Utopia*. Would he perhaps continue his predecessor's scheme without interruption, or possibly devise another of his own? Such conservative voices spoke predominantly for the interests of Common Pleas, which had lost a larger volume of business to Chancery after 1515 than any other court of common law.[22] Allied against the conservatives were two influential groups: a few progressive sergeants and apprentices, and those barristers specializing in Chancery and Star Chamber work. Another ally was the septuagenarian Christopher St German, an intellectual dynamo throughout the 1530s and most learned defender of equity and Chancery.[23] But most firmly committed to Wolsey's system were the common lawyers practising in Chancery and Star Chamber. Numbering some thirty or so in all,[24] no group was more concerned at the possible new direction of events, calculating a serious decline in their own business should the conservatives be permitted to have their way.

To state the question in its simplest form, More's promotion to the chancellorship in 1529 triggered a self-motivated debate between common lawyers with King's Bench and Common Pleas practices on the one hand, and Chancery and Star Chamber practices on the other. We know about this debate, because it generated a literature. By November 1530, St German had published both the remarkable Dialogues which comprised his *Doctor and Student*, a treatise which elegantly defended the equitable initiatives of More's time.[25] An English edition of the First Dialogue (which in 1523 and 1528 was offered only in Latin) was issued in 1531; the Second Dialogue was first written and published in English alone. By publishing in the vernacular in 1530 and 1531, St German gained himself a wide readership, both Dialogues being sold in rival English editions within a year of initial publication.[26] But his success so disturbed conservative opinion that an anonymous Sergeant at the

22 Blatcher, ch. 2.
23 See below, pp. 151–6. The most recent account of St German's career in the 1530s is by Mr Barton, in his introduction to St German's *Doctor and Student*, ed. T. F. T. Plucknett and J. L. Barton (Selden Society: London, 1974), xi–xiv.
24 As n. 18 *supra*.
25 The best edition is by Plucknett and Barton, as n. 23 *supra*.
26 *Doctor and Student*, ed. Plucknett and Barton, pp. lxix–lxxvi.

laws of England quickly penned a strident *Replication* in answer.[27] Long recognized as a propaganda piece of telling asperity and obvious (if sour) sincerity, the historically important feature of this tract is that it included a reference to St German's Second Dialogue, and could not thus have been written before November 1530.[28] The older view that its thrust was against Wolsey, leaving More in the clear, is therefore improbable: the evidence is all the other way.[29]

The *Replication*, unlike *Doctor and Student*, aimed at a straightforward and practical approach. St German's was a philosophical as much as a legal treatise; his account of the chancellor's right to exercise jurisdiction rested on an application to English law of the (mainly) Aristotelian principle of *epikeia* — a method of interpreting positive human law in accordance with the presumed intention of the legislator. The principle of interpreting strict law flexibly in the interests of justice was in English practice called 'conscience' or 'equity'. St German himself tended to regard conscience as an objective ideal implanted in man by the workings of the 'natural power or motive force of the rational soul . . . moving and stirring it to good and abhoring evil'.[30] But in practical terms, conscience was the moral principle which gave the chancellor the cognitive and coercive authority to pronounce decisions in his courts and bind litigants to observe them. Evil must be searched out, and parties could not be allowed to escape the consequences of their wrongful acts because of the excessive rigidity of strict law.[31] Although St German was accused of condoning arbitrary and irresponsible methods of legal interpretation, he was misunderstood by his critics, since his overall purpose was to show that common law, and not any other sort of law, governed the consciences of Englishmen.[32] Thus he argued that the use of *epikeia* in construing law was not a criticism of the law itself; Chancery was merely ensuring that common law was applied according to its true effect and intention. Against this, the *Replication* held that Chancery procedure, backed by the writ of *subpoena*, 'voided' good common law by subjecting

---

27 'A Replication of a Sergeant at the Laws of England', in *Doctor and Student*, ed. W. Muchall (London, 1815).

28 *Ibid.*, 10. D. E. C. Yale, 'St German's *Little Treatise Concerning Writs of Subpoena*', *The Irish Jurist*, vol. x (1975), 324–33, esp. 326 n. 13.

29 For the older view, see R. J. Schoeck in *The Law Quarterly Review*, vol. lxxvi (1960), 503.

30 *Doctor and Student*, ed. Plucknett and Barton, 81.

31 For practical examples, see below, chs. 3–4.

32 Cf. *Doctor and Student*, ed. Plucknett and Barton, xlvi. 'A Little Treatise Concerning Writs of Subpoena', in *Doctor and Student*, ed. W. Muchall (London, 1815), 43.

parties to a discretionary process which was uncertain, 'contrary to all good reason and all good policy'.[33] Suits by *subpoena* were not only against common law, they were against reason's law, God's and the commonwealth.[34]

But the Sergeant's principal target was the lord chancellors of England. For the most part, they had been prelates with 'but superficial knowledge in the laws of this realm'.[35] When one was approached by a suitor:

> Regarding no law, but trusting to his own wit and wisdom, [he] giveth judgment as it pleaseth himself, and thinketh that his judgment being in such authority, is far better and more reasonable than judgments that be given by the king's justices according to the common law of the realm.[36]

By way of illustration, the Sergeant drew an analogy with the vision of the White Horse in White-Horse Vale at Uffington in Berkshire. Just as an observer sees the horse well at a distance but less well as he nears it, so the 'unlearned' chancellor understands less as he approaches and then trespasses on the corpus of the common law.[37] Since this attack was made after, rather than before 1529, the clear implication was that Thomas More, a common-law chancellor, was guilty of professional apostasy by exercising an equitable jurisdiction at all. It was a most reactionary view, and its author, whose credentials as a sergeant-at-law St German in fact doubted, concluded that a sufficient standard for conscience was to stick to strict common law alone.[38]

> Me thinketh that the law ought not to be left for conscience in no case; for the law commandeth all that is good for the commonwealth to be done, and prohibiteth all things that are evil and against the common weal. Wherefore if you observe and keep the law . . . and eschew all things that is evil . . . you shall not need to study so much upon conscience, for the law of the realm is a sufficient rule to order you and your conscience what you shall do in every thing, and what you shall not do.[39]

To fulfil the common law was to be 'perfectly virtuous' — an

33 'Replication', 5–6.
34 'Replication', 6–7.
35 'Replication', 7–8.
36 Ibid.
37 Ibid.
38 'Replication', 9.
39 Ibid.

assertion we must ascribe to invincible ignorance.

Who was the *Replication*'s author? Although definite proof is unobtainable without better sources, the tract's finale (on uses) closely resembles an Inner Temple reading by Thomas Audley.[40] Speaking in 1526, Audley argued that uses (i.e. trusts)[41] were founded on covin and deceit, and were part of a plot to subvert common law and start up a new law called conscience. Unlike common law, conscience was uncertain; it depended on the 'arbitrament' of one man, the chancellor alone. In particular, it would frustrate the certainty of men's title to land, since uses overthrew certainty by 'divers subtle wits'.[42] But whether Audley or another was the author, St German knew him to be a practising lawyer, asking whether or not 'he that made the same treatise hath sometime devised such uses as hath been necessary for his clients'.[43] All we can do in the present state of research is to note the new target of conservative polemic as shown by the *Replication*. Whereas Audley's Inner Temple reading simply argued that Chancery posed a potential threat to common law in 1526, the *Replication* went much further, confronting a common-law chancellor with personal responsibility should the threat not abate. This was the novel element which the situation of 1529 introduced. It is in this context that the *Replication*'s appeal to the judges must be read: 'And so in conclusion after my conceit, if this be not reformed by the great wisdom and policy of my lords and masters the judges of this realm, the law of this realm will be undone'.[44] The judges were exhorted by the Sergeant to rise in defence of the English legal system as it had evolved since Henry II's reign.

The *Replication* prompted a swift reply from St German under the title *A Little Treatise Concerning Writs of Subpoena*, a succinct essay in support of the progressive view of Chancery.[45] St German offered first an informed historical justification of Chancery's jurisdiction, after which he gave specific examples of cases where application of the principle of *epikeia* by the chancellor was essential to reason and

---

40 Cambridge University Library MS. Ee. 5. 19, fos. 1–17. I am most grateful to Dr J. H. Baker for drawing this reference to my attention. Dr Baker has subsequently discussed Audley's reading in his edition of *The Reports of Sir John Spelman*, vol. ii (Selden Society: London, 1978), *198–200*.
41 Uses are explained below, pp. 53–4.
42 MS. Ee. 5. 19 (*ut supra*), fo. 7.
43 This remark did not get into print, but is in St German's autograph (B.L. Harleian MS. 829). See Yale, 'St German's *Little Treatise*', 326.
44 '*Replication*', 14.
45 Printed in *Doctor and Student*, ed. W. Muchall (London, 1815).

justice.[46] For instance, a party could have no remedy except in Chancery against an action at law by a former creditor upon an uncancelled bond in respect of a debt actually repaid.[47] Although the general rule that written obligations could be discharged only by written receipts was salutary, since few persons would otherwise pay debts without first attempting 'untrue surmise' of repayment, the equity of Chancery's intervention to relieve repaid but uncancelled debts was obvious. As St German thought, 'it should more commend the common law that it suffereth remedy to be had in this case in the Chancery, than it should do if it should clearly prohibit it'.[48] He agreed, nevertheless, that it was undesirable that Chancery should intervene indiscriminately to remedy legal loopholes.[49] Cases existed where relief had to be left to the private consciences of the parties.[50]

> When a man that hath right cannot come to his right at the common law but that this should follow an inconvenience or a contradiction in the court, for eschewing whereof the common law will give him no remedy, and then if he should have a *subpoena* the same inconvenience or contradiction would follow in the Chancery, no *subpoena* lieth.[51]

For instance, a writ of *subpoena* could not lie against a statute, nor against the maxims of common law.[52] One such maxim was that judgments given at common law could not be annulled except by writ of error, attaint or certification of *novel disseisin* — a maxim given statutory sanction in 1285 and 1402.[53] Chancery should thus avoid reviewing common-law decisions, even if proved erroneous or unjust. The law would otherwise 'have no end, and thereupon would fall many inconveniences'. The chancellor could, however, enjoin a party about to obtain an inequitable verdict or judgment.[54]

St German concluded by denying the Sergeant's claim that the chancellor's conscience was uncertain and arbitrary.[55] Conscience,

---

46 'A Little Treatise Concerning Writs of Subpoena', 16–23.
47 *Ibid.*, 20–24; see below, pp. 70–3.
48 'A Little Treatise Concerning Writs of Subpoena', 24.
49 *Ibid.*, 23–34.
50 *Ibid.*, 23–34.
51 Not printed, but quoted by Yale from St German's autograph in 'St German's *Little Treatise*', 331 n. 30.
52 'A Little Treatise Concerning Writs of Subpoena', 30.
53 *Ibid.*, 31.
54 See below, ch. 4.
55 'A Little Treatise Concerning Writs of Subpoena', 42–3.

although rightly grounded upon God's law and reason, was not destructive of the English system, because the chancellor was informed by no other human law than common law.[56] Conscience was necessarily complementary to law, but anything explicitly void in law was automatically void in conscience too.[57] It was also absurd, said St German, to argue as the *Replication* did that common law alone was sufficient to guide a man and his conscience. A simple objection was that common law 'will not always give him remedy when he hath right'.[58] However, St German and the Sergeant shared one point of confluence. The development of a 'rival' forum for litigation based on Chancery and Star Chamber had raised tricky questions arising from excessive competition between jurisdictions, both at common law and equity, and between individual courts within the equitable forum. Unregulated competition between parallel jurisdictions raised, as it seemed, a truly awful prospect of perpetual litigation, especially in real property suits. St German accordingly held that this was the possible danger to be avoided by the lord chancellor, it being the element of overlap which would introduce uncertainty into the legal system.[59] Chancery and Star Chamber, whatever they were allowed to do, must never be permitted to rock the foundations of common law, whatever the equities of individual cases or however indefensible in conscience the maxims of law were as rational principles.[60]

Yet the reality was that general legal business had already begun to transfer into Chancery and Star Chamber, notably real property suits.[61] These were years bedevilled by litigation about land: the difficulties of making family settlements, the problems of mortgages, forged deeds, false claims, and a busy traffic in pretended titles had combined to ensure a ready supply of litigants in all the courts. But Chancery and Star Chamber now seemed best able to provide the legal services that men of property needed to keep their affairs in order. Doctrinal distinctions apart, the advantage of the 'rival' forum lay in its use of English bill procedure, notably in the answer which the defendant had to exhibit on oath; this combined with a meticulous analysis of written proofs and powers of recov-

---

56 *Ibid.*
57 *Ibid.*
58 'A Little Treatise Concerning Writs of Subpoena', 44–5.
59 *Ibid.*, 30–31, 39–40; *Doctor and Student*, ed. Plucknett and Barton, 107–113.
60 Cf. C. M. Gray, 'The Boundaries of the Equitable Function', *The American Journal of Legal History*, vol. xx (1976), 192–226.
61 Metzger, 'Das Englische Kanzleigericht unter Kardinal Wolsey, 1515–1529', 214–88, 332–41; Guy, *The Cardinal's Court*, chs. 3–4.

ery and discovery.[62] Many cases succeeded in Chancery which, though theoretically remediable, would have failed at common law — a major attraction. A lamentable truth played down equally by the *Replication* and St German was that litigants — the most potent force for change in all the courts — did not themselves care whether their judgments were in accordance with God's law, common law, reason or conscience, as long as they met immediate personal needs and were enforceable. Parties wanted tangible results, not lectures in jurisprudence. They would flock to whichever court was offering a public service, oblivious of altruism.

As regards legal doctrine, the 'rival' forum's rise was the consequence of common law's failure to adapt. In both its civil and criminal aspects, common law was derived from an admixture of feudal practice and the king's peace which enabled it to tackle ancient but not current socio-legal problems.[63]Common law had become settled in an age of force rather than of cunning; it was conspicuously underdeveloped by 1529 in respect of fraud, perjury, the rules of evidence, maintenance, champerty, embracery, subornation and conspiracy. In a lawyer's words, 'as English society was becoming increasingly sophisticated economically and socially, so wrongdoing was becoming more sophisticated. Or at least, contemporary man apprehended better the nature of that wrongdoing'.[64] Acts of covin and oppression, notably pretended title and multiple pursuit of actions designed to get an opponent to sell interests in land cheaply, were more significant offences in Tudor society than disseisin, forcible entry and trespass. But because the law had not adapted, many aggrieved parties had no recourse other than to petition the chancellor to compel wrongdoers to act in accordance with good conscience. Traditionally, he had acceded to such requests if he believed them to be genuine. Conscience was a chancellor's sufficient warrant to scrutinize the moral acceptability of men's taking advantage of their supposed 'legal' rights and to enjoin them from doing so unfairly.[65]

But the question was, must chancellors continue indefinitely to remedy the whole gamut of defects in the legal system? To some extent, the central courts of common law were tinkering hesitantly with historic forms of procedure, or grudgingly admitting

62 W. J. Jones, *The Elizabethan Court of Chancery* (Oxford, 1967), 446; Guy, *The Cardinal's Court*, ch. 4.

63 T. G. Barnes, 'Star Chamber and the Sophistication of the Criminal Law', *Criminal Law Review* (1977), 316–26.

64 *Ibid.*

65 See below, chs. 3–4.

innovations based on *assumpsit* or new kinds of action on the case under Henry VIII.[66] King's Bench had greatly helped itself by evolving a comprehensive bill procedure, modelled on that of Chancery, which enabled it to poach much useful business from Common Pleas during the sixteenth century.[67] Nevertheless, the proverb was still 'where there is no remedy there is no wrong', and three obstacles stood firmly in the way of a concerted policy of law reform by common lawyers themselves: their undue reverence towards their traditional craft, their fears both of change and criticism, and the rivalry between courts which fostered too many vested interests.[68] The irony was that, failing constructive proposals designed to bring Tudor law into line with current social conditions, the *Replication*'s prophecy of doom might soon be fulfilled. Successive chancellors would have no choice but to elaborate Wolsey's scheme by which law enforcement and crime prevention became the particular function of Star Chamber, while civil disputes likewise came increasingly there and into Chancery. A major programme of law reform was needed in 1529, and if the common lawyers could not reach agreement on this, they would necessarily be compelled to continue co-operating tacitly at worst, actively at best, in a process by which all their business could become lost to the 'rival' forum except that in treason, felony and the more archaic actions concerning freehold property. As such, More's tenure in Chancery and Star Chamber marked a decisive era for lawyers. It remained, however, to be seen whether More would succeed in making a smooth transition.

66 Blatcher, *The Court of King's Bench*, 24–6.
67 *Ibid.*, chs. 7–8.
68 *Ibid.*, 101.

3

MORE'S WORK IN THE COURTS: REAL PROPERTY SUITS

THOMAS MORE'S suitability for the lord chancellor's judicial work had been an important consideration at the time of his elevation to office, and the official expectation that he would become energetically involved in the management of Chancery and Star Chamber was soon fulfilled. From the beginning, More resolved to continue Wolsey's general policy by which the needs of litigants were met as far as possible by equitable procedure in the absence of improved facilities at common law. In Chancery, the level of litigation began to rise steeply: Sir Thomas was presented with 2,356 suits in the thirty-one months of his office, an average of 912 per annum.[1] At first sight, this represents an increase of seventy per cent over Wolsey's annual average of 535 suits, but averages and percentages are not always meaningful. Business in Chancery (and Star Chamber) tended to increase steadily over the years, though at differing rates of growth. Chancery litigation in the last year of Wolsey's tenure had most probably risen to an actual figure of around 600 suits, while that for the first year of More's was approximately 725 suits, for the second year 890 suits, and for the final seven months 740 suits. But in any event, More's chancellorship saw the most substantial period of growth in Chancery litigation since the reign of Edward IV. The new litigation was, nevertheless, similar in subject-matter to the old: of More's suits, 1,122 (47.6%) were disputes over real property or chattels real; 363 suits (15.4%) were purely mercantile, concerning merchant debts, equitable debt/detinue, bonds or recognisances; and 871 suits (37%) were miscellaneous, ranging from forgery and fraud, to false imprisonment, defamation, extortion, tithes disputes and testamentary squabbles.[2]

In Star Chamber, too, the high level of work achieved by Wolsey's enforcement policy and encouragement of civil litigation was maintained by More. Approximately 120 suits had passed through the court during Wolsey's last year, and papers extant in

1 C 1/601–94.
2 Strictly, the backlog of Chancery suits left by Wolsey should be added to complete this analysis of More's suits, but it is quite impossible to identify which of Wolsey's cases were still pending in October 1529.

the Star Chamber archive suggest that some 400 suits were filed under his successor.[3] However, Star Chamber bills of complaint (unlike those of Chancery) were addressed to the king not the chancellor, and are often impossible to date as a result. Analysis has to be based on the enforced sample of 167 suits which can be positively assigned to More's period of office.[4] The sample is nonetheless sufficient to confirm that the nature of the litigation received in Star Chamber by More was identical to that which had been taken under Wolsey.[5] Of the 167 identified suits, 73 (43.7%) concerned real property or chattels real, and 94 (56.3%) alleged riot or trespass, maintenance or barratry, perjury or false verdict, municipal or economic disorder, official malpractice or individual wrongdoing. Commercial suits, apart from a number involving aliens or foreign ships and cargoes, were rarely found in Star Chamber; they seem to have gone normally to Chancery or Admiralty.[6]

The scope of the work discharged by More as lord chancellor was thus directly comparable to that undertaken by his predecessor. More's policy included no jurisdictional innovations, no changes of direction within the existing jurisdictions. He was, though, presented with a higher annual quota of litigation in Chancery (and perhaps Star Chamber too) than any previous chancellor, even discounting the substantial backlogs left by Wolsey. As before, the bulk of this litigation — a dominant 47% in Chancery and 43% in Star Chamber — was in the sphere of real property. Litigants were consistently being advised by legal professionals to bring their unquiet titles and claims to land into the chancellor's courts for adjudication, in Chancery under colour of detention of deeds, in Star Chamber under pretext of riot or forcible entry. Few suits were genuine which purported to be no more than actions to recover deeds unconscionably detained, or informations plus claims for damages consequent upon rioting. Both formulae were accepted methods of inviting the trial of title to land by the chancellor, the pleadings drawn by lawyers and scriveners in either case following stereotyped patterns.

3 STAC 10/4, Pts. 2–5.
4 STAC references to these 167 suits are given in Appendix 1.
5 For a fuller analysis of Wolsey's suits in Star Chamber, see J.A. Guy, *The Cardinal's Court: the Impact of Thomas Wolsey in Star Chamber* (Harvester, Hassocks, 1977).
6 For a commercial suit brought by aliens in Star Chamber, STAC 2/26/347, 21/210, and Ellesmere MS. 2652, fo. 11v. The case was finally heard by More on 16 May 1531.

About 1520 in Chancery, for example, John Wynneswold filed a model complaint to Wolsey.[7] He alleged that his great-grandfather had been seised of several freehold estates in Allesley in Warwickshire, which 'be descended and of right owe to descend to your said orator'. But the title-deeds to the properties 'be come to the possession and custody of one Richard Colman'. Despite repeated requests for their delivery to the plaintiff, Colman refused to comply 'contrary to the law, right and good conscience'. Since Wynneswold did not know the 'number certain of the said evidences, nor whether they be contained in bag, box, chest ensealed or other encloser', he was without remedy at common law. He therefore sought a *subpoena* against Colman, commanding him to appear in Chancery and make answer to the matter. Complaints like this seem plausible enough, until defendants are found filing counterclaims to the property and thereby justifying possession of the deeds. Colman's argument was that the plaintiff's distant ancestors had in truth been seised of the disputed land, but that his grandfather had bargained and sold it to Colman's grandfather for ten marks. Colman thus retained the deeds 'for the conservation of his inheritance, as lawful is for him to do'. Actions would then proceed to a trial of title, it being the policy of successive chancellors actually to test the titles of the parties and award the deeds claimed accordingly. As such, the court could confer upon the successful litigant a secure title in practical terms. By depriving claimants of the documents necessary to a common-law action, equitable decrees were able to ensure the retention by a recipient of an existing possession, and were often sufficient to give possession to a successful demandant, especially when supported by an injunction to the tenant requiring him to allow his rival peaceful possession and the cessation of litigation elsewhere. At other times, decrees simply observed that the demandant had failed to prove a valid claim, or noted that the tenant had established his title by charters and witnesses, the suit being dismissed *sine die*.

The position in Star Chamber was very similar. In Trinity term 1530, William Brundley of Wistaston in Cheshire filed a bill before More which asserted that his father had died seised of a freehold estate of twenty-four acres, the property by right descending to himself as son and heir.[8] He 'entered and was thereof seised' for fourteen years until forcibly ousted by Hamnet Cheynn and other 'riotous and misruled persons to the number of sixteen', servants to

7 C 1/590/38.
8 STAC 2/6/251–54, 25/18.

John Fulshurst, a claimant to the property. The intruders held themselves in possession by force, and began burning the plaintiff's timber. Brundley thus prayed a *subpoena* summoning Fulshurst and the rest into Star Chamber. From the start, More treated this suit as one of unquiet title, referring it to local commissioners to hear and end without official investigation of the supposed rioting. Such cases of 'riot' or 'forcible entry' were, in fact, equivalent to actions of trespass *quare clausum fregit* and actions on the statutes of forcible entry at common law. The fictitious entries, ousters and damage necessary to the mechanism for claiming land at law were translated into the bills of plaintiffs in Star Chamber, both to invite the court's attention and to elevate suits to the domain of royal jurisdiction and beyond the claims of local courts.[9] Again the chancellor would usually order that the respective titles of the parties be formally investigated, either at the centre or (as in Brundley's case) before local persons of status. Possession would likewise be settled by a decree in favour of the better claimant, and would be enforced under threat of further proceedings in Star Chamber for contempt.

Much of the litigation on real property in More's time (perhaps as much as two-thirds in Chancery) involved at some stage an enfeoffment to uses. The practice of executing family settlements by this means had become ubiquitous in the fifteenth century, the advantages being considerable. As Coke observed, 'there were two Inventors of Uses, Fear and Fraud; Fear in Times of Troubles and civil Wars to save their Inheritances from being forfeited; and Fraud to defeat due Debts, lawful Actions, Wards, Escheats, Mortmains, etc.'[10] A simple form was when a landowner enfeoffed a group of friends to his own 'use', and after his death to that of his heir upon whom a freehold estate was to be settled by reconveyance. The feoffor could thus conserve the heir's assets by avoiding the incidents of *primer seisin*, relief and wardship, despite some statutory reassertion of feudal rights in the reign of Henry VII.[11] Uses were, however, most often employed to execute the wishes of feoffors after their deaths, achieving in effect the devising of land by will which feudal law forbade. A settlor in the early sixteenth century would enfeoff his friends to his own use during his life, and thereafter 'to the use of the performance of his last will' as declared either

9 Guy, *The Cardinal's Court*, 53–5.
10 Quoted in E.W. Ives, 'The Genesis of the Statute of Uses', *English Historical Review*, vol. lxxxii (1967), 674. Cf. C. St German, *Doctor and Student*, ed. T.F.T. Plucknett and J.L. Barton (Selden Society, London, 1974), 222–5.
11 By 4 Hen. VII, c. 17, and 19 Hen. VII, c. 15.

then or subsequently.[12] Provision could be made for his widow or another before the ultimate beneficiary entered, and it was possible for a man who settled on himself with remainders over to leave a reversionary interest in his feoffees, their heirs and successors, obliging them to make final disposal of the land according to his expressed wishes. All this caused a good deal of confusion, but the real drawback was that the courts of common law only offered limited remedy against feoffees who defaulted on their agreements. Common law would protect the right of the feoffor or his heir to re-enter a property if such a condition had been declared at the time of the enfeoffment. But the interests of other beneficiaries enjoyed no legal sanction. It was the chancellor, following the example of the ecclesiastical courts after 1450, who began the slow but steady process by which other interests became guaranteed on the ground of conscience.[13]

Four examples of suits in Chancery under More (all, as it happened, involving uses) will illustrate the range of circumstances in which the chancellor protected interests in land. In the first case, More defended a clear title against unconscionable conduct on the part of the defendant. William Huddeswell had decided in 1524 that, should he die without direct issue, his property at Richmond in Yorkshire should pass to his kinsman, Edward Huddeswell.[14] He chose two feoffees, who stood seised to his use until his death, when they reconveyed the land to Edward. William's nephew, Christopher, then made a claim and took possession by force. Edward obtained a judgment in *novel disseisin* at the local assizes, but this was insufficient to quieten Christopher who held some deeds to the property. Edward asked to have these, but Christopher refused 'against all right and good conscience'. Edward accordingly filed a complaint before More in Chancery. Christopher answered that the feoffees were, in fact, seised to the use of William and his heirs, so that the use descended to him as nephew and heir. He had entered the land to take his lawful profits and was surprised by Edward's action at the assizes. As a sub-plot, his counsel Robert Chidley (Inner Temple) alleged, too, that this action had been corrupt, since Edward had retained all possible local lawyers to his side and had tampered with the jury. Chidley conceded that Edward had indeed

12 E.g. C1/686/7.
13 For fuller discussions of this complex subject, see S.F.C. Milsom, *Historical Foundations of the Common Law* (London, 1969), 169–88, and M.E. Avery, 'The History of the Equitable Jurisdiction of Chancery before 1460', *Bulletin of the Institute of Historical Research*, vol. xlii (1969), 129–44.
14 C1/642/21–3; CP 40/1045, *ro*. 104.

obtained seisin by deed of feoffment, but his enfeoffment was to the use of Christopher and his heirs. After hearing both sides and seeing the evidence, More decided in favour of Edward. On 28 October 1530, he ordered Christopher to be bound in a recognisance of 100 marks as a guarantee of Edward's peaceful possession.[15] Three days later his final decree confirmed this solution, requiring also that Christopher surrender his deeds of claim to Edward.

Other circumstances in which More was asked to protect interests in land arose out of the dishonesty of one or more feoffees to uses. Nicholas Phillip's bill complained that although four out of five feoffees to his use were willing to execute their estate to him, one John Lilley had refused against 'all right and conscience'.[16] Having neither 'ability nor power' to enter, and having no remedy at common law, the plaintiff begged More to compel Lilley to agree with his co-feoffees. No decree is extant in the case, but a writ of *subpoena* was issued, ordering the defendant's immediate appearance in Chancery to explain his alleged breach of trust.

Much Chancery litigation under More was caused by discontented heirs whose legal rights of succession to land by descent had been delayed or denied by the erection of uses. William and Joan Stone filed a bill claiming that John Stephen of Ardleigh in Essex had enfeoffed himself with others to his own use and the performance of his will.[17] Joan was the testator's daughter, and the will granted her half her father's land to herself and her heirs. The other beneficiary was her brother John, and it was he who was said to have seized possession of his father's deeds and evidences. John junior had next taken his sister's profits 'against all right and good conscience', and had disputed the boundaries of his land. The plaintiffs begged More to intervene, knowing neither the certainty of the documents they lacked nor even the names of the feoffees to Joan's use. Sir Thomas duly summoned the defendant by *subpoena* and investigated the case during 1530 and 1531. However, a final end was not reached until 11 July 1533, when Sir Thomas Audley decreed for the plaintiffs' peaceful possession of their half of the land, ordering the defendant to surrender the deeds wrongfully seized to them and to pay costs as taxed by the court.

The most demanding real property litigation which More faced in Chancery was that in which several interests were at stake. An interesting case involving the separate interests of a settlor, his feoffees, his heir and a claimant was that brought by Robert Nor-

15 C 244/173/37B.
16 C 1/663/35.
17 C 1/679/22–3.

wich (himself a Chancery barrister), Thomas Blake, William Bocking and John Warnes.[18] The background was that Warnes had enfeoffed himself and his co-plaintiffs to the use of himself and his heirs in respect of land at Swafield in Norfolk. The complaint was that muniments concerning the property had come into the possession of William Burwell, who detained them contrary to 'all right and conscience'. The reality was, in fact, that Burwell had brought an action of trespass on the statute 8 Hen. VI, c. 9 against Warnes and his tenants in Common Pleas, aiming to recover the land on the strength of the muniments. The parties had been deemed to be at issue in Common Pleas, a *venire facias* was returned, and Burwell was about to receive a favourable judgment. The feoffees therefore sought a *subpoena* against him, with an injunction ordering cessation of his action of trespass added, in order that their legal title to Warnes's land might be asserted. Both *subpoena* and injunction were granted by More, and Burwell appeared in Chancery to file his answer. His argument is no longer extant, but the reference to 8 Hen. VI, c. 9 suggests that he claimed a prior title, alleging that Warnes had disseised him by force and then declared an enfeoffment to uses to defraud him of his right. After scrutiny, this plea (if such it was) was found to be bad, and More decided that his line of approach should be the conscientious protection of the use, being encouraged in this view by written testimony on oath that Burwell had deprived Warnes of his profits by force.[19] Warnes himself, however, had died before the day of final hearing. More's decree (dated 22 November 1530) provided accordingly that his heir should succeed to the full enjoyment of the use. Burwell was to abandon his claim against the feoffees, handing all his documents to them, and was not to vex either them or the heir with lawsuits or invasions of quiet possession. He was also to pay costs and damages as assessed by the court to the feoffees, who were to transmit the money to Warnes's executors.[20]

Most litigants whose suits resulted from conflicting interests in land or involved uses addressed themselves to Chancery under More, that court being the established centre of equitable procedure in the reigns of Henry VII and VIII. Wolsey's policy had, however, attracted a growing number of property disputes into Star Chamber. The basis on which lawyers recommended one court or another to their clients remains obscure, but the records show that

18 C 1/548/32.
19 SP 1/34, fos. 439–43 (*LP* iv. 1349).
20 This decree, endorsed on the bill of complaint, is visible under ultra-violet light.

unusual complexity of claim, suspected chicanery or harassment, and genuine acts of violence by defendants numbered among the criteria employed by professionals when making the decision to proceed in Star Chamber.[21] A case which contained all these elements was that brought before More by Robert Eland, who complained in 1530 that Henry Savile and his servants 'in manner of war arrayed' had expelled him from his manor of Carlinghow in Yorkshire, contrary to law, justice and good conscience.[22] The plaintiff had attempted to recover possession by an action of forcible entry at common law, but found his opponent 'so cruel' and endowed with 'so great power' locally that no jury would find against him. When Eland was threatened that he would be 'beaten, maimed and slain' should further suit be made, he appealed to More for protection both for his person and his right to Carlinghow.

On the face of it, the case was a notorious instance of misconduct by an overmighty subject in his locality. Savile's denials that any violence, threats or maintenance had occurred were simply too perfect to be true. But his reasoned explanation that an unquiet title was at stake was quite accurate, and the parties joined issue on Eland's claim that he and his ancestors had enjoyed a freehold estate for 150 years in special entail by descent from Sir John and Eileen Eland and their heirs male. More's reaction to these pleadings and the suspected violence was to issue an injunction against Savile under penalty of £100, requiring him to restore quiet enjoyment to Eland without fail while the question of title was referred to two judges, Anthony Fitzherbert and William Shelley.[23] Such procedure was common in Star Chamber and Chancery: it restored the *status quo ante bellum*, and shifted the initiative in promoting the suit on to the defendant, who needed to prove a title superior to the plaintiff's in order to secure dissolution of the injunction. Superior proof seemed unlikely at first sight in Savile's case. The plaintiff showed his descent in male line from Robert Eland, second son of Sir John Eland (*ob.* 1350) by his third wife Eileen, as was required by his assertion of the special entail.[24] Against this his opponent could only claim descent at six generations distance from Sir John Savile, who had married Isabel, daughter of Thomas, second son of Sir John Eland senior by his first wife Alice. Nevertheless, the defendant pleaded a fine of 1372 by which Eileen and her second husband were

21 Not all the violence alleged in Star Chamber was fictitious by any means; see Guy, *The Cardinal's Court*, 18, 58–9.
22 STAC 2/14/45–6, 18/214, 19/130, 360.
23 Ellesmere MS. 2652, fo. 10.
24 Cf. the pedigree in C 142/45/24.

to hold the manors of Brighouse and Carlinghow from Sir John
Savile and Isabel, with the remainder to Thomas, Eileen's eldest son
and Robert Eland's brother, with the reversion to Sir John and
Isabel and Isabel's heirs.[25] Contrary to the terms of this alleged
settlement, Robert Eland (the plaintiff's ancestor) had succeeded his
brother Thomas (the remainderman) in defiance of the reversionary
interest due to Sir John Savile and Isabel (the defendant's ancestors).

No sooner had these facts come to light than prospective inter-
pleaders arrived upon the scene. William and Elizabeth Sandon (in
Elizabeth's right) and John Lindsey claimed that they themselves
had been co-seised in Carlinghow until riotously ousted by a combination of the present defendant and his opponent's brother.[26]
Both Carlinghow and Brighouse, their counsel said, had been the
subject of 'continual suits, claim and entry' for years. When the
Sandons and Lindsey had recovered possession at common law,
they were expulsed again, this time by Robert Eland himself.
Hearing now of his Star Chamber suit against Savile, they wished
to show title as co-heirs of John and Elizabeth Fulneby, Elizabeth
having been daughter and (in their submission) sole heir of Eland's
great-grandfather. They also sought a sequestration of Carlinghow
by More's order, with the profits to be paid to their use until Eland
was removed from possession and a final order taken in the matter
of their own quiet enjoyment. But these requests were not granted.
It was objected by Eland that the Sandons and Lindsey were already
at issue with him on a writ of entry *sur disseisin in le post* in Common
Pleas, and More believed that the outcome of that action would
settle the whole dispute between them.[27] His injunction for Eland's
possession was effective only against Savile for the duration of the
Star Chamber suit, and did not prejudice the rights of other
claimants. As to Savile himself, it was open to him to bring a new
action either at common law or in Star Chamber against whichever
of his rivals was successful in Common Pleas, though this does not
seem to have actually happened. His efforts against Eland in Star
Chamber meanwhile surceased without resolution of the conflicting claims, and the greater part of the time already spent by More
and the judges upon the dispute was wasted. This was perhaps a
pity. Short of a comprehensive reform of property law and con-
veyancing practice by which the basis of entitlement became
relieved of historical and genealogical uncertainties, the only way

25 C.T. Clay, 'The Family of Eland', *The Yorkshire Archaeological Journal*, vol.
    xxvii (1924), 240–8.
26 STAC 2/18/214.
27 A search for this action in the records of Common Pleas was unsuccessful.

for a chancellor to proceed was to resolve opposing claims as they arose. On the other hand, few chancellors other than Wolsey were actively seeking out work, and it was rare indeed at this date for a judge to see his role in the courts as extending beyond the requirements of the particular parties before him. The usefulness of Star Chamber in Eland's case had been to regulate Savile's tendency to violence by injunction, and More's ultimate relegation of the suit for self-solution at common law at least freed him from the accusations of officiousness often levelled at his predecessor.

Nevertheless, More actively pressed Star Chamber suits on real property to a conclusion when reason and justice demanded, which should at last refute the ancient myth that his appointment to office was Henry VIII's reaction to Wolsey's policy in the courts.[28] Had More, a common lawyer, been informed in October 1529 that his task was to calm supposed strife caused by Wolsey's ignorance of legal procedure, he must immediately have foreclosed on the Council's equitable meddling in substantive property issues. The trial of freehold titles in conciliar courts was contrary to several medieval statutes, but was justified on grounds of the 'policy and good rule' of the realm.[29] More agreed as lord chancellor that the statutory limitation was impossible to respect in the sixteenth century, as Morton and Wolsey had realized, if the Council was to maintain intact its traditional reputation for equitable proceedings. For instance, he gave his personal attention to a complex sequence of cases in Star Chamber and Chancery over the disputed estates in Lincolnshire and East Anglia of lord Willoughby de Eresby (*ob.* 1526). After the baron's death, his widow lady Mary had maintained unilaterally the right of her nine-year old daughter, Catherine, as heir general against that of her uncle, Sir Christopher Willoughby, as heir male, thereby obliging Sir Christopher to make claim to the whole inheritance as the best means to secure promptly the lands covenanted to him on his marriage to Elizabeth Tailboys in 1512.[30] More's reaction was to place those estates which could be identified as settled by the late baron in the possessión of the intended beneficiaries, while sequestrating the profits from the remaining properties pending a final resolution of the disputed titles by himself, the chief justices and the master of the wards, such resolution to be achieved after scrutiny of all relevant documents

---

28 See above, pp. 40–3.
29 The statutes included 5 Edw. III, c. 9; 25 Edw. III, St. 5, c. 4; 28 Edw. III, c. 3.
30 *The Complete Peerage,* rev. by G.H. White, xii, Pt. II (London, 1959), 673, 701–2.

obtainable by the equitable process of discovery.[31] The ensuing litigation mostly outlasted More's tenure of office. One portion, however, was ended with a Star Chamber decree of 18 February 1531 by which More shared a group of manors in Norfolk and Suffolk between lady Mary and Sir Christopher.[32] This decree was enforced by injunctions under penalty of £500 against both contestants, requiring them to ensure vacant possession of the lands awarded within ten days.[33]

Other property disputes over which More assumed control by Star Chamber order or decree included those between Sir Thomas Cornwall and George Zouche (heard on 6 December 1529),[34] John Bussy and Dr Marshall, rector of Scotton in Lincolnshire (1 February 1530),[35] Anthony Daubeney and Sir John Holford of Cheshire (3 February 1530),[36] and the abbot of Haughmond and the Higginses of Shropshire (11 July 1530).[37] In the first of these cases, More prefaced his order for sequestration with a short justification of Star Chamber's role in proprietal matters. The claims of the parties to the manors of Hoo and Aylesford in Kent had resulted in competing entries upon the lands:

> By reason whereof divers riots, unlawful assemblies and other misdemeanours have been committed, and be like eftsoons to ensue to the commotion and disturbance of the king's subjects and the breach of his peace in those parts unless remedy be provided.[38]

Here More repeated the essence of Wolsey's sentiment, expressed in August 1517, that men with rival titles to property must learn the 'new law' of Star Chamber, 'that they shall beware how from thenceforth they shall redress their matter with their hands'.[39] But like Wolsey, too, More was willing to pronounce Star Chamber decrees on proprietal issues exacerbated neither by violence nor other misdemeanour. On 15 February 1530, for instance, Gregory Curson was awarded quiet enjoyment of the manor of Knotting in Bedfordshire according to a lease made to him by Thomas lord

31 STAC 2/17/399, 18/182, 21/17, 22, 30; STAC 10/4, Pt. 2; C 1/589/38, 691/26, 689/32; C 54/400 (recognisance of 28 November 1531).
32 STAC 2/17/399.
33 *Ibid.*
34 STAC 2/18/330.
35 STAC 2/17/405; Ellesmere MS. 2652, fo. 8v.
36 STAC 2/12/150.
37 Ellesmere MS. 2659.
38 STAC 2/18/330.
39 SP 1/16, fo. 16v. (*LP* ii. App. 38).

Cobham, whether or not the attorney-general subsequently recovered the land against the lessor (as seemed likely).[40] The decree was 'for divers considerations', from which one presumes that More shared identical concern for the rights of *bona fide* lessees as was expressed in an act of the Reformation Parliament (21 Hen. VIII, c.15), though in circumstances not covered by that statute.[41]

The most difficult and controversial property litigation which came before More in Star Chamber was that which exposed embarrassing defects in the legal system. Perhaps the best example of this is the series of suits over an estate at Lillingstone Lovell in Oxfordshire, which began when John and Ellen Ward complained to Wolsey that Nicholas Wentworth had forcibly ousted them from their land without cause.[42] According to the complaint, one Richard Clare had enfeoffed Giles Pulton and others to his own use and that of his will, by which the feoffees in default of Clare's direct issue were to stand seised to the use of John and Ellen and Ellen's heirs in fee. Richard died without issue, and the Wards entered by licence of the feoffees, remaining in possession until wrongfully expulsed, as they asserted, by the defendant. As expected, Wentworth in answer claimed a better title to the land by bargain and sale made to him by Richard Clare. He denied that the plaintiffs were the beneficiaries of the settlement they had described, and traversed that Pulton and others were feoffees to their use. The parties were deemed to be at issue, and Wolsey referred the case to Chief Justice Ernley for examination and report. Since Wentworth could prove neither that Clare had been sole seised at the time of the supposed sale, nor that he himself had no prior notice of the erection of the use claimed by the plaintiffs, Wolsey decreed on 2 July 1519 that the Wards should resume possession until Clare's enfeoffment to uses had been disproved in Star Chamber.[43]

Naturally reluctant to return without obtaining better proofs, Wentworth began to make his own researches into the evidence. He suspected by 1528 that Thomas Poynour, his former steward, had dishonestly 'made and forged the said surmised feoffment' to Giles Pulton and others out of malice, and was counselled by William Whorwood (Middle Temple) to begin an action of forging of false

40 STAC 2/2/159–60.
41 On the act, see below p. 123.
42 The documents from which this story is reconstructed are STAC 2/19/239, 20/44–5, 88, 91, 128, 133, 139, 141, 24/48, 31/fragments; SP 1/183, fo. 17v. (*LP* xix. I. 19); SP 1/243, fo. 16 (*LP Add*. 1443). Some internal contradictions in the documents have had to be resolved as seemed most likely.
43 STAC 2/31/fragments.

deeds in Common Pleas.[44] The suspect was arrested and Wentworth presented his case. Poynour then pleaded craftily that the deed was good and not forged, and that since Wentworth had enjoyed no interest in the land at the time of the supposed forgery, he had no ground of action. The parties came to issue and the case was referred by *nisi prius* to the local assizes. Poynour there showed the jury a sealed indenture dated 1512 reciting a feoffment by Thomas Clare, Richard's father, to Pulton, Richard Clare and others in favour of himself and his heirs by descent, and the jury, relying on this evidence, gave a verdict in Poynour's favour. Now Wentworth saw that this indenture was itself authentic, but guessed that Thomas Clare's feoffment as recited in it was a fabrication. He also guessed that Poynour had suborned witnesses and tampered with the jury. However, there was nothing he could do to avoid the verdict, the original feoffment not itself being at issue between the parties and not discoverable. He did sue out a writ of attaint against the jurors, but later accepted the advice of the local J.P.s that this was a waste of time and money.

John and Ellen Ward died shortly after this, and Wentworth made another entry upon the land, believing Wolsey's former decree to have been dissolved by their deaths. At once Richard and Alice Budd filed a complaint before More in Star Chamber, claiming that the estate had descended to Alice as Ellen's daughter and heir, and that they were forcibly excluded by Wentworth's entry against right and good conscience.[45] Richard and Alice rested their title on Wolsey's decree, a claim which Wentworth traversed by arguing that it had given no inheritance to Ellen's heirs, nor was it binding beyond the time that he found the proof needed to invalidate Richard Clare's alleged enfeoffment to uses. Wentworth told More that it was 'openly published and known' in the country that Thomas Poynour was a common forger. But this assertion lacked adequate proof, and Sir Thomas referred the case to the chief justices for scrutiny in Easter term 1531.[46] A full examination of the rival claims followed, and it emerged that Thomas and Richard Clare's successive deeds of feoffment to Giles Pulton and others were indeed at base. The question was, were the deeds genuine? More hesitated. He did not like Wentworth's evidence, which was at best the 'common voice and fame' of Oxfordshire and Bucking-

44 A search for this action in the records of Common Pleas was unsuccessful.
45 STAC 2/20/44–5, 128, 133.
46 STAC 2/31/fragments.

hamshire.[47] In addition, Richard Clare's deed had been subscribed by Ernley in 1519, the presumption being that the signature constituted a judicial *imprimatur*.[48] More decided that on balance the facts did not justify the criticism he would incur by reviewing the validity of Poynour's common-law verdict. In this respect, he was more scrupulous than Wolsey might have been in similar circumstances. He pronounced a decree for quiet enjoyment of the land in favour of the Budds and their heirs, excusing himself from a 'final determination' of the title itself 'for lack of opportunity of time'.[49] However, he added that this decree could be reversed if Wentworth showed 'better matter' in Star Chamber on the alleged forgery, and ordered the disputed documents to be held meanwhile in Star Chamber as 'suspect deeds'.

For once, More's caution was detrimental to justice. Ten years later, Wentworth was able to lay before Audley the confessions of Poynour's father, mother and wife, and additional proof of the ex-steward's forgeries appeared by the depositions of twenty more witnesses.[50] The mother admitted that her son did 'forge the deed . . . whereby Ellen Ward won the land from Wentworth'. Having concocted the fake document, Poynour had hung it 'upon a rake's head in the smoke to cause it seem old'. He had also forged a will and went twice to consult genuine documents before getting the seal engraved. He had forged an acquittance, 'which he believed the better for such common law as he heard in the country'. Furthermore, he had indeed procured witnesses to commit perjury before the jury in Wentworth's action of forging of false deeds. In the end, then, the truth came out and remedy was provided: 'the visor', in Wentworth's phrase, was 'pulled off craft's face'. But his success took twenty-five years to achieve, and he had to persist to the point where 'honest vehemence' was mistaken for sheer wilfulness. In Wentworth's 'vehemence', we may perhaps detect a family characteristic inherited by his famous sons Peter and Paul, who as M.P.s began an active Parliamentary tradition which ran in almost unbroken sequence from the mid-Elizabethan period to the Rump Parliament. Nevertheless, Wentworth senior's case of Lillingstone Lovell revealed the extent to which forgery, perjury and chicanery could frustrate right and evade the law under the early Tudor

47 Such evidence might have been deemed sufficient to punish Poynour, but was wholly inadequate to bind a title to land.
48 STAC 2/31/fragments. Wentworth argued that the signature was added merely to ensure that the deed remained unaltered.
49 STAC 2/31/fragments, 19/239.
50 STAC 2/31/fragments; SP 1/183, fo. 17v.; SP 1/243, fo. 16.

system. It showed, too, the problems faced both by litigants and the courts when lands obtained by fraudulent title devolved or descended to unsuspecting parties. Wentworth could obtain little enough help from the courts in his pursuit of justice, and More himself came none too well out of the story. His interpretation of his role as successor to Wolsey made him shirk antagonising the critics of equitable procedure, and he ducked the issue raised by Wentworth's accusation. The basic problem, however, remained the defectiveness of the existing system: what was needed most in England was a public investigatory and prosecutional function to combat all types of crime at local level, a function allocated to J.P.s by the Marian and Elizabethan statutes. Stiff measures against such sophisticated offences as forgery, perjury and fraudulent conveyances were also an urgent requirement.[51] It was thus a pity that next to nothing could be achieved in these respects prior to 1563 and 1585,[52] owing to the conservative attitude of common lawyers in the House of Commons.[53] The lamentable truth was that sixteenth-century professionals had ultimate interests only in the continuing success of their own private practices.[54] The wider furtherance of public justice would long rate a low priority in English legal history.

51 Cf. G.R. Elton, *Reform and Renewal* (Cambridge, 1973), 150–7.
52 The years of 5 Eliz. I, cc. 9, 14; and 27 Eliz. I, c. 4.
53 E.g. Elton, *Reform and Renewal*, 155–6, concerning Cromwell's project which became 32 Hen. VIII, c. 9.
54 For instance, practitioners also tended to exploit the poor relations between the courts for selfish ends, a tactic most effective in sensitive property suits. Reason and justice demanded co-operation not conflict between equitable courts and those of common law, but even those lawyers working otherwise towards this goal in government would assert the ascendancy of ancient courts and procedures in Chancery and Star Chamber when the tactic offered them a temporary professional advantage. As Wolsey's heir, More's desire not to stir up professional unrest by his work in the courts was perhaps exceptional, but the same issue continued to vex all chancellors down to Nicholas Bacon.

4

MORE'S WORK IN THE COURTS: COMMERCIAL SUITS

AFTER More's real property work as lord chancellor, the largest single category of business with which he was confronted in the courts was the commercial and mercantile litigation brought into Chancery, commercial suits being defined as including any case in which a pecuniary transaction was the principal issue at base.[1] Three hundred and sixty-three suits filed in Chancery under More concerned merchant debts, equitable debt/detinue, bonds or recognisances, all of which came from plaintiffs anxious to obtain relief which the chancellor alone could provide. These commercial suits amounted in practice to a heavier load in relation to More's other legal duties than might appear from simple statistics.[2] This was because a fair proportion of the real property and other suits in Chancery never actually reached the lord chancellor himself, being either withdrawn by their promoters at an early stage or compromised out of court with the help of the masters and clerks.[3] But the commercial litigation in Chancery was rarely abridged prior to its perusal by the bench,[4] and it relied heavily, too, on procedures of *certiorari*[5] and *corpus cum causa*[6] restraining actions in other courts, methods over which it was More's policy to exercise stringent personal control whenever possible.[7] A rough projection is that the ratio between real property and commercial suits involving More himself was in the region of 7:4, although the evidence is too

---

1 In the latter half of the fifteenth century, mercantile and commercial litigation had predominated over real property suits. For example, between 1480 and 1483 some 60% of the litigation in Chancery concerned equitable debt/detinue, merchant debts or involved aliens. N. Pronay, 'The Chancellor, the Chancery, and the Council at the end of the fifteenth century', in *British Government and Administration*, ed. H. Hearder and H.R. Loyn (Cardiff, 1974), 92.
2 The figures for litigation in Chancery under More were given on p. 50.
3 This is clear from the endorsements, or lack of them, on plaintiffs' bills of complaint, the usual place for procedural and decretal record in Chancery at this date.
4 As the endorsements on bills show.
5 *Certiorari*: a writ granted to remove proceedings from an inferior court.
6 *Corpus cum causa*: a writ to secure the physical production in court of a person in custody together with the record of his case.
7 See below, pp. 89–92.

defective to give such a calculation more than tentative emphasis.[8]

More's commercial work is best discussed in terms of the remedies which litigants appealed to him to supply. Broadly speaking, five forms of relief were most in demand: the discharge of debt under deed entered into by way of fraud, usury or other moral impediment; intervention against an action at law by a creditor upon an uncancelled bond in respect of a debt in fact wholly or partly repaid; intervention in favour of the representative of an absent alien harassed by his principal's creditors; the examination of imperfectly fulfilled parol agreements and bargains with a view to obtaining either specific performance, or the apportionment of blame with compensation and damages; and the physical production of a plaintiff held prisoner in gaol together with the record of his case, in order to secure his immediate release on bail[9] with subsequent trial of the case in Chancery. These remedies were sought either individually or in combination, the last of them appearing jointly with either of the first two when it was a disputed bond or obligation that had led to the plaintiff's committal to gaol.

Examples will again best illustrate the circumstances in which More was petitioned to supply these forms of relief. A wide variety of acts of covin and exploitation was presented by plaintiffs seeking, first, the discharge of debt under deed, to which the chancellor responded on the ground of conscience. As such, this was an area of work which placed heavy demands upon More's powers of analysis and judgment. Not only was the cancellation or moderation of men's bonds a controversial matter — for who would pay either debt or rent should obligations become easily dischargeable?[10] The chancellor had also to ascertain the elements of moral impediment in the original transaction from its own intrinsic nature, the evil conscience of the defendant not being triable by direct evidence. As in later law, the intention to dishonesty was subordinated to the fact: moral impediment had to be proved from the attendant circumstances, and could not be presumed.[11] Another important limitation at this date was that the chancellor was not yet able to relieve

---

8 I estimate that More was personally involved in around 1,000 of the 2,356 suits filed in Chancery during his tenure (42.4%), and that some 440 were real property suits and some 250 were commercial suits. But although informed by endorsements and the files, this projection is unprovable.

9 The word 'bail' here is technically a misnomer. Plaintiffs were set at liberty upon providing 'sufficient security' for their reappearance in court later. In modern parlance, however, this is bail, and the word is used for convenience.

10 Cf. 'Replication', in *Doctor and Student*, ed. W. Muchall (London, 1815), 3–7.

11 W.J. Jones, *The Elizabethan Court of Chancery* (Oxford, 1967), 423.

plaintiffs from the consequences of their own folly, inexperience or carelessness:[12] folly had no remedy in conscience, since it was not the plaintiff's position which was under critical review but the defendant's moral turpitude.[13]

If, however, folly was itself no reason for redress, it was agreed that the exploitation of youthful inexperience, perhaps by professional confidence tricksters, tended to be more 'unconscionable' than fraud perpetrated upon mature persons in the normal course of their affairs, and it can be no coincidence that a high proportion of the plaintiffs who sought substantial or total discharge from their legal obligations by bill in Chancery claimed to be minors. A plea of nonage undoubtedly bolstered up many suits which would otherwise have been dismissed by the court on sight, and the validity of the claim was probably central to many suits in which fraud or usury was averred, as was also the case in later practice.[14]

Thomas Heton complained in Michaelmas term 1529 that Robert Farmer, a London leatherseller, had craftily enticed him by 'fair words' into two fraudulent and usurious bargains for credit.[15] Heton had been 'minded to have some money to apparel himself against Easter', and was obliged like other young men about town to make 'chevisance' to obtain it — i.e. he had to make an illicit bargain with a usurer.[16] Prior to 1546 when an act limiting interest to ten per cent in effect legalized the practice,[17] usury was unlawful at common law and by statute, with the result that backstreet moneylenders ran profitable businesses, though the risks were high. Farmer, whom the plaintiff now described as 'a common seducer of young men to bring them to their undoing', 'sold' him first some worsteads valued at £20, on the moneylender's assurance that his associate, inevitably named Smith, would buy them back later in the day for £15 or £16 cash. However, it turned out that Smith would only offer £12. Heton refused to resell at that price, but was given no choice: Farmer had not delivered the cloths and simply gave his victim £12, claiming to have resold direct to Smith himself. Heton next bought a ring for £4, Farmer promising to buy it back at any time within a year for £3 6s 8d. But again the purchase

12 Cf. *ibid.*, 444.
13 Cf. C. St German, *Doctor and Student,* ed. T.F.T. Plucknett and J.L. Barton (Selden Society: London, 1974), 185.
14 Jones, 434–5.
15 C 1/642/55–62; C 244/172/49B, formerly C 47/119/86/10.
16 Literally, *venir à chef de quelque chose*; in this sense, an unlawful bargain or contract with indirect gain in point of usury.
17 37 Hen. VIII, c. 9.

turned out to be worth only £1 6s 8d. For these transactions, Heton
was bound by statute staple in £30 to pay £24, upon which repayment he defaulted. Farmer then sued for £30 in the Mayor's Court
of London, and Heton was committed to Ludgate prison. As a
plaintiff to More, the latter now sought the moderation of his debt
from £30 to the 'true duty' (the actual cash value of the goods
purchased), which he assessed at £13 6s 8d. Pleading that the bargains were fraudulent, usurious and contrary to an act of 1495 (11
Hen. VII, c. 8), he sought release from £16 13s 4d of the £30, adding
that the king was entitled to the moiety of Farmer's advances by
way of forfeiture.

As presented by John Skewys (Lincoln's Inn), Heton's suit is
instructive. Too old to plead nonage, the plaintiff buttressed his case
by portraying his opponent as a professional confidence man. He
emphasized that the bargains were contrary to a penal statute,
insinuating thereby that the case was of public importance, and he
attempted effect by exaggerating the extent of Farmer's unconscionable gain, since £6 of the 'lost' £16 13s 4d was not usury but the
penalty for Heton's default on his obligation. Such techniques
confirm that subtle presentation was indeed necessary to a suit's
success in this difficult area, although it is also a truism that the
Chancery bench had familiarized itself over the years with all the
arts of the lawyers' craft. More's reaction to Skewys's pleading was
to authorize a *corpus cum causa* to the mayor and sheriffs (on 1
December 1529), ordering both Heton and the record of Farmer's
case against him to be brought into Chancery on Saturday next (4
December).[18] The case was on that day added to the Chancery list,
and four sureties were found the following Monday to assure
Heton's daily appearance in court until such time as judgment was
pronounced, thereby permitting his release on bail. What More's
final decision was is unknown. As so often happens, we simply hear
that he bound Heton on the 6th to pay Farmer 'all such sums of
money' as he should later adjudge.[19] But this does tell us something.
By accepting the suit for judgment, More showed that he could
contemplate releasing part of Heton's debt, otherwise the case
would have been left pending in the Mayor's Court. The later
arguments of counsel reveal, too, that the thrust of the plaintiff's
case came to focus on the extent to which Heton had been 'seduced'
by an older man of evil experience, an approach to which added
momentum was given by a motion from Skewys that Farmer had

18 C 244/172/49B.
19 *Ibid.*

committed 'wilful perjury' in his written answer.[20] This illustrates the rule that it was the state of the defendant's conscience, irrespective of the plaintiff's naivety or folly, which dictated the chancellor's eventual response.

As More well knew, the rule had particular significance for suits in which the plaintiff's motivation was itself suspect. For instance, a young servant of Catherine of Aragon, Richard Fisher, complained in mid-November 1530 that he had become bound by obligation in £15 to John Chandler, a London draper, though under twenty-one at the time.[21] Subsequent conflict between the parties as to the nature of their bargain had resulted in Chandler's starting an action of debt in the Mayor's Court. Fisher had been arrested and the matter was at issue on the question of nonage. Fisher accordingly begged More to direct a *corpus cum causa* to the mayor and sheriffs, commanding them to bring his person and the record of his case into Chancery, with a *subpoena* to Chandler ordering his simultaneous appearance. Both requests were granted: issued on Monday 21 November 1530, the writs summoned the parties for the following Wednesday, when the plaintiff and his sureties were bound to his further appearance the following Tuesday.[22] The case was again adjourned for future judgment, but an important detail had already emerged. Fisher had become bound to the draper 'at his father's request', his father being a draper too. The suspicion is inescapable that his plea of nonage in reality disguised an attempt by Fisher senior to avoid the penalty for defaulting on a commercial transaction in accordance with a scheme pre-arranged with his son. Juveniles were not always as innocent as they pretended, and it has been rightly observed that 'it is sometimes difficult to determine who was fooling whom'.[23] Strict emphasis on the state of the defendant's conscience at least reduced the possibility that the chancellor, by offering relief, might actually abet acts of moral dishonesty by young plaintiffs and their confederates.

Not all plaintiffs were, of course, young or inexperienced, and some were mere practitioners of that ancient litigants' art — the judicial try-on. Such a try-on was brought to More in Hilary term 1531 by Richard Blachus, rector of Ewhurst in Surrey, who 'confessed' that he had gained presentation to his benefice 'contrary to God's law and all Christian laws' by giving the patron, a past prior of Merton, an obligation in £20 to pay £3 a year to him and his

20 C 1/642/56.
21 C 1/633/4; C 244/173/47, formerly C 47/119/87/33.
22 C 244/173/47.
23 Jones, 434.

successors.[24] Blachus later denied this bargain, being 'grounded upon simony', but the present prior had commenced an action of debt for forfeiture of the £20. The rector thus petitioned for the dissolution of the obligation by decree in Chancery, and a *subpoena* was issued against the prior, ordering his appearance on 10 May 1531 to justify himself in the matter. This he did, and More's evaluation was published two days later by decree. The prior had shown an exemplification of a Common Pleas' judgment made in Edward IV's reign, which proved that a customary annuity of £3 was owed to him from the profits of the rectory. This fully vindicated his conduct and defeated the plaintiff, who perhaps hoped that a new prior would remain ignorant of the common law record. More thus dismissed the case from court.[25]

Whereas fraud, usury or other moral impediment was necessarily stressed by plaintiffs seeking the amelioration of bonds into which they had become ensnared, those suitors seeking the second category of relief, namely direct intervention against actions at law in respect of debts wholly or partly repaid, took their stand on the argument of undue advantage. The theory in this type of case was that the creditor manipulated his superior legal position to gain excess profit, which was unconscionable and liable to redress by *certiorari* or *subpoena*.[26] The most common circumstance was that in which a debtor by obligation paid his debt on his day, but failed to take either a written acquittance or the return of the obligation which bound him. Notwithstanding his payment, the creditor then brought an action of debt on the obligation, and the debtor could have no remedy at common law. By law, the debtor was required to pay the money again. Alternatively a debt might have been partially repaid, but being unsatisfied in full on the appointed day, the creditor had sued at law for repayment of the whole amount as if nothing was paid, perhaps with a penalty for default added. A later Chancery exponent explained the approach of the various courts to bonds and other instruments.

> The question at law is whether it were sealed and delivered or the like, and that being found by verdict, judgment followeth that the whole sum shall be paid; whereas the Chancery examineth not the sealing and delivery of the bond, but what was at first due, what hath been paid since, what doth remain unpaid; and

24 C 1/610/16.
25 *Ibid.* (endorsement).
26 Jones, 424–6.

accordingly doth order the party to take but what is justly due unto him, with his damages and costs, and will not suffer him to take £800 because he had a judgment for so much, where it was proved that all was paid but £20.[27]

In offering this remedy, the chancellor did no more than correct the undue advantage which the creditor enjoyed because of the way the law had developed, the ground of his intervention being to cleanse the creditor's conscience. Nevertheless, the matter was aired in discussion between the Sergeant at the laws of England and St German. The former upheld the 'good common law' rule that matter in writing must be answered by 'matter in writing or by matter of record'.[28] St German argued, interestingly, not that the legal rule was too rigorous or inequitable; the common law judges knew rather, he said, that payment of a debt was itself sufficient discharge of obligation in reason and conscience. But different courts used different customs. What was law for some was not necessarily binding in others.[29] St German aimed to reconcile the reasonableness both of common law and Chancery in such cases, as indeed was necessary. It would not do to criticize the rule about obligations under seal, which had anyway started life as a rule of proof before it was elevated into a proposition of substantive law; nor could the chancellor contemplate taking any point of reference other than that of the creditor's unconscionable conduct in bringing his action of debt.[30] Chancery would otherwise have found itself remedying the negligence and folly of thousands of debtors, and its relief would quickly have become a perverted factor on which men might hope to count in advance when making bargains.[31] No man could be allowed to be unlucky to more than a very moderate extent.

Plaintiffs seeking relief within this second commercial category stated their cases with unusual brevity. Anne Ardern complained that she had years ago paid £5 to Thomas King, a London blacksmith, in satisfaction of her obligation, but King, notwithstanding repayment, had begun an action of debt against her in the Sheriff's Court to get the money a second time.[32] Anne had been arrested and

27 Quoted by Jones, 446.
28 'Replication', 5.
29 'A Little Treatise Concerning Writs of Subpoena', in *Doctor and Student*, ed. W. Muchall (London, 1815), 20–4. D.E.C. Yale, 'St German's *Little Treatise Concerning Writs of Subpoena*', *The Irish Jurist*, vol. x (1975), 329–30.
30 Cf. St German, *Doctor and Student*, ed. Plucknett and Barton, 77–9.
31 Jones, 445–6.
32 C 1/602/39.

imprisoned, and was about to be condemned to pay again 'contrary to right and good conscience'. She was a 'poor widow', and the creditor drew advantage from the fact that, having 'none acquittance to discharge the same obligation', she had nothing to plead in common law. She thus begged More to direct a *corpus cum causa* to the sheriffs of London, issuing a *subpoena* summons also to King, prior to hearing her matter in Chancery. The woman's bill was presented to More at Chelsea, and he at once granted her requests, commanding the case to be brought on within a few days.[33]

An equally simple case concerning a debt partly paid was brought by William Hood of Shrewsbury in Trinity term 1530.[34] The plaintiff had owed John Bailey and Richard Waters twenty marks by obligation for twelve colts he had purchased. Only £5 of the debt remained unpaid at the time of default, but the creditors were suing Hood for the full twenty marks in the Town Court at Shrewsbury. Having the advantage because the debtor 'hath none acquittance proving the payment of the said £8 6s 8d', and because they themselves were much 'friended and of such power and acquaintance' in the town, the creditors were about to have judgment pronounced in their favour. Hood, professing himself willing to pay his outstanding debt, accordingly sought a *certiorari* to the bailiffs of Shrewsbury, ordering them to stop his case and send it into Chancery, 'there to remain until your lordship shall further examine the premisses and order it according to right and good conscience'. The writ was duly issued, but with an unknown result.[35]

A third suit was that also sent to More at Chelsea by Richard Boys, a London skinner.[36] He had assisted Arthur Gravele, a grocer, by becoming bound with him in a joint obligation in £8 to William Hancocks, a vintner. Gravele had then defaulted and an action of debt was begun by the creditor. A new agreement was next devised by which Gravele paid the vintner £4 cash and delivered him a second obligation in £4, guaranteeing four future quarterly payments of 20s. The vintner was to surrender on his part the original obligation in £8 to Boys. But the last was not done, despite frequent requests by the plaintiff, and Hancocks next started a second action of debt on the same obligation in the Sheriff's Court of London. Boys was gaoled and about to be condemned in £8 'contrary to all right and good conscience', having 'none acquittance nor other means by plea to discharge the same obligation'. He

33 *Ibid.* (endorsement).
34 C 1/644/22; C 244/173/17, formerly C 47/128/5/27.
35 C 244/173/17.
36 C 1/610/8.

therefore besought the chancellor to have him brought quickly into Chancery by *corpus cum causa*, with a *subpoena* requiring the vintner's simultaneous appearance and answer. Again these requests were granted by More's personal order, but with an undiscoverable final result.[37]

The third variety of commercial relief offered by More in Chancery was the simplest and least debated, constituting intervention in favour of the representative of an absent alien harassed by his principal's creditors. Such a case came before More on 3 August 1530, after the end of Trinity term, and he resolved to hear it without delay in conformity with the proverb that 'Chancery is always open'.[38] Edward Lightmaker had been deputed by his father Harry, a Steelyard merchant, to manage his London affairs while he was abroad. John Lacy, a City grocer, Ralph and John Gifford, clothmen, and James Dupré, a foreign merchant, had then claimed to be his father's creditors, and Edward could not disprove this, having no access to the relevant ledgers and accounts. The outstanding total amounted to £125, though Edward believed that most of this money was not yet due or payable in Flanders. Meanwhile, he had been imprisoned in the Counter for six weeks, and would remain there unless awarded a *corpus cum causa*. Before the case was brought on, the plaintiff (filing a new bill) modified his plea, bolstering his story of misfortune with an additional claim of nonage.[39] More was impressed, and Edward was discharged from the Counter. The hearing of the four creditors was then adjourned until Michaelmas term, by which time Harry Lightmaker's return should have made further litigation unnecessary.[40]

The fourth area of Chancery's commercial work was that in which the chancellor examined imperfectly fulfilled agreements and bargains, usually parol agreements, with a view to ordering either specific performance or apportioning the defendant's culpability with compensation and damages. Just as the assessment of fraud and usury in the first category of business demanded keen analysis and judgment on More's part, so this was the area which involved him in fine problems of mercantile practice, pecuniary calculation and moral evaluation. At a time when one faulty transaction could ruin a trader whose suppliers (or purchasers) let him down — goods were often marked up and resold in the sixteenth century before they were physically received — there was no shor-

---

37 *Ibid.* (endorsement).
38 C 1/653/44–45; C 244/173/25, formerly C 47/119/86/35.
39 C 1/653/45.
40 C 244/173/25.

tage of suitors seeking relief, notably specific performance which could not be obtained at common law.[41] Much commercial litigation arose from the fluctuating cost of raw materials in the sixteenth century. Purchasers wanted specific performance of bargains to supply goods of known quality at stated prices, and the chancellor was able to decree a *restitutio in integrum* in place of the inadequate damages obtainable at common law. Thomas More dealt, too, with unresolved suits arising from the dislocation of European trade by Wolsey's wars. An ex-diplomat skilled in international law and mercantile practice, he was the ideal man to undertake these complex duties, and his thoroughness and fairness were apparent. As in all areas, however, the ground of his intervention was that of conscience: Chancery's jurisdiction existed to cleanse the consciences of wrongdoers rather than to safeguard the particular interests of the wronged, although the two might overlap.[42] Yet wrongdoing need not have been done deliberately or maliciously to require conscientious correction. The result was that accident and misadventure were again treated as akin in effect to moral dishonesty, sharp practice and fraud, as was inherent in the theory of undue advantage.[43]

Even so, the courts had also to face up to economic reality. Edward Collin, a Devon cordwainer from South Molton, complained to More in Easter term 1531 that he had made a verbal agreement with Baldwin Turner, a tanner, for the regular supply of good-quality leather.[44] The price of leather had then risen by 34%, and Turner would no longer adhere to the agreed terms. Although Collin went to the tanner's shop to choose his leather and mark it, the tanner sent him other, inferior stock. This situation was common enough, arising whenever a supplier could no longer hold out against clients prepared to pay higher prices. But the evidence of bad faith on the defendant's part was somewhat threadbare. The bargain was old and imprecise as to duration. It turned out that the plaintiff had bought good leather for a decade at the agreed prices, and it was his own legal action which smelt most of sharp practice. More's prudent reaction was to refer the case to the 'mediation of neighbours' for self-solution. When this did not work, the suit was added to the backlog of cases left for Audley to sort out in 1532 and 1533.[45]

41 Jones, 426–7.
42 Jones, 424.
43 *Ibid.*
44 C 1/621/7–9.
45 C 1/621/7 (endorsement).

Within a jungle of conflicting interests, the suit on which attention must focus is that of *Vaughan* v. *Parnell*.[46] Noted on its own merits as a rare battle of wits and wills, the case later rose to fame by the charge of corruption levelled against More by the defeated defendant, and by the latter's selection as a member of the jury at the ex-chancellor's trial in July 1535.[47] After inconclusive litigation in the Mayor's Court of London and in Chancery under Wolsey, the plaintiffs, Geoffrey and Richard Vaughan, had united in a new bill to More against John Parnell,[48] a City draper and informer,[49] for his breach of agreement in failing to complete a bargain in cloths and woad. On 12 February 1528, Parnell had sold Richard 1,000 kerseys at 24s 4d each, total value £1,216,[50] with delivery to be made by Whitsunday following (31 May). Richard was to pay £840 in cash and the rest in woad, and duly began to discharge this obligation by sending Parnell 303 bales of Toulouse woad. According to Richard, this was worth 15s a hundredweight, making a cash value of £420. While awaiting delivery of his 1,000 kerseys, Richard resold them, together with 165 others which were part of 300 previously bought off Parnell at 24s 6d each. Richard's sale was to foreign merchants, and he contracted to deliver the goods at the next mart at Antwerp. The deal, he said, was to his 'great lucre' — namely, £200 profit.

Richard next went abroad, leaving his master, Thomas Cromwell, to receive the 1,000 cloths and ship them to Antwerp.[51] But Parnell failed to deliver, despite Cromwell's repeated offers to pay the outstanding £840 in cash. Cromwell offered the vendor a month's respite to collect the cloths together, but had no success. As a result, Richard was arrested in Antwerp for non-performance of his bargain with the foreign merchants, which put him to trouble and expense on top of his lost profit. Returning to London, he sought re-delivery of his 303 bales of woad, but Parnell, being 'a great usurer and a man of evil conscience', refused pointblank. This, the plaintiffs said, deprived them of working capital, and they

---

46 C 1/587/15, 41–2, 685/39–41.
47 Roper, 61–3; Harpsfield, 343–4, 349–50. There can be no real doubt that the same Parnell was the man on the jury. A busy litigant and informer, Parnell regularly turns up in the records of the central courts, described alternatively as 'citizen' or 'draper'.
48 C 1/685/39.
49 For Parnell as an informer, CP 40/1063, *ro.* 791; for an action of debt brought by Parnell against Richard Vaughan, CP 40/1063, *ro.* 17; for a cross-suit by Parnell in respect of Geoffrey Vaughan's suit to Wolsey, KB 27/1082, *ro.* 37.
50 The figure should be £1,216, although £1,260 is in some of the documents.
51 On the relationship between Vaughan and Cromwell, G.R. Elton, *Reform and Renewal* (Cambridge, 1973), 38–46.

appealed to More both for re-delivery of the woad, and for compensation for their lost profit and the damage to their business caused by Parnell's bad faith.

More ordered a *subpoena* to be served on Parnell, and litigation began between the parties. But the defendant was obstructive, and was rebuked by More on 9 February 1530: he was to answer the charges directly, without prevarication.[52] Parnell was getting an advantage by way of delay, and More ruled accordingly that the Vaughans should have the benefit of testimony taken in their earlier suits to Wolsey. This was in spite of a technical bar that they were not both parties to the suits in question, having brought separate actions prior to 1529.[53] Parnell did not like this at all, because it hastened the case considerably and saved his opponents the cost of bringing witnesses into court a second time. More then called in expert valuers and assessors to assist him.[54] These specialists could do little in terms of ending the dispute, but could clear up points of commercial detail. For instance, Parnell held that Richard's Toulouse woad was of poor quality, worth 8s not 15s a hundredweight, reducing its total value to £224. Experts could put a true price on such commodities, provided they could get access to the defendant's warehouse.

After much argument, the case came to judgment on 20 January 1531, only fifteen months after it had begun. More decreed that all existing agreements between the parties should be null and void, that Parnell should pay the Vaughans £128 for the woad plus £50 damages for their lost profit, and that the Vaughans should pay him £20.[55] Why the last provision was included is obscure; the decree has been heavily mutilated and the bare facts alone can be made out.[56] No doubt the case was even more complex than it appeared, and the Vaughans were plainly at fault in some undiscovered way. This was evidently true as far as the Toulouse woad was concerned, since an award of £128 valued it at 4s 6d a hundredweight — a far cry from 15s. More had discounted the Vaughans' estimated profit, too, by three-quarters. As such, his decree must appear to represent the height of fairness. Alas Parnell, who in his role of informer was used to making money out of his litigation, did not agree, bearing More a grudge which he repaid at the time of the Nun of Kent affair by telling the Boleyns that the decree had been corrupt. More, he

52 C 1/685/39 (endorsement).
53 *Ibid.*
54 *Ibid.*
55 *Ibid.*
56 The decree is best read under ultra-violet light.

alleged, had accepted a 'great gilt Cup' as a bribe.[57] This was quite
untrue: the cup had been brought to Chelsea by Geoffrey Vaughan's wife *after* the decree, and More had anyway sent it back.
Malicious accusations of this type normally went unheeded, especially when made by disappointed litigants as infamous at Westminster as Parnell. However, in its desire to get the edge on More in
January and February 1534, the Council took up the matter; and,
although Sir Thomas might joke (as ever), the peril of his situation
was indicated by the fact that the earl of Wiltshire — as Roper says
the 'preferrer of this suit' — could or would not understand the
relevance of More's statement that the cup arrived after, not before,
the decree for the Vaughans. As to Parnell's selection as a member
of the fateful jury,[58] Henry VIII, pursuing More to the death in
1535, had required Cromwell upon his allegiance to secure a guilty
verdict, and we must recognize this additional proof of the
thoroughness of Wolsey's ex-counsellor.

The fifth category of relief in Chancery under More has already
been observed as an integral element in the suits brought by Heton,
Fisher, Ardern, Boys and Lightmaker. By awarding a *corpus cum
causa* against an inferior jurisdiction, the chancellor could order the
physical production in Chancery of a plaintiff held prisoner in gaol,
together with the record of his case, and allow his immediate release
on bail with subsequent trial of his case in Chancery.[59] This secured
the plaintiff's discharge from the hazards of a Tudor prison, while
transferring his case to a superior court of record offering the
equitable remedies which might enable him to defeat his opponent.
Writs of *corpus cum causa* (or *certiorari* when the plaintiff was not held
in gaol) thus enabled Chancery to offer what was, in effect, a
jurisdiction appellate from the plethora of local and private courts
which formed the bottom three-quarters of the existing judicial
framework — a valuable function both in terms of good justice,
centralization and the uniformity of practice so badly lacking in the
English system as a whole. Another benefit was that the service
operated outside the usual law terms, facilitating release from
prison during the long summer months when writs of *habeas corpus*
could not be returned into King's Bench.[60]

As would be expected, procedure by *corpus cum causa* was most

57 Roper, 61–3.
58 The list of jurors is printed in Harpsfield, 349–50.
59 For an analysis of the process at an earlier period, see P.M. Barnes, 'The
Chancery Corpus Cum Causa File, 10–11 Edward IV', in *Medieval Legal
Records edited in memory of C.A.F. Meekings* (London, 1978).
60 C 244/170–75, *passim*.

often adopted in cases of imprisonment for debt, and writs authorized by More were addressed to the Mayor's and Sheriff's Courts in London, the Mayor's Courts in Exeter, Oxford, Cambridge, Bristol, Northampton, Norwich and Kingston-upon-Thames, the Town Courts at Ipswich and Shrewsbury, and the manorial courts of Wolsey and Queen Catherine.[61] When the plaintiff was brought into Chancery, he would present the gist of his case and offer security for his appearance in court at future hearings or whenever required by the chancellor. He and his sureties would be examined, and bound (if approved) in penal recognisances guaranteeing whatever arrangements the lord chancellor devised. The plaintiff was then set at liberty upon the conditions laid down in the recognisance by which he was bound over. Should he fail in a subsequent appearance in court, the penalties of the various recognisances would be deemed forfeit and leviable by action of debt at Chancery's common-law side, and the plaintiff would be returned to gaol pending hearing of his case.

Procedure by *corpus cum causa* could not, however, be invoked unless the plaintiff's bill alleged sufficient matter cognizable by Chancery's equitable jurisdiction.[62] More would refuse to issue a writ unless good reason for relief was presented, and would remit cases back to the inferior jurisdiction on seeing that he had awarded a writ on inadequate grounds. For example, John à More (no relation to Sir Thomas) was granted a *corpus cum causa* on 27 May 1530 which secured his release from Exeter gaol.[63] He was brought before the chancellor on 1 July following,[64] but his plea was ruled insufficient and he was sent back to the Mayor's Court.[65] All the same, à More had some sort of argument against his opponents, since Sir Thomas bound one of them over to co-operate with the mayor and his officials so that the case could be ended within a month.[66] This was unusually creative: unable under the rules to offer relief in Chancery itself, Sir Thomas assisted a litigant by hastening proceedings in a local court, using his prerogative power as lord chancellor.

---

61 C 244/172–73, *passim*.
62 This discussion is concerned with the equity side of Chancery alone, the 'Latin' or common-law side being insignificant by More's time, and (in terms of its issue of writs *habeas corpus cum causa*) restricted to cases of privilege.
63 C 244/173/14, formerly C 47/96/8/1.
64 The delay until 1 July was unusual; it would be fascinating to know whether the politics of Henry VIII's letter to the pope were responsible. See below, pp. 129–30.
65 C 244/173/20B.
66 *Ibid*.

On other occasions, More exercised caution and refused to release prisoners on bail until security had been offered for the satisfaction of their creditors. Richard Hunt complained in Michaelmas term 1530 that he had been imprisoned by the sheriffs of London in the Counter, that they had no lawful reason for holding him, and that they would not allow his release on sureties.[67] He was granted a *corpus cum causa* on 31 October and brought into Chancery on 5 November, when it appeared by the sheriffs' return that he had in fact been taken for a debt of £4.[68] More ruled that bail would not be allowed unless money or plate was deposited into court sufficient to satisfy the creditor should he prove his case. Hunt handed over 'a cross of gold with stones', a jewel which was returned to him when he later defeated the creditor at a Chancery hearing.[69]

More's caution within this last leading category of Chancery's business was one of his personal hallmarks. This was appropriate in view of the appellate nature of the area's function, but especially because the Sergeant at the laws of England had attacked the chancellor's own judicial conscience, which he held to be arbitrary and uncertain. The argument that a chancellor might interrupt due legal process upon conjecture, or make a decision without proof which turned out to be ill-founded, was a weighty one which applied even more to *corpus cum causa* and other interim hearings than it did to final decrees — the former being prior to the full testimony of witnesses, the main method of Chancery proof. It was a criticism not entirely refuted by St German's assurance that chancellors were 'bound in conscience' either to amend erroneous decisions or make restitution out of their own pockets.[70] More accordingly applied rigorously the traditional Chancery procedures of surety, security and scrutiny, cultivating in the process a distinctive policy of self-involvement, scrupulousness and discretion. In the last resort, his great contribution was exactly this: to rejuvenate the ancient theory that judges had a personal duty in conscience to see right done by all whose business was entertained in the courts they directed.

67 C 1/639/11.
68 C 244/173/38, formerly C 47/119/87/19.
69 *Ibid.*
70 '*A Little Treatise Concerning Writs of Subpoena*', 36–40.

5

MORE'S POLICY AS CHANCELLOR

HAVING considered More's daily work as lord chancellor, we may attempt a reconstruction of his policy as Henry VIII's chief magistrate. We have seen that the succession to Wolsey, the need for law reform, the debate over Wolsey's 'rival' courts of equitable procedure, and the resultant tension and division within the legal profession itself were four elements integral to the crisis of 1529. Where did More stand on these issues, and what did he do about them? Answers to these questions have to stem from existing historical orthodoxy; for unlike More's work in the courts, a subject studiously ignored by his biographers, his overall policy as a judge has received much literary treatment. Significant studies are those by William Roper (More's son-in-law),[1] Nicholas Harpsfield,[2] the unidentified Ro: Ba:,[3] Thomas Stapleton,[4] lord Campbell,[5] R.W. Chambers[6] and Miss E.M.G. Routh.[7] As a *point d'appui*, the arguments of these writers must be evaluated, happily a simple task since all accounts subsequent to Roper's are, in fact, derivative. Successive scholars did little more than gloss the relevant passages of his *Lyfe of Sir Thomas Moore,* compiled in 1557. The aspects of More's policy which have been treated are his integrity, his devotion to duty and respect for due legal process.

On More's integrity, the biographers recite first Roper's account of the tongue-in-cheek complaint made to Sir Thomas by William Daunce, another son-in-law.[8] Under Wolsey, the story began, many members of the chancellor's household, even doorkeepers, had got great gain. But Daunce could not profit by assisting friends

1 W. Roper, *The Lyfe of Sir Thomas Moore, knighte,* ed. E.V. Hitchcock (Early English Text Society, London, 1935).

2 N. Harpsfield, *The Life and Death of Sir Thomas Moore, knight, sometymes Lord High Chancellor of England,* ed. E.V. Hitchcock (Early English Text Society, London, 1932).

3 Ro: Ba:, *The Lyfe of Syr Thomas More, sometymes Lord Chancellor of England,* ed. E.V. Hitchcock and P.E.Hallett (Early English Text Society, London, 1950).

4 T. Stapleton, *The Life and Illustrious Martyrdom of Sir Thomas More,* ed. P.E. Hallett (London, 1928).

5 John lord Campbell, 'Life of Sir Thomas More', in *Lives of the Lord Chancellors and Keepers of the Great Seal of England* (London, 1856), ii. 1–77.

6 R.W. Chambers, *Thomas More* (London, 1935).

7 E.M.G. Routh, *Sir Thomas More and His Friends* (New York, 1963).

8 Roper, 40–2, 115–17.

to obtain audience of More, who had made himself fully accessible to all suitors. The slur on Wolsey was mean, since Daunce well knew that the cardinal had made a real effort to make impartial justice available to all, although it is true that his servants had devised an unauthorized fee system for introducing litigants into his apartments. In reply, though, More congratulated Daunce for his scrupulousness, but mentioned other ways in which a judge could help his intimates: by showing favour by word or letter; by appointing a biased commission to hear and end a suit; or by urging an arbitrament upon parties with unequal claims, thus ensuring partial success for the one who would have lost in a judgment.[9] Far from revealing a proclivity to mild favouritism which so scandalized Campbell, More's response was, in fact, a witty rebuke to Daunce for his lack of subtlety. Why get caught up in anything as unsophisticated as bribery? More's wit carried the greater irony in that the practices he cited were rampant among J.P.s in the sixteenth century, and were not unknown in the central courts at Westminster. In any event, his reported conclusion was uncompromising:

> Howbeit, this one thing, son, I assure thee on my faith, that if the parties will at my hands call for justice, then, all were it my father stood on the one side, and the Devil on the other, his cause being good, the Devil should have right.[10]

Roper gave further instance of More's attitude by reference to a 'flat decree' he made in Chancery against Giles Heron, a third son-in-law, when the latter presumed too much of his favour and 'would by him in no wise be persuaded to agree to any indifferent order'.[11] The theme is then developed in terms of More's refusal of presents from litigants.[12] The taking of bribes by judges and officers was a heinous offence, punishable in a judge by attainder or impeachment in Parliament. The custom was, nevertheless, for litigants to offer New Year gifts of plate or trinkets, game, wine or cheeses to lawyers, arbitrators, court officials, and even magistrates. A related practice was that by which successful litigants were expected to treat members of juries and inquests to expensive dinners after verdicts had been given. In many instances, the distinction between gratitude, anticipated or otherwise, and intended corruption was marginal. The test employed by Star Chamber, the court which specialized in cases of judicial perversion, was whether

9 Roper, 41–2.
10 Roper, 42.
11 Roper, 42–3.
12 Roper, 61–4.

or not the gift was made or promised prior to the judgment or
verdict. On this basis, only the third occasion on which More was
proffered a gift represented an outright threat to his integrity. He
was wise to refuse both the Vaughan cup and the £40 in gold which
Mistress Crocker attempted to present to him at New Year. However, these gifts postdated the litigation which prompted them: to
have accepted would have been rash, but not corrupt. The affair of
the Gresham Cup was quite different.[13] One Master Gresham,
probably John Gresham, a prominent citizen and mercer of London, had sent 'a fair gilt cup' to Sir Thomas for New Year, even
though his suit in Chancery was still awaiting judgment.[14] More
could not possibly have taken the cup; to accept was bribery. Yet
the situation offered scope for a merry jest of the type More could
never resist. Gresham's cup was aesthetically pleasing, but its legal
worth was its monetary value alone. What ploy was better than to
send back another cup which was of inferior craftsmanship but
greater monetary value? By the exchange Sir Thomas won the
better cup, rebuked ·the donor and preserved his integrity. Alas
these subtleties were not widely appreciated, and we may agree
with Lord Justice Russell that More's conduct was strikingly
injudicious.[15] His political rivals in Council were watching the
chancellor like hawks, suspecting his participation in the organised
opposition within and without Parliament to Henry VIII's divorce.
As Roper and Chambers commented, 'it was well for More that he
kept his hands clean'; at the time of his projected attainder in
Parliament, 'it would, without doubt . . . have been deeply laid to
his charge, and of the king's highness most favourably accepted'.[16]

On the subject of More's devotion to duty, the biographers again
follow Roper. Not only did Sir Thomas undertake his formal,
morning sittings in Chancery and Star Chamber, he would also sit
'in his open hall' at Chelsea 'every afternoon': 'to the intent that, if
any persons had any suit unto him, they might the more boldly
come to his presence'.[17] More's rule was to peruse all bills of
complaint himself, confirming by his signed endorsement whether
or not they alleged 'matter sufficient worthy a *subpoena*'.[18] According to Stapleton and Ro: Ba:, his diligence on the Chancery bench
was such that more suits were dispatched 'in shorter space than

13 Roper, 63–4.
14 The case was perhaps C 1/635/8.
15 Chambers, 270–1.
16 Chambers, 269; Roper, 61.
17 Roper, 43.
18 *Ibid.*

were wont to be in many years before or since'.[19] Although suits had been depending there for many years, More cleared away the backlog and kept pace with current litigation. One morning, the chancellor sat 'when there was no man or matter to be heard. This he caused to be enrolled in the public acts of that court'.[20] The incident, says Miss Routh, launched the popular rhyme:

> When More some time had Chancellor been
>   No more suits did remain
> The like will never more be seen
>   Till More be there again.[21]

We shall return to these various claims.

Roper is again the source for biographical discussion of More's respect for due legal process. Roper praised first Sir Thomas's great reverence for his father, the King's Bench judge. When passing through Westminster Hall into the court of Chancery, the chancellor used to seek his father's blessing in a scene of touching deference.[22] If, too, they met at law readings in Lincoln's Inn, Sir Thomas 'would offer in argument the pre-eminence to his father, though he, for his office sake, would refuse to take it'.[23] The meat of Roper's case is, however, the episode concerning injunctions. More, we are told, soon encountered what Chambers called 'the friction which had arisen between common lawyers and the Chancellor by reason of Wolsey's injunctions'.[24] But injunctions were essential to the smooth operation of Chancery and Star Chamber, and More resolved to reconcile legal opinion to their use. He accordingly instructed John Croke, one of the Six Clerks of Chancery, to prepare a docquet 'containing the whole number and causes of all such Injunctions as either in his time had already passed, or at that present depended in any of the king's Courts at Westminster before him'.[25]

> Which done, he invited all the Judges to dine with him in the council chamber at Westminster: where, after dinner, when he had broken with them what complaints he had heard of his Injunctions, and moreover showed them both the number and causes of every one of them, in order, so plainly that, upon full debating of those matters, they were all enforced to confess that

19 Ro: Ba:, 69.
20 *Ibid.*
21 Routh, 175.
22 Roper, 43.
23 *Ibid.*
24 Chambers, 272.
25 Roper, 44.

they, in like case, could have done no other wise themselves. Then offered he this unto them: that if the Justices of every court (unto whom the reformation of the rigour of the law, by reason of their office, most especially appertained) would, upon reasonable considerations, by their own discretions (as they were, as he thought, in conscience bound) mitigate and reform the rigour of the law themselves, there should from thenceforth by him no more Injunctions be granted. Whereunto when they refused to condescend, then said he unto them: 'Forasmuch as yourselves, my lords, drive me to that necessity for awarding out Injunctions to relieve the people's injury, you cannot hereafter any more justly blame me.'[26]

Roper's narrative is convincing in this area. More's public humility before his father, although somewhat ostentatious, would have appealed to his sense of occasion. His handling of the dispute over injunctions also rings true. We know that he was careful to secure the approval of the judges for those of his Star Chamber decisions which were potentially controversial, and he took the trouble to cancel those outdated injunctions of Wolsey's still on the file after his accession to the chancellorship.[27] The preparation by Croke of a docquet containing More's injunctions would have been something easily achieved by reference to the relevant *contrabrevia* held in Chancery;[28] the postprandial debating of queries in the Exchequer Chamber or Star Chamber was likewise a traditional judges' proceeding. These episodes must have occurred almost exactly as described by Roper, and More's argument on injunctions has clear implications for our perception of his role as successor to Wolsey.

But while the literary account of More's policy as chancellor has undoubted standing, it is historically inadequate. Its approach is too subjective, being exclusively concerned with edifying aspects of More's tenure which ennoble his character rather than assess his actual contribution, and a number of myths await imminent debunking. Roper's purpose was to write a sixteenth-century saint's life, and his method (and those of his imitators) was primarily polemical. The aim was to assemble a strategic mixture of evidence and anecdote to refute propaganda unfavourable to More's character put out by Henry VIII after 1535, and to 'prove'

26 Roper, 44–5.
27 C 263/3/9A, 11, 13A. The relevant suits are C 1/566/11, 510/22, 484/11. The first injunction settled a possession *pendent lite*; the other two restrained actions in Common Pleas.
28 Now class C 263 at the P.R.O., from which most files are alas incomplete.

that Sir Thomas was not guilty of the lax, high-handed practices attributed *ex post facto* to the disgraced Thomas Wolsey. Henrician propaganda had naturally vilified More's alleged treachery at home and abroad to justify his and Fisher's executions. As to the fallen Wolsey, More had signed the Parliamentary articles which had accused the minister (unfairly) of hindering justice by long delays in ending suits, by interruption of due legal process and ignorance of ancient procedures, and by lack of respect for good common law and its judges.[29] It was necessary for the early biographers to stress that More truly deserved his European reputation as a righteous judge; even, too, to demonstrate that he did not sin where he had condemned sin, and that he had avoided the errors of his 'unlearned' predecessor. In short, the biographers have emphasized issues of controversy alone, not least the issues of the 1550s when Roper was writing, and have seized on More's legal career as a source of supply to demonstrate his integrity and conscientiousness.

Discussion of More's policy must consider instead his response to the crisis of 1529. Most striking is the fact that Wolsey's initiatives were fully maintained by his common-law successor. The goal of both men was the better provision of impartial and efficient justice, and they agreed that this meant developing an equitable forum based on Chancery and Star Chamber. Wolsey began the development as an end in itself, but it is arguable that the growth of Chancery's business under More was a direct consequence of his selection in 1529. The prospect of a common-law chancellor handing down equitable decrees was seen by litigants as giving doctrinal validation to the 'rival' courts, thus boosting public confidence in their proceedings. Even so, there was more at stake than the provision of new and better courts. The wider importance of More's continued support for Chancery and Star Chamber was, rather, that his decision impelled the common lawyers on the long course by which their own justice would one day be reformed. This was because he was himself a common lawyer: whereas Wolsey had run his courts as an extension of his personality, More appeared to use them as an official blueprint for the future of English royal justice.

In the event, More's hands quickly became tied by the greater crisis of Henry VIII's divorce. The common law and its institutions were deprived of the considered review which should have come their way, and the basic deficiencies in the existing legal system became obscured amid the statutory programme of the 1530s. The last point should be better known. The legislative measures accom-

29 *LP* iv. 6075; see below, p. 125.

panying the Henrician Reformation which allegedly rejuvenated the realm as Thomas Cromwell's contribution to reform of the Tudor common weal did nothing to alleviate the most significant and troubling legal problems of the sixteenth and seventeenth centuries. These were that men of property lived in daily fear that they might be compelled to ride to Westminster and defend themselves expensively against unjust charges filed by false accusers. Landowners 'could not sleep at night for fear that technical flaws in their titles might jeopardize their entire inheritances'. Litigants who had obtained a verdict in one court could never know when they would be sucked back into a whirlpool of retaliatory lawsuits in other courts. Honest subjects could rarely go to law in the happy knowledge that eirenic ideals of justice would prevail, owing to the high prevalence of perjury, subornation, embracery and other corrupt practices in the central as well as the local courts of justice. In the 1620s, Sir Edward Coke would conveniently, if arbitrarily, delineate four main groups of interrelated abuses: straightforward human malevolence, corrupt practices in the courts at Westminster, problems concerning the relationships between central and local jurisdictions, and abuses which undermined legal certainty and security of property and caused 'multiplicity' of suits.[30] But the Tudor and Stuart mind tended to attribute these grievances to the greed of individuals, rather than to fundamental flaws in the commonwealth's structure, with the result that ministers, councillors and practising jurists continued to believe until the 1870s that remedy lay in traditional methods of moral persuasion and Parliamentary tinkering. In the Tudor period, successive lord chancellors were simply left to work things out empirically. If Thomas More ever dreamed of imposing Utopian reform on English justice, he was thus born three centuries too soon.

As a practical alternative, More began instead to rationalize and extend the partnership between Chancery and common law which had distinguished Wolsey's term of office. But before long he ran into trouble, perhaps inevitably, with the professional lawyers, the point of conflict being (as Roper knew) his use of injunctions restraining litigation at common law. The intermittent controversy between the chancellor and the judges over injunctions had not ended with Wolsey's disgrace: not surprisingly, since More's practice in awarding them was identical to that of his predecessor. Both men issued injunctions in Chancery and Star Chamber at similar

---

30 S.D. White, *Sir Edward Coke and the Grievances of the Commonwealth* (Manchester, 1979), 50–85.

rates within the categories long customary. Not all injunctions, however, were equally controversial. Of the forms at More's disposal, those most resented by common lawyers, especially the judges and sergeants of Common Pleas whose work was often affected by them, were classified as common injunctions. These were directed against litigants and their lawyers, ordering them under penalties ranging up to £200 to abandon proceedings on the specified matter in another court. Yet More did not inhibit himself from awarding common injunctions in the interests of justice. As we have seen, his daily work frequently required their employment to stop inequitable litigation at law on title to land or debt under deed.[31] For instance, one Friday afternoon (19 August 1530) Sir Thomas granted a litigant four such injunctions from his house in Chelsea, staying actions in Common Pleas about an estate at Walden in Essex.[32] Well indeed, too, might these examples have been resented, since this was one of the rare occasions when More was fooled. The party's case in Chancery turned out to be a try-on, and his opponents were freed to resume their actions in Common Pleas on 5 November following.[33]

At the famous meeting in Star Chamber, More showed the judges each of his injunctions, arguing the grounds on which it had been awarded and convincing them that, in his place, they would have reached a similar decision on the evidence before them. This part of the debate culminated in a triumph for More. But not so the latter part. More's final proposition was that injunctions would be unnecessary if the common-law judges would 'upon reasonable considerations . . . mitigate and reform the rigour of the law themselves'.[34] Such mitigation, he suggested, required the grant of no new powers. The authority of the judges to interpret legal rules equitably was already inherent in their offices, being a responsibility owed to their own judicial consciences. In fact, there were areas of practice in which common-law judges already accepted that they had a discretion ungoverned by law, and Chief Justice Fineux had commonly said that 'who so taketh from a justice the order of his discretion taketh surely from him more than half his office'.[35] More believed firmly that judges were to follow their consciences, vis-

---

31 E.g. C 263/3/14–18; C 1/671/27 (endorsement). Cf. W.J. Jones, *The Elizabethan Court of Chancery* (Oxford, 1967), 462–73. See above, chs. 3–4.
32 C 263/3/14–17.
33 *Ibid.*
34 Roper, 45.
35 *The Reports of Sir John Spelman,* ed. J.H. Baker, vol. ii (Selden Society: London, 1978), 41.

ualizing a marriage between equity and common law. He aimed to
harmonize the one with the other, ensuring that the reforming ideal
took shape as a vital member within a living organism, rather than
as a surgical knife to be wielded at uneven periods and with uncertain consequences. He knew from his days in private practice, as did
St German, that rigid adherence to common-law rules by the judges
would ultimately discredit the legal system. Judges who were slaves
to the rules often gave judgment against both truth and their own
knowledge — something that could not happen in the equitable
forum, where the chancellor could 'never be bound to give judgment against his own knowledge nor against that that appeareth
evidently to stand against conscience'.[36]

More thus appealed to conscience. As St German had explained
in *Doctor and Student,* 'laws covet to be ruled by equity'.[37]

> And for the plainer declaration what equity is, thou shalt under-
> stand that, since the deeds and acts of men for which laws be
> ordained happen in divers manners infinitely, it is not possible to
> make any general rule of the law but that it shall fail in some case.
> And therefore makers of laws take heed to such things as may
> often come, and not to every particular case, for they could not
> though they would. And therefore to follow the words of the law
> were in some case both against Justice and the commonwealth:
> wherefore in some cases it is good and even necessary to leave the
> words of the law, and to follow that [which] reason and Justice
> requireth; and to that intent equity is ordained, that is to say *to
> temper and mitigate the rigour of the law.*[38]

Equity must follow the law.[39] More and St German agreed on this,
although they agreed on little else in the 1530s. This was the idea
behind More's belief that the judges must model their own judicial
consciences upon the chancellor's. Sir Thomas saw that English
jurisprudence would derive more benefit from the equitable
development of common law, with a corresponding reduction of
Chancery and Star Chamber doctrine into a species of law, than
from an unregulated trend towards rivalry between competing
jurisdictions.[40] However, the judges resolutely refused to accept

36 D.E.C. Yale, 'St German's *Little Treatise Concerning Writs of Subpoena*', *The Irish
  Jurist,* vol. x (1975), 331–2, esp. n. 31.
37 *Doctor and Student,* ed. T.F.T. Plucknett and J.L. Barton (Selden Society,
  London, 1974), 95.
38 *Ibid.,* 97 (my italics).
39 *Ibid.,* 99.
40 *The Reports of Sir John Spelman,* vol. ii. 43.

these arguments. Only then did More, in frustration and anger, gibe: 'Forasmuch as yourselves, my lords, drive me to that necessity for awarding out Injunctions to relieve the people's injury, you cannot hereafter any more justly blame me'.[41] On returning to Chelsea, he confided to Roper a sentiment which echoes down the centuries:

> I perceive, son, why they like not so to do, for they see that they may by the verdict of the Jury cast off all quarrels from themselves upon them, which they account their chief defence.[42]

More's plea for reform went unheard. His subsequent policy as lord chancellor was accordingly that of streamlining the system he had inherited from Wolsey, and the problems he tackled were practical in nature. One of Wolsey's failings had been possession of an almost naive belief that if private parties, especially those at issue over property growing from unquiet title, were given exhaustive and meticulous 'justice' and 'equity', good order could be preserved. In common with many of his contemporaries, Wolsey did not gauge rightly the persistence of what Professor Barnes dubbed 'the new-style litigant, bent less upon asserting a right than not forgoing an advantage, less on winning than not losing in court, and always questing for another court in which to continue battle with his adversaries'.[43] Wolsey believed his courts of Chancery and Star Chamber to be ultimate tribunals of impartial justice; even before his disgrace, however, each court was *en route* to becoming 'largely just another forum for the assiduous litigant'. Wolsey's facility of free access to Chancery and Star Chamber was a necessary (perhaps unfortunate) consequence of his promulgation of an enforcement policy. Thomas More resolved not to restrict access to the courts, but he attempted the beginnings of a policy of strict scrutiny of bills prior to the issue of writs of *subpoena* or *corpus cum causa*.[44] Wolsey had sometimes tended to be a plaintiffs' judge as well as a litigants' chancellor, and the indiscriminate issue of writs was an abuse which showed little sympathy for the interests of defendants.[45] It also meant that frivolous suitors and time-wasters took up a quite

41 Roper, 45.
42 *Ibid.*
43 T.G. Barnes, 'Star Chamber and the Sophistication of the Criminal Law', *Criminal Law Review* (1977), 316–26.
44 E.g. C 1/602/39, 40; 605/17, 33; 610/8; 611/32; 620/4; 621/35; 622/37; 639/14; 642/1, 16; 644/23; 653/8; 671/27; 683/41; 685/10, 22.
45 J.A. Guy, *The Cardinal's Court: the Impact of Thomas Wolsey in Star Chamber* (Harvester, Hassocks, 1977), 81.

disproportionate amount of the courts' time, in turn exacerbating the delays which preceded the hearing of other cases. Sir Thomas's policy was thus considerably more responsible than Wolsey's. Roper claimed that More subjected 'every' bill of complaint to personal scrutiny, approving the sufficiency of the plaintiff's case by his signed endorsement, but this is a wild exaggeration.[46] Only a tenth of the extant fiats for process carry More's approbatory scrawl. The comprehensive policy outlined by Roper may have been desirable (and it no doubt appealed to Roper's own contemporaries in the 1550s), but it was impracticable: the pressure of work in the courts, Parliament and the Council was too great for a Tudor lord chancellor to vet all bills himself. More's idea was, nevertheless, a step in the right direction — a determined, if short-lived effort to revert to the stricter practices of the fifteenth century. However, he did not insist that plaintiffs should offer pledges to prosecute, as under the old system;[47] nor did he require bills of complaint in Star Chamber to be signed by counsel, as later became standard practice.[48]

A useful concession allowed by More to defendants in Chancery was his willingness to consider whether or not they should be allowed *ab initio* to appear by attorney rather than in person. This obviously could apply only to Chancery; a Star Chamber defendant was required not only to be sworn to the truth of his answer but was examined in court upon the plaintiff's interrogatories, and personal appearance was essential. In Star Chamber, criminal allegations were usually at stake, despite the essentially civil issues at base. In Chancery, however, the bulk of sixteenth-century litigation was civil. As More well knew, appearances by attorney were allowed in civil actions in the common-law courts, and he plainly wished to introduce this rule into Chancery procedure in appropriate cases. He noted *per se vel per atturnatum* in his own hand on the dorse of many bills of complaint authorizing issue of process against defendants.[49] The concession was a helpful innovation; one which was retained by More's successors and which, by enabling defendants to

---

46 Roper, 43. For writs issued on bills unscrutinized by More, examples are: C 1/633/1, 2, 4, 12, 17, 25, 29; C 1/638/1, 9, 13, 15, 28; C 1/639/11; C 1/642/5, 14, 17, 21, 26, 27, 31, 32, 34, 36, 37, 40; C 1/653/1, 16, 21, 27, 32, 33, 37–9, 42–6, 49; C 1/685/5, 6, 8, 11.

47 E.g. C 1/601/48, 51, 52, 54, 55; C 1/602/39, 40; C 1/605/5, 8, 11; C 1/639/14; C 1/642/1; C 1/662/6.

48 Guy, *The Cardinal's Court*, 80–1.

49 E.g. C 1/602/46; C 1/612/36, 37, 39–41; C 1/614/32; C 1/615/26, 42, 43; C 1/618/23, 28; C 1/619/32; C 1/622/37; C 1/639/10, 14; C 1/682/36; C 1/685/2.

swear to their answers out of court, saved many people the time, trouble and expense of travel to London.

More's finest improvement on Wolsey's scheme came perhaps in his tough enforcement policy.[50] In Star Chamber, the Council had already gone some way towards combating the failure of defeated parties to obey its decrees in civil suits, but the problem of bad losers still remained in 1529. Its solution was clearly crucial. While retaining penal recognisances as the basic method of enforcement both in Chancery and Star Chamber,[51] More also commanded obedience to his proprietal decrees by issuing injunctions.[52] Penalties for non-compliance were set as high as £500, leviable on the party's lands and goods, and double damages might be imposed.[53] When faced by direct disobedience, More invoked the ancient procedure by which writs of assistance were addressed to the sheriff, ordering him to execute a decree forcibly and arrest any person offering resistance pending his appearance before the Council.[54] Contemners of More's decrees were gaoled automatically when apprehended, and Sir Thomas was also the first lord chancellor to prescribe that contempts committed in Chancery were punishable summarily in Star Chamber. This was the reality behind Roper's garbled story of his 'flat decree' in Chancery against Giles Heron, when the latter presumed too much.[55] More refused to proceed further with Heron's suit, and bound him in 1,000 marks (£666) to his appearance in Star Chamber, when he was to suffer such order as seemed expedient. The alternative was to submit to the lieutenant of the Tower, to remain 'true prisoner' during the king's pleasure.[56] These terms as set out by More were unusually stiff: a flagrant contempt must have been committed by Heron. More's strict attitude likewise gave substance to the concept of finality in equitable decrees. Wolsey had often been tentative, sometimes even irresolute, hoping that parties would agree to settle their differences in a spirit of fair compromise. Sir Thomas, in contrast, favoured the severity of common-law theory of the 'final' end, an approach which was attractive to plaintiffs seeking restraint of obstructive defendants.

50 Cf. Guy, *The Cardinal's Court*, 134–5.
51 E.g. C 54/400, m. 26; C 244/173/5B, 8D, 20B, 28B, 37B; STAC 2/2/160.
52 STAC 2/12/65, 17/399, 17/403, 18/330, 19/178; STAC 10/4, Pt. 2; B.L. Harleian MS. 2143, fo. 70; Ellesmere MS. 2659.
53 STAC 2/18/332, 19/178; Lansdowne 639, fo. 22.
54 STAC 2/17/405, 19/178; STAC 10/4, Pt. 2; Ellesmere MS, 2757.
55 Roper, 42–3.
56 C 54/400 (entry for 18 December 1531).

As expected, More applied the full range of his abilities and sense of duty to his work as lord chancellor. The records confirm Roper's claim that he made himself available to litigants at Chelsea in the afternoons, as well as in court in the mornings. It is clear, too, that he immersed himself in legal minutiae as much as time allowed.[57] His Chelsea activities included the binding of Star Chamber defendants to good behaviour, and bailing them pending fine before the Council, the issue of writs of *subpoena* and *corpus cum causa*, and the making of orders and injunctions.[58] The evidence does not permit us to confirm that More sat at home awaiting suitors 'every afternoon', as Roper asserted — one has to be sceptical in these matters — but we cannot doubt that he made unusual efforts to be accessible. The stories of Stapleton and Ro: Ba: must, however, be laid to rest. It is possible that More worked harder and faster at determining suits in Chancery than his predecessors or successors; this statement cannot be tested without better sources. But the claims that More cleared away suits which had stood unresolved for many years, kept abreast of current litigation, and left no backlog on his resignation are myths. It is certain that much of Chancery's business under More, and a good deal of that which had accumulated under Wolsey, was not concluded when Audley succeeded to the great seal — the records establish this beyond doubt.[59] Similarly, More did hear suits which were twenty years old, but there is not the slightest evidence to suggest that he was any more successful in ending them than his predecessors.[60] The longevity of much civil litigation in Chancery and Star Chamber was not caused by the dilatoriness of the bench, but by the intractability of the parties — their stubbornness and refusal to settle. Without the co-operation of both sides to a suit, legal proceedings could rarely be curtailed by the courts.[61] As to the inference that More sat one day in Chancery 'when there was no man or matter to be heard',[62] this (if it happened at all) could only have been a freak of timetabling. Nor could More have caused anything to be 'enrolled' in the public *acta* of the Chancery court: the story is anachronistic, since the initiation of decree and order rolls was a reform implemented at the time of Sir

57 E.g. C 1/609/15 (endorsement).
58 E.g. C 1/639/26; STAC 2/18/330; C 244/173/33; C 263/3/14–17.
59 E.g. C 1/602/21; 606/31–3; 610/2; 621/10; 633/13–16; 644/32; 671/1; 682/10; 685/2, 25.
60 STAC 2/15/296–300; 26/122, 417; 29/fragments; C 244/172/48B.
61 Guy, *The Cardinal's Court,* 97–105.
62 Ro: Ba:, 69.

Thomas Wriothesley's elevation to the chancellorship.[63]

Discussion of the legal component of More's public career is here completed, and the remainder of this book is concerned with more exciting, purely political issues. Yet it must never be forgotten that Sir Thomas More was not only meant to be a lawyer, he was that above all else. It was as a judge, not as a politician that his reputation stands highest. This was not least as successor to Wolsey, though More may himself have doubted such an assessment. As a prisoner in the Tower, he could see the futility of it all: most men lived not for justice but for greed and 'worldly fantasies'.[64] They sought after 'outward goods' for their 'worldly wealth', and 'riches, honour and renown, offices and rooms of authority' for their 'worldly pleasure'.[65] As he had written while still in private practice, society was in reality nothing better than a conspiracy of rich men (especially lawyers), pursuing their own interests against the rest.[66] Society was surely a farce: when the men of influence desired it, the laws could be rendered no better than cobwebs 'in which the little nits and flies stick still and hang fast, but the great humble bees break them and fly quite through'.[67] This, however, was More the philosopher not the practical jurist. It was also a view which was unduly pessimistic. Wolsey's concept of impartial justice, irrespective of social status, had begun to penetrate the English legal system at all levels, even though the final accomplishment of his goal was not achieved until the late nineteenth century. More had maintained and strengthened the machinery of Chancery and Star Chamber, he had continued to grapple with the socio-legal problems of the period, and he was prepared to innovate where necessary in the pursuit of speedier or more effective justice. He had added practical realism to Wolsey's idealism, and so ensured a smooth transition from the age of clerical to that of common-law chancellors. For thirty-one months in office, it was a magisterial performance.

63 C 78/1–3. The rolls were begun in 1543–44, when the opportunity was taken to put some earlier decrees on record, e.g. C 78/2/56.
64 *The Complete Works of St Thomas More*, vol. xii, *A Dialogue of Comfort against Tribulation*, ed. L.L. Martz and F. Manley (New Haven, 1976), Bk. III, ch. 12.
65 *Ibid.*, Bk. III, ch. 13.
66 *The Complete Works of St Thomas More*, vol. iv, *Utopia*, ed. E. Surtz and J.H. Hexter (New Haven, 1965), 241.
67 *A Dialogue of Comfort*, Bk. III, ch. 12.

PART THREE

MORE AND POLITICS

6

THE SITUATION OF 1529

SIR THOMAS MORE was appointed lord chancellor in the wake of the aristocratic *coup* which displaced Wolsey as Henry VIII's chief minister. He was selected after lengthy discussion between king and Council at Greenwich, being a compromise candidate between the duke of Suffolk and Cuthbert Tunstall.[1] Unlike Wolsey in 1515, More possessed no power-base at the time of his elevation. He had played no part in the manoeuvres by which Wolsey was unseated. On the contrary, his political status was no greater than that of a councillor, former royal secretary, diplomat, ex-Speaker of the House of Commons, and one whose voice had authority in the City of London. More was talented but hardly powerful in 1529. He was the man of the moment because a layman was required as chancellor, because he knew best the judicial work of Council and Chancery, and because he was not Wolsey's protégé. Most notably, More could not rival the two dukes in politics: Suffolk, who had aspired to succeed Wolsey, and Norfolk, the premier English peer and lord treasurer since 1524.

Norfolk, not More, would soon emerge as Wolsey's heir in the political beargarden. Eustace Chapuys, Charles V's new ambassador to England, discovered on arrival at Court in August 1529 that Norfolk's star rose as Wolsey's declined,[2] and wrote in September that power was guarded jealously by the two dukes and viscount Rochford (Anne Boleyn's father), the principal architects of Wolsey's destruction.[3] Norfolk was himself Anne Boleyn's uncle, his sister Elizabeth being her mother, so that Henry's infatuation combined with Anne's native political fluency made the duke's situation promising. Aged fifty-six in 1529, Norfolk was finally in the ascendant — or so he thought. His ambition stretched even to a dynastic alliance with the Tudors. Chapuys heard with astonishment that marriage was mooted between Henry's daughter Mary (later queen), formerly reserved for Francis I's second son, and Norfolk's son.[4] On 21 October 1529, the ambassador hastened to Norfolk's house, hearing news that the government was now in his

1 See above, pp. 31–2.
2 C[alendar of] S[tate] P[apers] S[panish], *1529–1530* (London, 1879), 132, 135.
3 *Ibid.*, 135.
4 *Ibid.*, 182 (p. 279).

sole charge. The duke was gratified by the visit, protesting smugly — and insincerely, as he hoped — that English affairs were managed by the whole Council.[5] Chapuys at once urged the emperor to address letters of friendship to Norfolk and Suffolk (in that order), and to provide pensions at least equal to Francis I's. Meanwhile, More was resident at Court in September 1529, but his duties were confined to finalising details of the treaty of Cambrai prior to its ratification.[6] Within a month he had begun work as lord chancellor, but it was still to Norfolk that Chapuys and others gave attendance in political matters.[7] Though feeling his way, the duke was acting as chief of the Council. Throughout November and December 1529 it was he with whom Chapuys discussed both the divorce and Charles's need for money to relieve the Turkish seige of Vienna.[8] For instance, the envoy was asked on 7 December to meet 'the government' in London; he accepted, and found himself closeted with Norfolk.[9] More's name did intrude on the conversation, but only in connection with a report he was writing on mercantile disputes (could he ever get away from such work?). Sir Thomas was not personally present at the meeting; perhaps, though, his presence was inappropriate since Norfolk raised the divorce issue.[10] At any rate, Chapuys wrote after the meeting that the duke's power grew daily.[11]

If More was going to exert influence as lord chancellor, he had to work through the Council chamber, co-operating fully with those in power under Henry, especially Norfolk. But two limitations impeded his freedom to participate in the consultative process by which the royal will was translated into official policy. First, More could not attend all meetings of the Council. After the fall of Wolsey, formal Council sessions at which he presided as lord chancellor continued as usual in Star Chamber; however, policy meetings were now held at Court, too, where Henry and the Boleyns were. The divorce crisis marked Henry VIII's first prolonged attention to public affairs, the result being a major shift of political gravity away from Star Chamber towards the Court. In this respect, Anne Boleyn destroyed Wolsey's structure and altered the mechanics of government. More needed to be present at all

5 *Ibid.*, 194 (pp. 295–96).
6 *LP* iv. 5911, 5941.
7 *CSPS, 1529–1530*, 211.
8 *Ibid.*, 216, 224.
9 *Ibid.*, 228.
10 *Ibid.*, 228 (pp. 357–59).
11 *Ibid.*, 232 (p. 369).

Council meetings, including informal ones at Court summoned by Henry on impulse. But this was impossible in practice, since his judicial work in Chancery and Star Chamber detained him at Westminster during the legal terms, when he resided at his house in Chelsea.[12] A gap in the sources confounds any attempt to estimate what proportion of Council meetings More missed in this way, making it difficult in turn to calculate his relative isolation.[13] Assuredly, though, the drift to Court weakened the chancellor's hold over policy, since he could not be consulted when not readily available.

The second limitation on More's freedom to participate was that he had always to remain Henry's loyal servant at a time when the acid test of loyalty was support for the royal divorce. Shortly after becoming chancellor, More was tackled by Henry on this very point, a difficult but inevitable interview which More later described fully to Thomas Cromwell.[14] It began where an earlier interview had left off, and to understand the context we must briefly examine the circumstances of the former meeting. This took place at Hampton Court sometime between 12 and 17 October 1527, being the occasion when Henry first broached the matter of his marriage to More.[15] Conversing with Sir Thomas in the gallery, Henry had laid the Bible before him and read out conflicting texts from Leviticus and Deuteronomy.

> If a man shall take his brother's wife, it is an impurity. He hath uncovered his brother's nakedness; they shall be childless (Leviticus, xx. 21)

> When brethren dwell together, and one of them dieth without children, the wife of the deceased shall not marry to another; but his brother shall take her, and raise up seed for his brother (Deuteronomy, xxv. 5)

These were just two of several passages which, despite plain mutual contradiction, proved, as Henry always maintained, that his marriage with Catherine of Aragon was against divine law, which the pope cannot dispense.[16] Henry had married Catherine by virtue of Julius II's dispensation of the impediment of affinity which her

---

12 More's residing at Chelsea during term as chancellor, stated by Harpsfield p. 54, is confirmed by the attestations on judicial writs in the Chancery files.
13 The Ellesmere Extracts effectively cease with the fall of Wolsey.
14 Rogers, no. 199.
15 *Ibid.*; OBS 1419 (Henry VIII's Itinerary).
16 J. J. Scarisbrick, *Henry VIII* (London, 1968), 152–4, and ch. 7.

former marriage to Henry's deceased brother, Arthur, had set up between them. [17] But this dispensation, according to Henry, was invalid. His marriage was against the Levitical law, which the king's supporters held to be absolute. Henry was living in sin, because the affinity between himself and Catherine which arose from his brother's marriage 'could in no wise by the Church be dispensable'.[18]

More had disagreed in 1527 with Henry's interpretation, though was careful to profess (unconvincingly) ignorance of theology and canon law.

> Whereupon his Highness, accepting benignly my sudden unadvised answer, commanded me to commune further with Master Fox, now his Grace's Almoner, and to read a book with him that then was in making for that matter.

This draft book was also shown to 'well learned men' at Hampton Court, who agreed on a revised form and contents which were later confirmed by Wolsey and the bishops at York Place.[19] 'Master Fox' was obviously Edward Foxe, a Cambridge theologian elected provost of King's College in 1528.[20] His public career, shaped throughout by the needs of royal policy, was also launched in 1528, when he and Stephen Gardiner travelled to Rome to secure a commission from Clement VII enabling the divorce to be tried in England.[21] In the effort to persuade the pope, Foxe and Gardiner took with them a book, the 'King's book', which Clement himself read and claimed (diplomatically) to find impressive.[22] Almost certainly, this was the polished version of the work which More was shown in draft.

When Henry interviewed More the second time in late 1529, the king appealed to him to open his mind and reconsider the case for annulment of the marriage.

> And if it so were that thereupon it should hap me to see such things as should persuade me to that part, he would gladly use me among other of his counsellors in that matter, and nevertheless he graciously declared unto me that he would in no wise that I

17 *Ibid.*
18 Rogers, no. 199.
19 *Ibid.*
20 *Athenae Cantabrigienses*, ed. C. H. Cooper and T. Cooper (Cambridge, 1858), vol. i. 66, 531.
21 *Ibid.* Foxe's career has been treated more fully in G. D. Nicholson's excellent doctoral dissertation, 'The Nature and Function of Historical Argument in the Henrician Reformation' (Ph.D., University of Cambridge, 1977), 113–19.
22 *LP* iv. 4120.

should other thing do or say therein, than upon that, that I should perceive mine own conscience should serve me, and that I should first look unto God and after God unto him, which most gracious words was the first lesson also that ever his Grace gave me at my first coming into his noble service. This motion was to me very comfortable, and much I longed beside anything that myself either had seen, or by further search should hap to find for the one part or the other, yet specially to have some conference in the matter with some such of his Grace's learned counsel as most for his part had laboured and most have found in the matter.[23]

More well knew that as a minister of state he had to make an effort to convince himself of the righteousness of Henry's cause. An attempt at self-conviction, which More now began in earnest, was the price of his tenure of office.[24] Henry's approval of his appointment as lord chancellor seems plainly to have rested partly on the miscalculation that he could win More round sooner or later to supporting the divorce. Evidently the king felt, too, that More's support would be the greater for being gained after close and impartial study of the merits of his case.

Henry assigned his own spiritual counsel to advise More following the second interview. Edward Foxe had been joined by Edward Lee, a theologian originally from Magdalen College, Oxford; Nicholas de Burgo, an Italian Augustine friar; and Thomas Cranmer, a theologian and fellow of Jesus College, Cambridge.[25] Cranmer had been recruited after a chance meeting with Foxe and Stephen Gardiner at Waltham in the late summer of 1529. He had given his opinion of Henry's case, and the king had approved of what was later reported to him. Cranmer thus became influential in directing the course of Henry's policy, arguing that, if Henry's marriage was against God's law, it was, in fact, no marriage at all. There had been no sacrament, and the parties had lived together in a state of concubinage. The king could therefore marry whom and when he chose, provided it was not within the forbidden degrees, and the facts of his case might be decided in England by the English Church. In other words, by proving that the Levitical law was absolute, by producing sufficient evidence that Catherine had consummated her marriage with Arthur, and by verifying the jurisdic-

---

23 Rogers, no. 199 (p. 495).
24 *Ibid.* (pp. 495–96).
25 *Ibid.* (pp. 495–96); *Athenae Cantabrigienses*, vol. i. 85, 145–54, 535; *Writings and Disputations of Thomas Cranmer*, ed. J. E. Cox (Parker Society: Cambridge, 1844), viii–xi.

tion of the English Church, Henry's cause would manifestly be gained.[26] With these ideas being floated around him, More now searched both the sources and the controversial literature on the divorce, reading 'as far forth as my poor wit and learning served me' and discussing what he found with Foxe and his group.[27] We do not know exactly what he read, but it would have included Cranmer's treatise *Articuli Duodecim*.[28] It probably embraced, too, the first sheets of a new 'King's book', which was prepared mainly in 1530.[29] This new manuscript was less of a finished work *per se* than a composite collection of materials towards a future definitive treatise on the divorce, and was compiled by Foxe, de Burgo and John Stokesley.[30] But despite prodigious study and 'diligent conference' with Foxe and the rest, More was quite unable to change his earlier opinion.[31] He did not reveal his precise doubts in 1529 or 1530; almost certainly, though, he would have agreed with Bishop John Fisher of Rochester and Cardinal Cajetan that the laws concerning degrees of marriage were merely judicial precepts. There was thus no obligation on Christians to obey them other than what flowed from the laws of the church, which the pope can dispense.[32] More probably understood the Levitical law, too, to mean not taking the brother's wife while he was alive; so that after he was dead, by the law of Deuteronomy, a man might marry his brother's wife.[33]

More decided to tell Henry that he was unable to change sides, and the king, as More claimed, accepted defeat with considerable grace — a rare (if impermanent) tribute to royal generosity.[34] The king, said More, would never 'put any man in ruffle or trouble of his conscience'.[35] But Sir Thomas now had to circumvent the divorce issue more than ever; as he later told Cromwell, he never did anything to obstruct Henry's cause.[36] More did not support the

26 W. F. Hook, *Lives of the Archbishops of Canterbury* (London, 1868), vol. vi. 438; Scarisbrick, *Henry VIII*, ch. 7.
27 Rogers, no. 199 (p. 496).
28 *Records of the Reformation*, ed. N. Pocock (Oxford, 1870), i. 334–99.
29 *LP* viii. 1054.
30 *Ibid.* Almost certainly, this manuscript was the *Collectanea satis copiosa* (B.L. Cotton MS. Cleopatra E. vi. fos. 16–135). The *Collectanea* was discovered by Dr Nicholson, who worked out its genesis and overriding influence over Henry's policy in his dissertation (*supra*, n. 21).
31 Rogers, no. 199 (p. 496).
32 G. Burnet, *History of the Reformation of the Church of England* (London, 1820), vol. i. I. 152–66.
33 *Ibid.*
34 Rogers, no. 199 (p. 496).
35 *Ibid.* (p. 496).
36 *Ibid.* (pp. 496–97).

divorce, but he could not oppose it and remain lord chancellor. He could keep quiet as one excused from advising on the matter. However, the limitation of this revised position was that almost all official policy would soon become inextricably linked to the divorce. The king's 'great matter' was More's matter too: it was the political issue of the moment, which dominated the minds of Henry's advisers until it was achieved in April 1533; it was the subject on which More had scrupulously to keep his own counsel as the means by which office might be retained. More's position was precarious indeed, calling for the utmost circumspection. Within months of accepting the chancellorship, a conflict had arisen between More's conscience and his integrity as Henry's 'good servant'. His tactics had at all times to be beyond reproach, displaying the loyalty More inescapably owed his sovereign lord. As he well knew, it was too easy otherwise for men as politically committed as Rochford to persuade the king secretly that More's words or actions were offensive, or even treasonable. Only upon resignation could More afford to proclaim himself the hostile conscience of Christendom.

After failing Henry on the divorce, More quickly resolved to serve him better in 'other things', as he put it.[37] High on his list of priorities was the detection of heresy, an enterprise of zeal for which Sir Thomas has been praised or blamed according to the sympathies of the commentator. It should thus be said at once that More's horror of heresy and utter conviction that it must be rooted out of the realm were genuine, in line with official policy and (by contemporary standards) perfectly legal.[38] No better apology for his extermination campaign can be found than his preface to Book One of *The Confutation of Tyndale's Answer*, a work published in January 1532.[39] More's argument was brief and cogent: Henry VIII desired nothing on earth as much as 'maintenance of the true catholic faith', being deservedly styled *Defensor Fidei*. Had not the king written his *Assertio Septem Sacramentorum* against Luther, and many times issued and re-issued proclamations against heresy and heretics?[40] Had he not personally sat in Star Chamber (on 25 May 1530), commanding as many J.P.s as could be assembled there to gather up

37 *Ibid.* (p. 496).
38 More's activities against heresy were later investigated by the Council at Henry VIII's request, but no fault could be found in them. *The Apologye of Syr Thomas More, Knyght*, ed. A. I. Taft (London, 1930), 143.
39 *The Complete Works of St Thomas More*, vol. viii, *The Confutation of Tyndale's Answer*, ed. L. A. Schuster *et al.* (New Haven, 1973), Pt. 1, 3–40.
40 *Ibid.*, Pt. 1, 27–28.

heretical books?[41] As Henry's 'unworthy' chancellor, More was morally obliged, as he reasoned, to follow the king's example. He must seek both to cleanse persons infected by heresy's foul contagion, and also to provide admonitory examples to those still in the clear. Strict punishment of heresy, More noted, was especially valuable as a deterrent. Even the burning of heretics was necessary in hard cases, when nothing would do but 'clean cutting out' of the part infected in order to safeguard the remainder of society. As the highest magistrate under the king, More also believed he had a fiduciary duty to suppress heresy by virtue of his chancellor's oath, and by 'plain ordinance and statute'.[42]

The statute More relied on was one of 1414 (2 Hen. V, St. 1, c. 7).[43] This had required him on admission to the chancellorship to swear to assist the church by arresting and presenting heretics for trial by the bishops, and by carrying out the judgments of the spiritual courts after convictions had been obtained. Regarding burnings, the established procedure was that the diocesan authorities alone tried accused heretics and pronounced sentences; but that, unless the convicted heretic abjured his opinions, or if after abjuration he relapsed, the secular arm (normally the sheriff) was then bound *ex officio*, if required by the bishop, to burn the victim publicly.[44] As lord chancellor, More automatically took overall charge of the proceedings of the secular arm, his one indispensable duty being to see that sheriffs complied with their legal obligation to commit condemned heretics to the flames. But Sir Thomas interpreted his oath in its broadest sense. He proved relentless in the work of apprehending and questioning suspects, on several occasions actually detaining men forcibly at his Chelsea house.[45] More was bitter, too, that his predecessor had neglected to exploit fully his investigative and other responsibilities, having a unique opportunity as legate *a latere* and lord chancellor. Rigidly orthodox and never tolerant of heresy, Wolsey had, nevertheless, been no irrational or vindictive bigot, showing kindness to both Hugh Latimer and Robert Barnes, and tending to impede the efforts of the

41 *Ibid.*, Pt. 1, 28 (the date of Henry's Star Chamber speech is given in Lansdowne 160, fo. 312v.).

42 *Ibid.*, Pt. 1, 28.

43 W. Blackstone, *Commentaries on the Laws of England*, ed. J. Stewart (London, 1844), vol. iv. 45–9; A. F. Pollard, *Wolsey* (London, 1929), 209–15; L. Miles, 'Persecution and the *Dialogue of Comfort*: a Fresh Look at the Charges against Thomas More', *Journal of British Studies*, vol. v (1965), 19–30.

44 Blackstone, vol. iv. 46–7. The procedure was set out in a statute of 1401 (2 Hen. IV, c. 15).

45 *Apologye of Syr Thomas More*, pp. 132–4; *LP* v. 574. See below, pp. 165–6.

zealots on the episcopal bench.[46] Wolsey was not a persecutor: he burned heretical books not men, and his legatine powers, far from launching an English Inquisition, were used to override the bishops' jurisdiction, enforcing the cardinal's preference for the perpetual imprisonment of convicted heretics, rather than for burnings. Wolsey was thus at odds with the harsher attitudes of bishops like Richard Fitzjames of London, Richard Nix of Norwich, and John Vesey of Exeter.[47] He had earned great praise for a holocaust of Lutheran books in May 1521; but his critics objected that the books should have been accompanied by their authors, and they murmured against an alleged infiltration of Lutherans into Wolsey's own college at Oxford.[48]

More's policy against heresy was to have significant implications for his career as lord chancellor, but these must be reserved for their proper place in the story.[49] For the present, it is necessary to appreciate that existing problems of heresy and anticlericalism in England were exacerbated unexpectedly in 1529 by the divorce crisis. The direct cause was the advocation of Henry's case to Rome by Clement VII.[50] Prior to that key event, heresy, anticlericalism and the king's marriage were issues entirely distinct from one another. Heresy, mainly Lollardy, had vexed the English Church for several generations, while anticlericalism had been endemic in Western society since the earliest times.[51] Henry's marriage question arose only in 1527, appearing at first sight to be a difficult but by no means insuperable exercise in international diplomacy. But the advocation transformed this situation. By the time the Reformation Parliament assembled on 3 November 1529, the once separate issues had welded themselves into a single crisis. Full texts of the pope's letters ending Wolsey's legatine court and citing Henry to Rome had been seen by the king in late August 1529, and troubled whispers soon leaked out.[52] Henry was outraged at being summoned before the Rota as an ordinary suppliant. He repudiated Clement's decision, which was both an indignity and a risk, since in Rome he might be denied the justice it was assuredly his wish to deny Catherine in England.[53] Henry was displeased enough to

---

46 H. C. Porter, *Puritanism in Tudor England* (London, 1970), 26, 37–8; *Athenae Cantabrigienses*, vol. i. 131; Pollard, *Wolsey*, 213–15.
47 A. Ogle, *The Tragedy of the Lollards' Tower* (Oxford, 1949), 261–62.
48 Pollard, *Wolsey*, 214–15.
49 See below, ch. 8, pp. 164–74; ch. 9, pp. 186–91.
50 Scarisbrick, *Henry VIII*, 226–8.
51 C. Cross, *Church and People, 1450–1660* (London, 1976), chs. 1–2.
52 *LP* iv. 5864.
53 *CSPS, 1529–1530*, 160 (pp. 221, 229); Scarisbrick, *Henry VIII*, 228.

allow Wolsey's overthrow, and he agreed next to bully the pope by putting pressure on the English clergy in Parliament. Election writs for Parliament were accordingly sent out in early October 1529 under the duke of Norfolk's supervision, and an alliance was threatened between the king and the latent (but powerful) anticlerical element among the laity which had built up over the years within the Church.[54]

This alliance was presaged shortly before Wolsey's court at Blackfriars had failed to pronounce a divorce for Henry. Planning their *coup* in the spring of 1529, the dukes of Norfolk and Suffolk had persuaded Thomas lord Darcy to collect evidence for use in attainder proceedings against Wolsey in Parliament, and also to sketch out the bones of the reaction to the cardinal's misrule.[55] Prepared in the form of a paper dated 1 July 1529, the dukes' scheme was an aristocratic backlash *par excellence*.[56] Its tenor was thoroughgoing anticlericalism. For instance, it was asserted that Henry VIII would gain in merit, honour and virtue by himself reforming *both* temporal *and* spiritual matters in the realm, irrespective of ecclesiastical liberty. All legates and cardinals could thus be excluded from England in future, 'their legacies and faculties clearly annulled and made frustrate'. The Church's fiscal exactions might be moderated by king or Parliament. A composite dossier of Church lands could be compiled, the titles of all properties being checked and registered, and the original purposes of individual benefactions to the Church being noted. The king's feudal rights might be fully enforced against the clergy, avoiding fiscal loss to the Crown. Furthermore, the legality of a total dissolution of English monasticism could be considered and debated by the king's learned counsel — 'for great things hang thereupon'.[57] Great things indeed: for Darcy's paper was compiled in 1529, not 1535 (the year of *Valor Ecclesiasticus*) or 1536 (the year of the first major stage of the Dissolution). On the other hand, the danger to the Church must be seen in perspective, since these most audacious proposals had no viable future as a Parliamentary programme in 1529. Such ideas as a full-scale Dissolution were too drastic even for Norfolk and Darcy to swallow in their entirety; especially Darcy, who later became a

54 *LP* iv. 5993; Scarisbrick, *Henry VIII*, 236–7.
55 SP 1/54, fos. 234–43 (*LP* iv. 5749).
56 See Appendix 2 for a transcript of this document. It is headed 'Memorandum, Parliament matters', and *Letters and Papers* fails to make clear that this page is quite separate from the rest of the document, which is the 'evidence' against Wolsey. The paper is in Darcy's hand.
57 See Appendix 2.

staunch opponent of heresy and royal supremacy, excluded from Parliament by Henry VIII and executed as a prime mover of the Pilgrimage of Grace.[58] Norfolk, Suffolk and Darcy had long aligned themselves as leaders of the aristocratic opposition to Wolsey, but it was Suffolk alone who hated the whole clergy as much as he despised Wolsey. While Darcy acted as the dukes' amanuensis in 1529, his own contribution to their composite Parliamentary scheme was moderate in scope, calling for legislation against usury and simony, better fortification of the Northern and Western Borders, and another look at English military organization.[59] Nevertheless, the writing was on the wall insofar as the paper did justice to Suffolk's views at the moment of Wolsey's destruction. It was Suffolk, too, who concurrently circulated literature at Court inviting Henry to strip the clergy bare and return to the ideals of the primitive church.[60]

How far Henry was listening to Suffolk before September 1529 is hard to tell. Thomas More, however, saw immediately that the proposed alliance with anticlericalism would invite the king to revise his whole religious alphabet. Worse still, it would encourage Lollardy among the lower classes, and Lutheranism among intellectuals and clergy. Since the mid-fifteenth century, Lollardy had crept back to prominence in London and the Thames valley, the Chilterns, Bristol, Coventry, Essex especially Colchester, Suffolk and Kent.[61] The bishops were barely holding the national situation in check. Lutheranism had by 1529 appealed only to a minority in the universities, in the City of London and at Court, but further dissemination had to be prevented by decisive repression, directed particularly against the trade in heretical books.[62] To this end Cuthbert Tunstall, bishop of London since 1522, worked busily, his panoply an integrated campaign of heresy trials, injunctions to his archdeacons, and police measures against printers and booksellers.[63] More had in 1528 taken charge under Tunstall of a polemical war against heretical literature, publishing in 1529 both his *Dialogue Concerning Heresies* and *Supplication of Souls*.[64] Meanwhile, Bishop

58 S. E. Lehmberg, *The Reformation Parliament* (Cambridge, 1970), 183, 254; J. A. Froude, *The Divorce of Catherine of Aragon* (London, 1891), 117, 289, 332, 346, 461.

59 See Appendix 2.

60 *LP* iv. 5416.

61 Cross, *Church and People*, ch. 2.

62 *Ibid.*, 53–60.

63 *Complete Works of St Thomas More*, vol. viii, Pt. 3, 1138, 1151, 1161–4, 1169–70.

64 *Complete Works of St Thomas More*, vols. vi–vii (forthcoming 1981–   ).

Fisher decried Luther in sermons by Wolsey's assignment as a heretic and traitor to the universal church.[65] But for two ineluctable reasons, the impact of these efforts would be reduced should Henry forge an alliance with anticlericalism. Firstly, heresy had been closely linked with treason since Sir John Oldcastle's revolt in 1414, but that association would evaporate should the king attack the clergy in Parliament.[66] Secondly, Wolsey had mobilised the prerogative and censorship powers of Star Chamber against heretical preachers and books,[67] against Lutheran merchants of the Hanse,[68] and to imprison or restrain summarily two national distributors of Tyndale's writings, Robert Necton and Humphrey Monmouth.[69] For example, he had caught Necton in September 1528, sent him to the Fleet, and then released him prior to trial by Tunstall on substantial bail, provided he presented himself daily for inspection in Star Chamber.[70] But were Henry to attack the clergy publicly, would Suffolk, or perhaps Norfolk or Rochford, divide the Council and withdraw Star Chamber's aid to the containment campaign? How far could things go?

More and his friends saw the dangers and were apprehensive. Justification, too, for their fears was soon furnished by the conduct of Henry VIII. Although the king's exact thinking in the summer and autumn of 1529 remains obscure, his mind was plainly wandering along new paths. He had recently read two books supplied to him by Anne Boleyn: William Tyndale's *The Obedience of a Christian Man* and Simon Fish's *A Supplication for the Beggars*.[71] Tyndale's was a work of propaganda, rooted in anticlericalism and designed to stimulate reform of the English Church under the king's direction. Henry claimed to like it; but More saw its true worth at once. It was nothing short of 'the worst heresies picked out of Luther's

---

65 Henry E. Huntington Library, San Marino, California, Rare book no. 89027.
66 More certainly felt that the anticlerical acts of the 1529 session of Parliament gave 'succour' to heretics.
67 Lansdowne 160, fo. 312.
68 L. Miles, 'Persecution and the *Dialogue of Comfort*', 21.
69 STAC 2/31/fragments (Necton's recognizance in 1,000 marks); B. L. Harleian MS. 425, fos. 8–12 (*LP* iv. 4282).
70 Necton's recognizance is dated 5 September 1528. He was released on his own security, and those of Thomas Necton of Norwich, grocer (200 marks), Thomas Meken of London, draper (£100), and Thomas Power of London, grocer (£100). Cf. *LP* iv. 4030.
71 *The Obedience of a Christian Man*, ed. H. Walter (Parker Society: Cambridge, 1848); *A Supplication for the Beggars*, ed. R. Peters (Scolar Reprint, 1973). There is no reason to doubt the tradition that Anne gave these books to Henry; see *Complete Works of St Thomas More*, vol. viii, Pt. 3, 1182–3, 1187–8, 1190–1; Scarisbrick, *Henry VIII*, 247.

works, and Luther's worst words translated by Tyndale, and put forth in Tyndale's own name'.[72] It could 'make a Christian man that would believe it . . . lose the verity of his Christendom'.[73] Fish's piece was simply a pithy but vicious attack on the wealth and greed of the clergy.[74] Did not the priests, Fish apostrophized, engross the nation's landed wealth, making vast fortunes from tithes and other exactions? Did they not also devour national resources like parasites, causing the impoverishment of the laity, while themselves living in idleness and vice, and spreading across England the leprosy and venereal disease they had caught from whores?[75]

> Who is she that will set her hands to work to get 3*d* a day and may have at least 20*d* a day to sleep an hour with a friar, a monk, or a priest? What is he that would labour for a groat a day and may have at least 12*d* a day to be bawd to a priest, a monk, or a friar?[76]

Henry VIII, Fish declared, should reform the clergy by act of Parliament; though only, he gibed, if he could — for were not priests stronger in Parliament than the king himself? Did not the bishops and abbots rule in the Lords, while the best lawyers in the Commons were bribed to support the clergy?[77]

Suffolk and Norfolk probably did not influence the king before September 1529, but in mid-September Henry was definitely listening to them.[78] An attack on the clergy was mooted at Court and much disturbed Chapuys, who alerted Charles V that Parliament was being summoned to exclude papal legates from England.[79] This (the first proposal made in Darcy's paper) the envoy significantly linked to Suffolk's 'old said saw' outburst at the Blackfriars' adjournment.[80] The door was wide open, said Chapuys, 'for the Lutheran heresy to creep into England'. Moreover, many people both at Court and in Parliament would follow Suffolk's advice and force a break with Rome.[81] Suffolk's policy, Chapuys continued, was threefold: to secure the trial of Henry's divorce in England, to satisfy the laity's grudge against the clergy, and to confiscate

---

72 *Complete Works of St Thomas More*, vol. viii, Pt. 3, 1182–3.
73 *Ibid.*
74 According to Fish, the clergy's corporate assets exceeded half the nation's wealth. Begging friars alone netted £40,000 per annum!
75 *Supplication*, fo. 4.
76 *Ibid.*, fo. 4v.
77 *Ibid.*, fo. 5.
78 *CSPS, 1529–1530*, 160.
79 *Ibid.*
80 *Ibid.*
81 *Ibid.*

wholesale church property.[82] A month later, the ambassador wrote that Suffolk was openly canvassing support for his plan to attack the English Church.[83] Meanwhile, Anne Boleyn and her father were pressing Henry to declare Clement VII a heretic.[84]

For Thomas More, it was clear that the advocation of Henry's divorce had loosed the king's mind upon a dangerous, even desperate course of action if it was carried out with any perception of its consequences. With Parliament in mind, the king next began to feign doctrinal heterodoxy for diplomatic gain at Rome. In other words, he not only projected an alliance with anticlericalism in September 1529, he pretended, too, to flirt with heresy. In doing this, he was simply attitudinizing: to play with Protestantism was one thing; to admit it into England was quite another for Henry, even assuming he could stomach its doctrines — which he could not. His position thus led him towards unpredictable behaviour. On 7 September 1529, for instance, he told Wolsey to release the prior of Reading, 'who for Luther's opinion is now in prison and hath been a good season at your grace's commandment'.[85] But the matter was heinous, for the prior had owned some sixty heretical books, and Wolsey did not comply.[86] All the same, Henry VIII had personally intervened in favour of a Lutheran heretic — a hitherto unprecedented act. On the other hand, the king reassured Cardinal Campeggio a few weeks later that he 'would never fail in doing service as a good Christian King'. He would crush Lutheranism and defend for ever the liberty of the English Church.[87] Was Henry sincere about this? The legate could not tell: he appeared so, but the king was an experienced deceiver, not least of himself.

A more revealing (and truthful?) statement was given by Henry on 28 November 1529 to Chapuys and others. His eyes twinkling with malicious irony, Henry delivered a lengthy monologue which attributed both war and heresy to the ambition of popes and cardinals. Had successive popes followed Scripture and the Early Church Fathers, they would have ordered the affairs of Christendom in a more seemly manner.[88] Luther was quite right to make this point; indeed, had Dr Martin confined himself to condemning clerical abuses, Henry would have joined him long ago. Just because

82 *Ibid.*
83 *LP* iv. 6011.
84 *CSPS, 1529–1530*, 224.
85 SP 1/55, fo. 122v. (*LP* iv. 5925).
86 *LP* iv. 4004.
87 *LP* iv. 5995.
88 *CSPS, 1529–1530*, 224 (where the month is mis-stated as October).

Luther had dabbled in heresy, 'that was not a sufficient reason for reproving and rejecting the many truths he had brought to light'. Henry would himself reform the English Church by act of Parliament, and Charles V should follow his example! Suddenly, Henry spat through his teeth:

> Now, I ask you, how can the Pope grant a dispensation for a priest to hold two bishoprics or two curacies at once, if he will not allow two women to one man? For here is the point . . . all doctors say that a dispensation in the former case is as necessary as in the other.[89]

Wisely perhaps, Chapuys would not wrestle with Henry in so tempestuous a mood. The opinions the king had expressed were, nevertheless, astounding when spoken by the author of *Assertio Septem Sacramentorum*. In his book eight years before, Henry had shown himself to be Luther's sternest and most uncompromising adversary. Especially shocking was the king's analogy concerning bigamy. Henry still smarted from Clement VII's refusal to allow him this solution — it was the course of action consistently recommended by the French — but the king's point was precisely the old Lollard argument that a layman could have two wives if a priest could have two benefices.[90] Henry's orthodoxy was manifestly under suspicion. Through William Benet, his ambassador at Rome, the king had repeatedly offered vague hints of schism if his divorce was not grantly swiftly — and in England. His remarks to Chapuys now read like a programme for Parliament.[91] By the end of 1529, the envoy could indeed only echo his earlier opinion that Parliament's anticlericalism was the result of the advocation of Henry's case to Rome.[92]

Within this context, Thomas More's motivation as lord chancellor assumes a strength of purpose. The crisis which threatened to disturb relations between *regnum* and *sacerdotium* in 1529 impelled him to a renewed appreciation of moral responsibility and public duty. As Roper suggested, there were three goals which, when achieved, would leave More content to be 'put in a sack' and 'cast into the Thames': a perpetual peace between Christian kings, the extermination of heresy, and a 'good conclusion' to Henry VIII's divorce suit.[93] The first of these aims was satisfied until 1538 by the

---

89 *Ibid.* (pp. 349–50).
90 Cross, *Church and People*, 43.
91 Cf. Scarisbrick, *Henry VIII*, 247.
92 *CSPS, 1529–1530*, 232.
93 Roper, 24–5.

treaty of Cambrai; the others characterized More's ambition as lord chancellor. The struggle against heresy and a Christendom unscarred by impending cataclysm were the things More most desired. It was thus imperative that Clement's advocation of Henry's case should not unleash the crude anticlericalism of men like Simon Fish or the duke of Suffolk. As More well knew, the international framework simply could not carry the strain. Either Henry would break with Rome, or he would have to be declared a schismatic. More would strive, then, to promote the welfare of the English Church and of all Christendom, despite his limited political position. He had achieved the office of lord chancellor and the succession to Wolsey, but the very situation which created his opportunity had cast him, too, as a potential opponent of Henry VIII. The wonder is surely not that More would ultimately fail, but that he ever believed he might succeed.

7

MORE, POLITICS AND CROMWELL'S RISE

MORE'S political baptism as lord chancellor was on 3 November 1529, when the Reformation Parliament assembled at Blackfriars amid a blaze of pomp and pageantry. As president of the House of Lords, More had to deliver a speech from the throne, outlining Henry VIII's needs and policy at the ceremonial opening of the first session.[1] We must thus examine what he said on 3 November, the synopsis here presented being a composite version of reports given by the Parliament roll, Edward Hall and Chapuys.[2]

Opening section
The king as a noble prince and shepherd of his people has for many years spared neither pains nor expense to achieve a general European peace, now obtained at Cambrai. This treaty has guaranteed the unity and quiet of Christendom, has eliminated risk of invasion from abroad, and has restored the prosperity of English trade, the benefits to trade being the result of unyielding royal endeavour. But this diplomacy inevitably cost the king much money, which now obliges him to seek Parliamentary cancellation of his debts.

Central content (longa et eleganter)
The king's vigilance as a good shepherd to detect in time anything hurtful or noisesome to his flock has warned him that the future welfare and tranquillity of the realm is under attack. Many existing laws have become outdated by continuance of time and social change, and new errors and heresies have sprung among the people because of their natural frailty. Parliament has thus been summoned to reform the realm, and will be asked to enact reformist legislation in appropriate areas.

Final section
Reform in church and state is necessary not least because of Wolsey's neglect in that regard. Just as King Henry is shepherd of his people, so there are a few rotten or faulty sheep who must be

1 S. E. Lehmberg, *The Reformation Parliament* (Cambridge, 1970), 76–8.
2 C 65/138, m. 1; *The Triumphant Reigne of Kyng Henry the VIII*, ed. C. Whibley (London, 1904), vol. ii. 163–4; C[alendar of] S[tate] P[apers] S[panish], *1529–1530* (London, 1879), 211 (pp. 323–25).

isolated from the rest of the flock, and Wolsey was the 'great wether' who craftily, scabbedly, and untruly juggled with his master. Fortunately, Wolsey has now received his deserts. He thought he could fool his king by cunning, but Henry saw through him as soon as his attention was no longer distracted by war. Wolsey has now been gently corrected,[3] which should also serve as an example to others.

More concluded by asking the Commons to choose a Speaker in the usual way, and Thomas Audley was selected after the customary adjournment.[4]

The first and last sections of More's speech were predictable enough. It had long been obvious that cancellation of Henry's debts would be required of his next Parliament in lieu of taxation, and it is arguable that the session of 1529 was finally convened for this purpose alone on the strength of the treaty of Cambrai.[5] But Parliament was originally to have been a stage for action against Wolsey, as Norfolk, Suffolk and Darcy had planned,[6] and a formal rehearsal of Wolsey's crimes of omission and commission plainly had to be included in More's address, even though the ex-minister had now already been destroyed by an alternative method to an act of attainder. It was a political necessity that More should explain to Parliament why a man who had ruled for fourteen years with Henry's full approval should suddenly have been overthrown. More's biographers have often expressed unease at their subject's attack on Wolsey, but Sir Thomas — never renowned for the courtesy of his polemic — was speaking not as a private person, but on behalf of the king.[7] Furthermore, the reasons given for the change of regime had to be dishonest. Parliament could hardly be told that Wolsey had been ousted for failing to obtain Henry VIII's divorce. Nor could it be told that the great cardinal was a financial disaster which England could afford no longer. Although the king's debts, mainly the loans collected for the invasion of France in 1522 and 1523, had been accumulated under Wolsey's administration, they followed directly from expensive wars supported in Council by the dukes of Norfolk and Suffolk, lord Darcy and viscount Rochford (Anne Boleyn's father) — the very men in power in 1529. It was thus impossible for

3 More was, of course, renowned for his use of understatement.
4 Hall, *Henry the VIII*, vol. ii. 165.
5 Henry asked for a list of the borough towns in the same week as the treaty, and four days after it the order directing Wolsey to make out writs of summons was enrolled in Chancery. *LP* iv. 5831, 5837.
6 See above, pp. 106–7.
7 Cf. R. W. Chambers, *Thomas More* (London, 1935), 240–3.

the dukes to criticize in Parliament policies they had earlier helped to promote; policies, too, which were possibly implemented against Wolsey's own better judgment.

In contrast, however, the central content of More's speech is interesting and important. Sir Thomas unveiled at length a two-tier programme against abuses arising from outdated laws in the temporal sphere, and against heresy in the spiritual domain.[8] Since More's private papers are lost,[9] it is a pity that neither the Parliament roll (which is a one-hundred word abstract) nor Hall (who was too busy gloating over Wolsey's fall) tells us exactly what he had in mind, because he evidently put forward specific proposals in perhaps unusual detail. At least, the roll's arcane summary supports this suggestion.

> De quibus quidem erroribus et abusibus longa et eleganter disseruit oratione, qua dictorum abusuum et errorum summam, causasque et occasiones eorundem, et quid pro eorum reformatione sit faciundum, singulari quadam eloquentia et facundia declaravit.[10]

The roll's comment is worth quoting, because it is possible evidence that More remained a Utopian reformer in 1529. But how much convention was there in such addresses to Parliament? We recall that Tunstall's speech of April 1523 had in similarly unimpeachable fashion explained the nature of good kingship, the benefits of good order, and the threat of foreign invasion (the real reason for calling that session).[11] Tunstall had then announced reform legislation, especially to remedy defects in the law and poor justice. Yet nothing was done, or was even intended then or later by way of reform in Parliament.[12] Statutory reform meant almost nothing to Wolsey, who worked in other ways. Did it mean anything to More either? The lack of any concrete evidence that it did would seem decisive, though we must consider in its proper place the actual legislation enacted by Parliament in 1529.[13]

What we can surmise with confidence is that in the nine days between More's appointment as lord chancellor and his speech to Parliament, Sir Thomas joined others in restraining the duke of Suffolk's recklessness. Working discreetly behind the scenes, More

---

8 C 65/138, m. 1 (poorly calendared in *LP* iv. 6043).
9 A fact often ignored by his biographers.
10 As n. 8 *supra*.
11 G. R. Elton, *Reform and Reformation* (London, 1977), 89–91.
12 *Ibid.*
13 See below, pp. 122–24.

helped drive a wedge between Suffolk and Norfolk, forming an attachment with the latter in the process. Suffolk had antagonized Norfolk in October 1529 by casting his ambition at the succession to Wolsey.[14] The union between the dukes, always a match of convenience, had achieved its purpose with Wolsey's confession on 22 October that he had offended in *praemunire* as papal legate, after which ancient aristocratic jealousies and rivalries could recover lost ground.[15] Suffolk was quickly styled president of the Council, an office dormant since Edmund Dudley's execution in 1510, and acted in that role with vice-cancellarian authority when More and Norfolk were temporarily absent from the centre.[16] But it was Norfolk who had now seized the reins as Henry VIII's chief minister, and as Anne Boleyn's uncle he did not need to defer to rivals. What Thomas More thus did was to exploit the fact that Norfolk predictably moved to a different position to Suffolk in late October 1529 with regard to the clerical estate. Once Wolsey was overthrown, the lord treasurer's former support for an attack on the English Church swiftly evaporated.[17] Norfolk was a staunch conservative, less passionate and more intelligent that Suffolk. His natural legerdemain also assured until 1546 his overriding ambition, which was political survival. Loyal to Henry and secure both at Court and in his dukedom, Norfolk's other aspirations did not extend beyond furthering his own interests at every opportunity. Conservative in religion above all, the duke declared his personal creed shortly after Thomas Cromwell's fall in 1540. He had never read the Bible 'nor ever would, and it was merry in England before this new learning came up'.[18] Unlike Suffolk, Norfolk did not hate the whole clergy as much as he despised Wolsey. Although he might agree, when angry enough, that clerical abuses should be denounced and the English Church stripped of its endowments, the project was one from which in cold blood he sprang back as conclusively as Henry VIII himself recoiled from Anne Boleyn's demand that the pope be named a heretic. Aware of the king's true opinions while shrewdly and selfishly formulating his own, Norfolk stopped short of policies which threatened to bring about schism. He thus favoured More, whom he thought loyal to Henry,

14 See above, pp. 31–2.
15 For Wolsey's surrender, *LP* iv. 6017.
16 J. A. Guy, *The Cardinal's Court: the Impact of Thomas Wolsey in Star Chamber* (Harvester, Hassocks, 1977), 133.
17 There is no further mention of Norfolk's pursuit of the matter by Chapuys, who was alert for such things.
18 *LP* xvi. 101.

sound on heresy, capable as an equity judge and diplomat, and (most important) no rival to himself in politics. We cannot doubt that Norfolk and More agreed perfectly that so drastic a plan as Darcy's draft would undermine traditional authority and release the flood-gates of heterodoxy and rebellion. As a *quid pro quo* for the duke's confidence, More could offer, too, his support for cancellation of the king's debts as a national priority. Sir Thomas thus enjoyed backing in Council and electoral influence for Parliament from Norfolk between 25 October and 3 November 1529. For instance, it was the duke who helped arrange the election of members of More's circle to the House of Commons.[19] It was Norfolk's weight which excluded— to More's utter relief— all reference to an anticlerical backlash from the chancellor's speech to Parliament. More and Norfolk, if not formally allied, were at least now working in harmony.[20]

But the first session of the Reformation Parliament was a relative failure for More. Either Suffolk's attitudes had become public knowledge by the time members settled down to work at Westminster, or More's announcement of Henry's desire to reform the realm had been misinterpreted by a House of Commons eager to hear what was uppermost in its own collective mind.[21] As burgess for Wenlock (Shropshire),[22] Edward Hall listed six main issues which now exercised the Lower House. All were anticlerical: excessive probate fees, mortuary fees, farming by clergy acting as surveyors or stewards to bishops and abbots, keeping tanning houses by monks, who also dealt in wool and cloth, non-residence and pluralism.[23] These grievances were the subject of noisy debate by the Commons. Neither More's circle nor anyone else's could moderate what was said, and discussions were almost entirely spontaneous. Such advance preparations as had been made were those of private interests: it was thus the Mercers' Company in London which had framed, in addition to articles on trade, motions on probate and mortuary fees.[24] Yet as More had perhaps feared, the Commons were emboldened by Henry VIII's recent attitudes. Religious affairs might formerly 'in no wise be touched nor yet talked of by no man except he would be made a heretic'.

---

19 Lehmberg, *Reformation Parliament*, 29.
20 *Ibid.*, 31.
21 *Ibid.*, 81.
22 *LP* iv. 6043 (2), p. 2692.
23 Hall, *Henry the VIII*, vol. ii. 166–7.
24 Lehmberg, *Reformation Parliament*, 81–2.

But now when God illumined the eyes of the king, and that their [the clergy's] subtle doings was once espied: then men began charitably to desire a reformation, and so at this Parliament men began to show their grudges.[25]

Assuredly, the Commons interpreted More's reform speech of 3 November in sectional rather than the national terms intended. Along with Suffolk, they focussed attention on the clergy alone.

After discussion by the full House, committees were appointed by the Speaker to consider the Commons' grievances with a view to drafting remedial legislation,[26] and these committees explored the six and other abuses in detail, producing three reform bills and two anticlerical petitions.[27] Two bills dealt separately with the matters of probates and mortuaries; the third tackled non-residence by occupation of farms, trading in cattle, hides, wool etc., and pluralism.[28] The mortuaries bill was the least controversial: having passed the Lower House, 'the spiritual Lords made a fair face' in the Upper, 'saying that surely priests and curates took more than they should'. According to Hall, they spoke thus 'because it touched them little'.[29] The other two bills were, in contrast, contentious. Led by Warham and Fisher, the bishops 'frowned and grunted' at the limitation of probate fees, Fisher delivering an outburst for which he was later reproved by Henry VIII.[30] He thought the bills would bring the Church 'into servile thraldom', and More may well have echoed in private his opinion that the Commons' motive was to bring the clergy 'into [the] contempt and hatred of the laity' as in Bohemia and Germany, where men had 'almost excluded themselves from the unity of Christ's holy church'.[31] The Commons, for their part, were incensed at the bishop's accusation that they acted out of 'lack of faith', sending Audley as Speaker to complain to Henry.[32]

After Fisher's rebuke, the two Houses named joint committees to consider the bills. It was then the clergy's turn to be outraged, since in one of these sessions 'a gentleman of Gray's Inn', probably Hall himself, replied to the bishops' prescriptive defence of their position, 'the usage hath ever been of thieves to rob on Shooter's Hill,

25 Hall, *Henry the VIII*, vol. ii. 167.
26 Lehmberg, *Reformation Parliament*, 83.
27 *Ibid.*, 83–6.
28 Hall, *Henry the VIII*, vol. ii. 167.
29 *Ibid.*
30 *Ibid.*
31 Lehmberg, *Reformation Parliament*, 87.
32 Hall, *Henry the VIII*, vol. ii. 167–8.

ergo is it lawful?'.[33] But these exchanges were interrupted by the need to consider in the Commons the government's bill to cancel the king's debts.[34] This had been introduced either by More or Norfolk in the Lords, where little opposition was encountered, but it was stiffly opposed in the Commons. The bill passed at last, the knights of the Council and other king's servants persuading enough members to carry the day.[35] Concessions were, however, required to appease resentment: some men had included their loans in their wills, others had made over the credit in payment of their own debts, 'and so many men had loss by it, which caused them sore to murmur'.[36] Henry VIII therefore granted a general pardon[37] —interestingly, this excepted all clergy who had violated the statutes of provisors and *praemunire*[38] — and rewarded the Commons by smoothing the way for its bills to reform ecclesiastical abuses. At the king's command, two new bills on probate fees and mortuaries were drawn 'indifferently' (probably by Henry's legal counsel), which Hall called 'so reasonable that the spiritual Lords assented to them all though they were sore against their minds'.[39] The acts did not condemn probate charges or mortuaries, but established scale fees according to the means of the payer.[40]

The Commons proceeded next to their third bill, against non-residence and the clergy's commercial undertakings, and pluralism. Quickly passing the Lower House, it was sent up to the Lords where it 'so displeased' the churchmen that they 'railed on the Commons . . . and called them heretics and schismatics'.[41] The bill was by far the most controversial of the session: it manifestly usurped Convocation's responsibility for church discipline. Some members of the Commons had already begun to challenge in committee the legislative independence of Convocation under the pope, even though ecclesiastical liberty was basic to the existing constitution as declared by chapter one of Magna Carta.[42] When raised by this bill, the point generated intense friction 'and the Lords spiritual would in no wise consent'.[43] The Commons therefore

33 *Ibid.*, ii. 168–9.
34 *Ibid.*, ii. 169.
35 Lehmberg, *Reformation Parliament*, 89–91.
36 Hall, *Henry the VIII*, vol. ii. 169.
37 21 Hen. VIII, c. 1.
38 Lehmberg, *Reformation Parliament*, 91.
39 Hall, *Henry the VIII*, vol. ii. 169–70.
40 21 Hen. VIII, cc. 5 and 6.
41 Hall, *Henry the VIII*, vol. ii. 170.
42 The challenge was exemplified by SP 2/L, fos. 203–4 (*LP* v. 1016 [3]).
43 Hall, *Henry the VIII*, vol. ii. 170.

protested to Henry, asking him to command the bishops to explain whether, according to canon law, the clergy might hold benefices in plurality or practise non-residence.[44] Probably at this time, too, the committees on grievances prepared (but did not send) petitions which Thomas Cromwell would later recast into the Commons' Supplication against the Ordinaries, during manoeuvres antecedent to the Submission of the Clergy in 1532. One petition began by roundly reminding the king that the clergy 'by themselves' in Convocation 'make laws and ordinances whereby without your royal assent, or the assent of any your lay subjects, they bind your said lay subjects in their bodies, possessions and goods'.[45] Meanwhile, Henry himself attempted to resolve the deadlock over non-residence and pluralism by ordering a committee of eight members from each House to 'intercommune'.[46] During an aggressive debate in Star Chamber by these sixteen, the Lords temporal sided with the Commons against the bishops, and in Hall's phrase 'by force of reason' (i.e. numbers) persuaded them to assent to a modified bill. Next day this bill was accepted in the Upper House.[47]

Since no original acts survive for the 1529 session of Parliament, we cannot be quite certain that this revised act against non-residence and pluralism (21 Hen. VIII, c. 13) was as great a triumph for the laity as Hall suggested.[48] However, it was a notable success for the anticlerical common lawyers who were now bent on assailing ecclesiastical liberty, because the act's enforcement clauses offered a threat to the church's cherished sovereignty — the first hint of the revolution to be crowned by More's resignation in May 1532.[49] Offenders (clergy guilty of farming, trading, non-residence or pluralism) were to be prosecuted by *qui tam* actions in the king's courts, and a small army of clerics was soon dragged through the Exchequer for misdoings which should strictly have come before the ecclesiastical courts alone.[50] Even worse, the act as passed declared null and void dispensations for pluralism obtained from Rome after 1 April 1530, and established fines of £20 for procuring such instruments in future.[51] For Thomas More, such measures were wholly unpalatable for reasons he later explained in his *Apol-*

---

44 *LP* v. 721 (2), wrongly dated in the calendar.
45 SP 2/L, fo. 203.
46 Hall, *Henry the VIII*, vol. ii. 170.
47 *Ibid.*
48 Hall was both a common lawyer and royal admirer.
49 Cf. Lehmberg, *Reformation Parliament*, 92–4.
50 J. J. Scarisbrick, *Henry VIII* (London, 1968), 252.
51 *Statutes of the Realm*, iii. 293.

ogy (1533).[52] On 3 November 1529, he had called Parliament's attention to abuses and outdated laws in the temporal sphere, but to heresy alone in the spiritual domain. He had limited Parliament's aid to appropriate areas — 'ubi expediens visum fuit'.[53] More held strongly that it was not for the laity to reform the English Church by statute, since the ecclesiastical laws were divinely instituted and pertained to the whole corps of Christendom.[54] The clergy of each province should instead reform themselves according to God's law by canons enacted in Convocation.[55] More admitted that the church's reluctance to reform itself had 'sore offended' God and inspired lay grudges against the clergy.[56] But whilst agreeing that clerics were far from blameless, Sir Thomas was adamant that the laity should not interfere in church affairs. On the contrary, *regnum* and *sacerdotium* should work in concert, each diagnosing and reforming its own faults. The two jurisdictions could thus co-exist and work in harmony, and the good men of both unite against the wicked members of either, notably heretics.[57] This catholic structure, More believed, was divinely ordained, consonant with reason and justice, the laws of England, the Scriptures, tradition and existing canon law.[58]

Thomas More thus saw the motivation behind the Commons' bills of 1529 as anticlericalism and heresy *simpliciter*. It was a crushing defeat for his early stand in the Council. Nevertheless, a victory for the resistance may have been won by Fisher, whose charge of 'lack of faith' on the Commons' part probably dissuaded the committees still preparing draft anticlerical petitions from reporting to the whole House and Henry VIII.[59] For obvious reasons, the Lower House of 1529 was sensitive to smears against its orthodoxy. After rebutting Fisher's accusation, the House could hardly continue to entertain quasi-heretical grievances.[60] The wider, explicitly jurisdictional aspects of the attack on the clergy

---

52 *The Apologye of Syr Thomas More, Knyght*, ed. A. I. Taft (Early English Text Society, London, 1930). Since this book was written, Taft's edition has been replaced by *The Complete Works of St Thomas More*, vol. ix, *The Apology*, ed. J. B. Trapp (New Haven, 1979).
53 C 65/138, m. 1.
54 *Apologye*, 162.
55 *Ibid.*, 163–4.
56 *Ibid.*, 163–4.
57 *Ibid.*, 58–9.
58 *Ibid.*, 58–9.
59 G. R. Elton, *Studies in Tudor and Stuart Politics and Government* (Cambridge, 1974), vol. ii. 127.
60 *Ibid.*

were therefore shelved for the moment, but not before Thomas Cromwell, present in the Commons as burgess for Taunton, had perceived the value of an approach which, starting from popular grievances based on wide consensus, led through one of Henry's tender points to the heart of ecclesiastical liberties.[61] The struggle would be resumed at a later date.

But while the Commons' anticlericalism was a set-back for More's ideals, it remains possible that the government made some progress towards the statutory reform of laws outdated by time and social change. The paucity of official business in the first session of the Reformation Parliament appears striking at first sight, but this may be an optical illusion created by a gap in the sources.[62] Seven statutes passed during the session which streamlined aspects of the legal system, and these should probably be treated as semi-official acts of reform. The distinction between public and private acts in Henry VIII's reign was a question independent of both legislative initiative and formal intent, so that any act designed to benefit the common weal (or *bonum publicum*) can be regarded as public.[63] Three such acts dealt with criminal procedure. Continuing the Tudor assault on abuses of sanctuary, felons and murderers who had taken refuge in churches were now to be branded on the right thumb with the letter 'A', and were to make their abjuration at a time fixed by the local coroner rather than after the traditional forty days. If they then refused to depart the realm at the time appointed, they were to lose all benefits of sanctuary.[64] Fraudulent embezzlement by servants of money, jewels, goods or chattels given into their charge was next made felony, providing the items were worth forty shillings or more.[65] The legal concept of custody, mooted earlier at common law, was simultaneously given statutory confirmation, with the result that servants were deemed not to have legally acquired such property as they physically possessed by virtue of their positions as servants.[66] It was a point which had been doubtful for years, with a consequent proliferation of offences. After the act, prosecutions for embezzlement lay at common law, relieving the party grieved of suing for redress by bill before Star

---

61 *Ibid.*
62 There are no drafts of acts passed or original acts extant for the 1529 session.
63 Cf. G. R. Elton, 'The Sessional Printing of Statutes, 1484–1547', in *Wealth and Power in Tudor England*, ed. E. W. Ives *et al.* (London, 1978), esp. 81–4.
64 21 Hen. VIII, c. 2.
65 21 Hen. VIII, c. 7.
66 J. W. C. Turner and A. LL. Armitage, *Cases on Criminal Law*, 3rd ed. (Cambridge, 1964), 379–80.

Chamber or Chancery. Temporary at first, the act was made permanent by Parliament in 1563.[67] A third statute provided that felons convicted of stealing should restore the stolen goods to their owner at the discretion of the judges, a reform of tantalising Morean interest if indeed modelled on the custom of the Polylerites as described by Hythlodaeus in *Utopia*.[68]

The other four acts reformed aspects of civil procedure. The first expedited land litigation at common law by allowing plaintiffs in an assize to abridge their plaints of any part upon which a bar was pleaded.[69] The second validated sales of land by executors wishing to satisfy the provisions of a testator's will, in cases where other executors refused to co-operate.[70] Land could not previously be sold by some executors only, although this breach of trust by the others resulted in unpaid debts and unperformed bequests, and caused much misery to widows and orphans. The third act protected tenants for years against eviction by new landlords who had obtained the freehold by fictitious recoveries.[71] Prior to 1529, a lessee's estate might have been defeated by a common recovery suffered by the freehold owner, which annihilated all leases for years then subsisting unless afterwards renewed by the recoverer. If ousted, the lessee's one former hope was a bill in Chancery, Star Chamber or the White Hall. After the statute, the termor was protected against recoveries, his interest now being secure. This was a far-reaching reform, guaranteeing enjoyment of the long lease, and thus enabling leases to be widely developed for arranging family settlements and mortgages.[72] Finally, a fourth act empowered landlords to collect their rents and customary dues even when (because of recoveries, secret enfeoffments and leases) they were no longer able to identify their tenants by name.[73] As this was a measure so pellucidly favourable to the landed nobility, it may perhaps have been promoted solely by individuals in the Lords, without the benefit of wider government assistance.

The extent to which More was engaged as a Utopian reformer in the various stages of this legislative package can never be discovered

---

67 By 5 Eliz. I, č. 10.
68 21 Hen. VIII, c. 11. *The Complete Works of St Thomas More*, vol. iv, *Utopia*, ed. E. Surtz and J. H. Hexter (New Haven, 1965), 77.
69 21 Hen. VIII, c. 3.
70 21 Hen. VIII, c. 4.
71 21 Hen. VIII, c. 15.
72 W. Blackstone, *Commentaries on the Laws of England*, ed. J. Stewart (London, 1844), vol. ii. 163–64.
73 21 Hen. VIII, c. 19.

without better sources. There is nothing concrete to suggest that he was involved, although any of the seven acts which was originally drafted by government counsel would have been approved by him at an early moment. The subjects of the acts, too, were all within his personal experience as a councillor under Wolsey. Far less convincing even than this, though, is a suggestion that More devised a comprehensive draft bill about titles to land in 1529.[74] The bill, which aimed at abolishing entails and outlawing uses (unless publicly registered), now looks to have been an amateur, not a professional document.[75] While it usefully provided for national registration of all conveyances (a goal still not achieved four centuries later), its procedures were complex and naive beside the known thinking of the Council a few years afterwards. For instance, the idea of recording uses in Common Pleas was clumsy and unrealistic, and the bill's ignorant surmise that the estates of peers were all entailed, coupled with its dream that absolute titles could be created simply by registration, indicated an amateur at work.[76] Nor was this bill the first draft of the later Statute of Uses, as has sometimes been stated. The real 'bill of primer seisin'[77] was a quite separate agreement on feudal incidents between Henry VIII and the peers, a matter which did concern More. He signed the agreement as lord chancellor, alongside the king, Norfolk, Suffolk, and twenty-eight other lords and councillors, and promised with the rest to secure its statutory enactment in the next session of Parliament.[78] However, events turned out differently.

One further question required More's attention in Parliament before he announced the end of the session on 17 December 1529, giving Henry's assent to the bills which had passed both Houses.[79] This was a last-minute attempt by Norfolk, Suffolk, Rochford and Darcy in late November to force the issue of Wolsey's attainder. Since mid-October, Henry's resolve had been that Parliament should not debate his ex-minister's failings and fate; rarely willing to murder in cold blood, the king knew it would be difficult to

---

74 *Essential Articles for the Study of Thomas More*, ed. R.S. Sylvester and G. P. Marc'hadour (Hamden, Connecticut, 1977), 115–16. The draft is SP 1/56, fos. 36–9 (*LP* iv. 6043 [6]).

75 E. W. Ives, 'The Genesis of the Statute of Uses', *English Historical Review*, lxxxii (1967), 677–80.

76 *Ibid.*

77 SP 1/56, fo. 14 (*LP* iv. 6043 [3]); B. L. Cotton MS. Titus B. iv, fos. 121–25 (*LP* iv. 6044).

78 *LP* iv. 6044.

79 Lehmberg, *Reformation Parliament*, 104.

pardon Wolsey if Parliament had already condemned him.[80] On 18 November 1529, Henry had gone as far as partially to reverse Wolsey's sentence for *praemunire*, receiving him back into royal protection — a softer attitude which was an unwelcome torment to those who had ousted the cardinal from power.[81] The factions of the previous spring thus momentarily realigned, and the dukes of Norfolk and Suffolk presented forty-four articles cast as a petition to the king on 1 December.[82] They asked that Wolsey be made a public example, never again to have 'power, jurisdiction, or authority hereafter to trouble, vex and impoverish this your realm'.[83] Most surprisingly, Thomas More was willing to sign this catalogue of Wolsey's alleged misdeeds, alongside Norfolk, Suffolk, Rochford, Darcy and others, and we thus have to ask ourselves how Sir Thomas could have reconciled this act of hypocrisy with his conscience. The petition's other signatories were all Wolsey's most bitter enemies,[84] and the articles were a veritable torrent of accusation. More had certainly disapproved of aspects of Wolsey's rule, and there were hints of animosity between the two men in the 1520s.[85] But Wolsey was in the right when he told Cromwell that most of the articles against him were untrue, while the few which were true revealed neither malice nor disloyalty to king or realm.[86] Why was More both prejudiced and unjust on this occasion? His address to Parliament had necessarily put out the official bromide on the fallen regime; surely, though, his support for Wolsey's attainder was quite a different affair? As an historian and judge, More knew the true score. Wolsey had been vainglorious 'far above all measure, and that was great pity, for it did harm and made him abuse many great gifts that God had given him. Never was he satiate of hearing his own praise'.[87] More's association with Norfolk's petition can only have sprung from a political deal with the aristocracy, in the context of a growing possibility that Wolsey would soon be pardoned and returned to power. Evidently, Sir Thomas opposed this development and signed the articles in order to preserve the *status quo*.

---

80 *Ibid.*, 102.
81 *LP* iv. 6059.
82 *LP* iv. 6075.
83 Lehmberg, *Reformation Parliament*, 103.
84 Except perhaps William Blount, lord Mountjoy.
85 See above, pp. 22–4.
86 *LP* iv. 6204.
87 *The Complete Works of St Thomas More*, vol. xii, *A Dialogue of Comfort against Tribulation*, ed. L. L. Martz and F. Manley (New Haven, 1976), Bk. III, ch. 10.

Even so, Norfolk's renewed fear of Wolsey's return to favour would ultimately wreck the former harmony between More and the duke during the coming months. Wolsey's continued presence on the political baseline put real pressure on the duke to justify himself as Henry VIII's chief councillor by resolving the divorce issue. By February 1530 Norfolk had not done this, and Wolsey — who professed willing to continue his career where he had left off — next received from Henry both a general pardon and part-restoration of his possessions.[88] Norfolk began to panic, denying Wolsey access to Henry (as Suffolk had done in 1529) and boosting action on the marriage question in Council.[89] The duke shook with apprehension at the mere thought of Wolsey's return to power. Caught and bowled in 1529, Wolsey looked like getting a second innings in 1530, and his earlier reputation for exacting vengeance when desired sent shivers of fear up Norfolk's spine. Wolsey was soon as active as ever at Esher and Richmond, on the one hand attempting to impress Anne Boleyn, on the other plotting avidly with the French, Charles V and the pope. He had first turned to Francis I and Louise of Savoy, his overtures being entertained in secret until the king and his mother perceived that their interest was already better served by the Boleyns. He had next approached the emperor, sending his Italian physician, Agostini, to open discussions with Chapuys during March 1530. But Norfolk got wind of these menacing moves, and threatened to tear his enemy apart if he did not 'make haste northward' to his diocese of York.[90] The situation was the more explosive in that it seemed to observers at Court that Henry now longed for his ex-chancellor's recall.[91] Wolsey delayed his departure for York as long as possible on the pretext of poverty, and a conspiracy was hatched by which Henry was to be admonished by the pope (under imperial mandate) to detach himself temporarily from Anne Boleyn to avoid international scandal. The pay-off for Wolsey was that Queen Catherine had agreed to bury the past and assist his return to power should the scheme work. Many people believed that Henry would respond to a conciliatory papal initiative; and here was a double danger for Norfolk, since he had so annoyed Catherine previously that, quite apart from his blood relationship to Anne, it was anathema that the Queen should recover her former influence, worst of all in formal

---

88 *LP* iv. 6213, 6214, 6220.
89 *CSPS, 1529–1530*, 257 (p. 450).
90 G. Cavendish, *The Life and Death of Cardinal Wolsey*, ed. R. S. Sylvester and D. P. Harding (New Haven, 1962), 130.
91 *CSPS, 1529–1530*, 232 (p. 368).

alliance with Wolsey.[92] Indeed a rehabilitated Wolsey might on these terms forge a common cause with Catherine's political partisans (including Thomas More?) to Norfolk's utter ruin.

In fact, Clement VII 'saw no reason to put his hand in the fire in order to pull out chestnuts for Wolsey'.[93] But it was still imperative to Norfolk's political survival in 1530 that progress be made on Henry's divorce, lest an impatient king recall the old regime or the Queen regain her influence, which amounted to the same thing. Norfolk's long-term position could, accordingly, never be Thomas More's. The divorce was the very objective to which More could not in conscience strive — quite the opposite. As we have seen, he had actually gained Henry's permission to be excused from advising at all on the matter.[94] Norfolk thus had to move sharply, and by June 1530 Sir Thomas was not merely prevented (as before) from attending impromptu Council meetings at Henry's Court because of his judicial obligations at Westminster, he was for the first time being formally excluded from certain pre-arranged policy sessions as one whose loyalty had begun to be suspect along with Fisher's.[95] More knew that he was driving himself towards a political cul-de-sac. Nevertheless, the damage might yet be made good, and More's situation was far from desperate in 1530. His scruples of conscience were a luxury Norfolk could not afford; on the other hand, More was not opposing an agreed or suggested royal policy at this date. He did not like the divorce, but he did not oppose it. He simply kept quiet, and did this plausibly, not least because Henry's case was still *sub judice*. Thus far, the king's methods had been sufficiently innocuous.

Several set-backs now confronted More. First, he was unable to retain Norfolk's backing in Council, so that a policy of Utopian reform became politically impossible, irrespective of More's enthusiasm and commitment. More did, however, retain majority support in Council for a continued attack on heresy and heretical books.[96] Secondly, More lost Tunstall's moral support by a decision (taken early in 1530) to translate the bishop to Durham. Replaced as lord privy seal in January 1530 by the earl of Wiltshire and Ormond, Anne Boleyn's father (created earl the previous month),[97] Tunstall was moved in February and given heavy duties

92 *Ibid.*
93 A. F. Pollard, *Wolsey* (London, 1929), 289.
94 Rogers, no. 199.
95 *CSPS, 1529–1530*, 354.
96 See below, pp. 165–74.
97 *LP* iv. 6085, 6163.

in the field of northern administration.[98] His successor as bishop of London was John Stokesley, a supporter of the divorce and Wolsey's enemy. Thirdly, the rise of an inner ring in the Council may be detected after the prorogation of Parliament in December 1529.[99] This consisted of Norfolk, Wiltshire, Stephen Gardiner (Henry's latest secretary), William lord Sandes (lord chamberlain), Robert Ratcliffe, earl of Sussex, Henry Courtenay, marquis of Exeter, Thomas lord Darcy, John lord Husy, and Sir William Fitzwilliam.[100] It marked the configuration of councillors to whom Henry looked for advice on his 'great matter'. In all other Council business, More was one of the inner ring as lord chancellor, but his overall position smacked of insecurity. Norfolk needed help not hindrance. He could not afford to patronize More, because royal policy on the divorce had become inextricably confused. Having made international noises through Benet and to Chapuys, flirted with heresy and permitted the Commons' anticlericalism in 1529, the king had at last run out of diplomatic steam.

Early in February 1530, Henry had sent an embassy led by Wiltshire, Stokesley and Edward Lee to Bologna (where the pope crowned the emperor on the 24th), in the hope of achieving an understanding on the divorce, but the mission had failed.[101] Charles V, now at peace with Clement VII, was less disposed than ever to yield. Clement thus responded by issuing a bull on 7 March which cited Henry to Rome and prohibited re-marriage by the king under pain of excommunication and interdict.[102] At home in Council, Norfolk proposed that Henry ignore the citation, but was reduced to asking Chapuys pointblank on 18 April what the emperor would do should Henry remarry in defiance of the pope with the approval of the English Church.[103] Would he declare war?[104] Chapuys replied that a foreign invasion would be unnecessary, since Henry's own subjects would rise in rebellion — a daring riposte which must indeed have given food for thought.[105] Of Henry's other councillors, Gardiner was reluctant to suggest anything beyond perfecting the tactics of delay at Rome in the hope of *deus ex machina*. Fitzwil-

98 *LP* iv. 6198, 6233. Pollard, *Wolsey*, 292.

99 Chapuys had heard something of this from Brian Tuke, though his rendering of the matter was garbled. *CSPS, 1529–1530*, 257 (pp. 451–52).

100 STAC 2/17/405; STAC 10/4, Pt. 2; Ellesmere MS. 2659.

101 Hall, *Henry the VIII*, vol. ii. 172.

102 *LP* iv. 6256.

103 *CSPS, 1529–1530*, 290 (pp. 510–11).

104 *Ibid.*, (p. 511).

105 *Ibid.*, (p. 511).

liam backed a familiar French suggestion that Henry commit bigamy and rely on a pardon.[106] Meanwhile, Cranmer (though not yet formally in the Council) advised that Henry take unilateral action in England with the authority of the English Church in Convocation, the course of action towards which he had been working with Edward Foxe, de Burgo and Stokesley.[107] Cranmer recommended, too, that Henry consult the universities of Europe for their opinions of his case.[108] We recall that Cranmer aimed to prove that the Levitical law was absolute, to garner sufficient evidence that Catherine had consummated her marriage with Prince Arthur, and to verify the jurisdiction of the English Church over Henry's case. The second of these *desiderata* lay conveniently to hand in the shape of evidence given for the king at Wolsey's legatine court; the first and third were under active research throughout 1530 by those already collecting materials for the new 'King's book'.[109] But what better now, thought Cranmer, than to validate the 'radical' approach — at least on the inability of popes to dispense the Levitical law — by gaining for the king the *imprimatur* of Christendom's most learned men? Much lauded by Henry, Cranmer's exercise was eagerly begun. However, Gardiner's plan was adopted as a stopgap measure, and the negotiations at Rome became distinguished by continued efforts to prevent Henry's case being heard there, and to recover it for English judgment.

With policy in this state of flux, it was obvious that Parliament could not be allowed to reassemble.[110] Scheduled originally to begin on 26 April 1530, the new session was put back to 22 June, ostensibly because of plague.[111] In June it was again postponed, this time to 1 October.[112] In Parliament's absence, Henry summoned a great Council at Windsor, where he exhorted his supporters on 12 June to sign a letter to Clement explaining the divorce as a matter of national policy.[113] The letter's tone was bellicose at first, and discussion was adjourned while the document was re-drafted.[114] Four days later, Henry was rewarded with signatures from most of those

---

106 For the disadvantage of this proposal, see G. Mattingly, *Catherine of Aragon* (London, 1950), 224.
107 See above, ch. 6.
108 Scarisbrick, *Henry VIII*, 255–8.
109 See above, ch. 6.
110 Henry VIII had no intention of allowing Parliament to initiate policy, or discuss his matrimonial affairs.
111 Lehmberg, *Reformation Parliament*, 105.
112 *Ibid.*
113 *CSPS, 1529–1530*, 354.
114 *Ibid.*

present, while others (notably Warham's and Wolsey's) were obtained afterwards by messenger.[115] More, Tunstall and Fisher were not summoned to the Council, and were·also excused from signing the letter. Despatched to Rome on 13 July, the document was still vaguely menacing, but was unspecific as to Henry's intentions should the pope fail to oblige on the divorce. It was thus a measure of Clement's strength of position that his answer was unruffled. Written late in September, the pope's reply noted that Henry had only himself to blame for the delay for failing to send a lawful proctor to Rome. Clement justified his past proceedings, and expressed benign surprise at the king's complaints. Did Henry think his past services to Rome entitled him to a verdict 'without regard had either to right or justice'?[116]

Henry did not relish this reply. But the matter was already unimportant.[117] The king had found a new adviser, a man qualified to consolidate an effective royal strategy at last. One source suggests that Thomas Cromwell may have become Henry VIII's servant as early as February 1530.[118] Hall guessed instead—but was he right?—that Wolsey's former counsellor changed allegiance while the cardinal prepared to travel to his diocese of York, a journey which finally began on 5 April 1530.[119] But whoever is correct, Cromwell had entered royal service by the spring of 1530, and was a sworn member of the King's Council by the end of that same year.[120] Stories of a decisive interview with Henry at which Cromwell waved a wand and emerged as chief adviser on the spot must, of course, be given wide latitude of interpretation. There were many interviews during a year or more. Cavendish spoke of Cromwell's rise as a gradual increase of power and mutual confidence, mentioning several meetings without ascribing importance to any particular one. He saw that Cromwell had 'a great occasion of access to the King for the disposition of divers lands' of Wolsey's colleges, 'by means whereof and by his witty demeanour he grew continually into the King's favour'.[121] However, what matters is when Cromwell gained a voice in government policy and thus

115 *CSPS, 1529–1530*, 366; *LP* iv. 6489, 6513; Cavendish, *The Life and Death of Cardinal Wolsey*, ed. R. S. Sylvester and D. P. Harding (New Haven, 1962), 143–4.

116 *Records of the Reformation*, ed. N. Pocock (Oxford, 1870), vol. i. 429–37.

117 *CSPS, 1529–1530*, 492 (p. 797).

118 G. R. Elton, *The Tudor Revolution in Government* (Cambridge, 1953), 83.

119 Hall, *Henry the VIII*, vol. ii. 174.

120 Elton, *Tudor Revolution*, 84–8.

121 *Life and Death of Cardinal Wolsey*, 129. For Professor Elton's latest views on Cromwell's rise, see *Reform and Reformation*, 136–8.

became More's rival. This looks to have occurred some months before, rather than after, Wolsey's death (on 29 November 1530). Amidst the political fluidity of 1530, two important initiatives may be detected between late August and the third week of October, and it is suggested that both were associated with Cromwell's rise to influence.[122]

The first concerned new claims advanced to bolster Henry VIII's kingly power. At the end of August 1530, Henry ordered his ambassadors at Rome to place before Clement the view that neither the king nor any fellow-Englishman could be summoned to a Roman court, because the custom and privilege of the realm pre-vented Englishmen being cited abroad by foreign jurisdictions.[123] In mid-September Henry treated a newly-arrived papal nuncio to a lengthy exposition of this English privilege,[124] and on the 25th the same nuncio was told by Suffolk and Wiltshire that 'they cared neither for Pope or Popes in this kingdom, not even if St Peter should come to life again' since Henry 'was absolute both as Emperor and Pope in his own kingdom'.[125] On 7 October the ambassadors at Rome were again instructed to declare England's privilege to the pope, Henry assuring them that Clement could not plausibly dissent. Questions might otherwise be asked about the nature of papal supremacy and how it was that the pope cited to Rome a ruler who was not only a prince and king but who acknow-ledged no superior on earth.[126]

Manifestly, these assertions exposed a thrust quite different from that of Henry's earlier letter to Clement. Although intimidatory in purpose, the document sent in July had in no way impugned papal jurisdiction over Henry's case. Yet in August the king had started to claim that he was not Clement's subject at all. These, then, were the crucial months in which Henry's caesaropapism was spawned, and the source of that remarkable political theory is now known to us, since Dr Graham Nicholson has brilliantly shown that the new claims were derived from Henry's study of a manuscript called *Collectanea satis copiosa*.[127] Almost indubitably, too, *Collectanea satis*

---

122 In working out these initiatives, I profited greatly from discussion with Professors Elton and Scarisbrick.
123 Scarisbrick, *Henry VIII*, 260–1; *St. Pap.*, vii. 261; *LP* iv. 6667, and App. 262.
124 *CSPS, 1529–1530*, 429, 433.
125 *Ibid.*, 445.
126 *St. Pap.*, vii. 261–62; *LP* iv. 6667.
127 G. D. Nicholson, 'The Nature and Function of Historical Argument in the Henrician Reformation' (Ph.D., University of Cambridge, 1977), 74–110, 145–6. The *Collectanea* is B. L. Cotton MS. Cleopatra E vi., fos. 16–135.

copiosa is none other than a fair copy of the composite research materials on the divorce which Edward Foxe, Nicholas de Burgo and John Stokesley had for some time been assembling in preparation for a new and definitive 'King's book'.[128] *Collectanea satis copiosa* was in fact but three-quarters complete in August and September 1530 — that is clear from its present structure, its paper and watermarks.[129] The point exactly, though, is that it was 'satis copiosa' by September; it was adequate both in argument and conviction to be shown to Henry, which was now done by Edward Foxe.[130] Moreover, Henry studied the *Collectanea* closely. As Nicholson discovered, the king's own hand is to be found in forty-six places on the manuscript, variously signifying his notes and queries, agreements or disagreements, and expressing (often) child-like pleasure or puzzlement. But for the most part, Henry greatly applauded the work of his scholars, since Foxe and his team, setting out *inter alia* to gain Cranmer's *desiderata*, had justified Henry's case from general theological and historical principles, not immediate diplomatic or political needs. The righteousness of Henry's cause was established by ingenious use of Scripture and traditional catholic sources — the Old Testament, the Early Church Fathers, the Donation of Constantine, Ivo of Chartres, Hugh of St Victor, the fifteenth-century conciliarists, and other authorities — against which the pope's recent proceedings were found to be a blatant usurpation. Another signal success was that Foxe had adequately verified the right of the English Church to pronounce Henry's divorce unilaterally, and without reference to Rome. But most importantly, Foxe had systematically derived from his sources a new and striking theory of English regal power, showing also how English kings had historically employed that power in handling the clergy. He imbued Henry with what amounted to a Byzantine sovereignty, part of which had been 'lent' to the priesthood by previous English monarchs. For instance, Foxe used the ancient *Leges Anglorum* to show that King Lucius I had in 187 A.D. become the first Christian ruler of Britain. In fact, the *Leges Anglorum* was a source less authoritative than it seemed, being a thirteenth-century interpolation of the so-called *Leges Edwardi Confessoris*. But it was a most pregnant source. It showed that the mythical Lucius had endowed the British Church with all its liberties and possessions, and then written to Pope Eleutherius asking him to transmit the

128 See above, ch. 6.
129 Nicholson, 289–95.
130 Nicholson, 114–22.

Roman laws. However, the pope's reply explained that Lucius did not need any Roman law, because he already had the *lex Britanniae* under which he ruled both *regnum* and *sacerdotium*:[131]

> For you be God's vicar in your kingdom, as the psalmist says, 'Give the king thy judgments, O God, and thy righteousness to the king's son' (Ps. lxxii, 1) . . . A king hath his name of ruling, and not of having a realm. You shall be a king, while you rule well; but if you do otherwise, the name of a king shall not remain with you . . . God grant you so to rule the realm of Britain, that you may reign with him for ever, whose vicar you be in the realm.[132]

In other words, Foxe was not merely justifying the king's divorce by his research; he was simultaneously announcing the doctrines of royal supremacy and empire. The result was that Henry, as he read *Collectanea satis copiosa*, became more convinced than ever before of the rights of his position. But not only should his suit for annulment of his marriage be dealt with promptly and in England, as he had thought previously. He must reassert, too, the imperial status of which English kings had been deprived by the machinations of popes. For England was an empire; it had been one in the ancient British past, and English imperial jurisdiction was a theological truth which no pope could conscionably disregard.

But the king had little notion of how Foxe's discoveries could be realized in terms of practical politics, and it was as a protégé of Henry's regal power that Thomas Cromwell now soared from unemployment to influence. Henry had been given much on which to ponder in August and September 1530. He had the ideological basis, in short, for the entire progress of the Henrician Reformation. Plainly, though, he needed time to think, to consult, and even to pray. He was meeting Cromwell regularly about Wolsey's (now Henry's) business affairs, and the king was impressed with Cromwell's briskness and acumen. The talk turned naturally enough to politics, as both Reginald Pole and Chapuys knew.[133] Cromwell next got to see *Collectanea satis copiosa*, as is shown by papers in his

131 Nicholson, 182–3. W. Ullmann, *Principles of Government and Politics in the Middle Ages* (London, 1966), 161–2.

132 E. Foxe, *Opus Eximium, de Vera Differentia Regiae Potestatis et Ecclesiasticae* (London, 1534), fos. 50–51. The full text is given and discussed in *The Church Historians of England: The Acts and Monuments of John Foxe* (London, 1853), i. II, 405–6. The document is quoted several times in *Collectanea satis copiosa*; Nicholson, 183.

133 Elton, *Reform and Reformation*, 136–7; *Tudor Revolution*, 72–4.

archive which relate to the *Collectanea* in its pre-published form (i.e. papers compiled before March 1531).[134] Meanwhile, Cromwell was steadily extending his political acquaintanceship — something Cavendish makes quite clear.[135] He was perhaps in touch with Norfolk and the Boleyns, and with Cranmer, who was already promoting his 'radical', unilateral divorce policy through Anne Boleyn and Wiltshire.[136] Quite possibly, too, Cromwell was in contact with Edward Foxe, whom he had known in Wolsey's household.[137] But Cromwell's greatest success was with Henry himself. Whereas Foxe, Cranmer and the rest were aware that — almost by accident — they had stumbled on Henrician caesaropapism as a political theory, they had nonetheless couched their findings in theological and legal language alone. Cromwell, however, saw immediate political advantages in Byzantine imperialism. With the anticlerical acts and petitions of the 1529 session of Parliament fresh in his memory, his reaction to *Collectanea satis copiosa* was swift and logical. What Lucius I had once granted, Henry VIII should take back by Parliamentary statutes founded on imperial ideology.

The idea was preposterous. But Cromwell had rightly grasped the mettle in terms of Henry's own psychology. If England was an empire, Henry VIII was its emperor. No one other than Henry, and least of all (or so one hopes!) Thomas Cromwell, thought England was an empire for a moment. Yet Henry found the notion most attractive, although, more ominously, he liked best the title 'Vicar of God'. After September 1530, Henry began to muse disconsolately upon England's lost privileges, of which the greatest was royal supremacy over the English Church. *Collectanea satis copiosa* had been a shattering revelation to the former author of *Assertio Septem Sacramentorum*, the book in which Henry had lauded papal authority against Thomas More's advice.[138] But the nub was even more galling. If Henry VIII was a Byzantine emperor, then his divorce could lawfully be tried by ecclesiastical judges appointed by himself in England, and responsible directly and solely to him. In

---

134 SP 6/1, arts. 27–33. To my knowledge, these documents have not previously been used.

135 *Life and Death of Cardinal Wolsey*, 126–30.

136 Elton, *Reform and Reformation*, 136–8.

137 *Ibid.*

138 Rogers, no. 199 (p. 498). Since this book was written, Richard C. Marius has argued that Henry VIII was, in fact, less pro-papal in 1521 than has been thought. 'Henry VIII, Thomas More, and the Bishop of Rome', in *Quincentennial Essays on St Thomas More*, ed. M. J. Moore (Boone, North Carolina, 1978), 89–107.

other words, Henry could, for example, commission the metropolitan archbishops and some other bishops to judge the merits of his case, and then certify before himself in Chancery. Judgment could thus be promulgated (after exemplification) in Chancery, enrolled on the Patent roll and proclaimed nationally by letters placard. The legality of this approach was, in fact, mooted in 1531 by Christopher St German, though not in all seriousness and strictly by analogue.[139]

St German — the common lawyer of whom more still will be heard — could not be serious because the overriding problem was one of consent and enforcement. Chapuys had known this when he told Norfolk in April 1530 that Henry's own subjects would rise in rebellion, should the king remarry in defiance of papal anathema.[140] Most of all, though, Thomas Cromwell knew it; and, as a dexterous common lawyer and committed Parliamentarian, he soon gave Henry the eventual solution. The king's caesaropapism could in practice be achieved only by a series of acts of Parliament; acts to which all subjects could be deemed to have given their consent, and which could thus be enforced by new and stringent treason laws. Cromwell's advice took, of course, months to communicate, and years to gain acceptance. It is, however, no coincidence that within weeks of Henry's reading *Collectanea satis copiosa*, and over two years before the Act of Appeals, the first Henrician attempt to draft an extended treason act was begun.[141] Enforcement was the key to the Henrician Reformation, and enforcement, above all else, was Thomas Cromwell's forte.

Starting in September 1530, then, Henry studied the pros and cons of an audacious proposal. Soon his innate conservatism, fear of the unknown and dislike of Parliament gave him inevitable doubts. Dislike of Parliament was the crucial obstacle, for Henry, although defeated years later by an admixture of political necessity and Cromwell's persuasiveness, always sought to avoid the presumption that his supremacy rested on mere acts of Parliament.[142] The king's imperial sovereignty was, after all, ordained by God and not man. Always, therefore, Henry preferred to work through 'his' clergy, a method at variance with Cromwell's preferences, and it is fair to say that Cromwell's principle of statutory reform by law made in Parliament never won Henry's wholehearted approval —

139 *A Little Treatise Called New Additions*, in *Doctor and Student*, ed. T. F. T. Plucknett and J. L. Barton (Selden Society, London, 1974), 340.
140 *CSPS, 1529–1530*, 290 (p. 511).
141 G. R. Elton, *Policy and Police* (Cambridge, 1972), 265–7.
142 Elton, *Reform and Reformation*, ch. 8.

not even after the Act of Appeals.[143] Indeed Henry's inner thoughts ever lingered in the medieval past. He hankered (strangely and contradictorily) after orthodoxy long after he had become a schismatic, while *Defensor Fidei* was the title dearest to his heart until the day he received a final *non omittas* from the greatest emperor of all. Henry, when honest with himself, agreed with Thomas More that the human positive law of the realm could not by itself displace the general law of Christendom: 'no more', as Sir Thomas pleaded in arrest of judgment, 'than the city of London, being but one poor member in respect of the whole realm, might make a law against an act of Parliament to bind the whole realm'.[144] But Henry was rarely honest, and practical politics would cast himself and More on opposite sides. In the last resort, the debate would thus not be about the royal divorce. Neither would it concern the powers of kings or popes, General Councils, Scripture or the decrees of the Roman Church. It would centre on the power of Parliaments and statutes as against Convocation and Rome: that is, English national sovereignty and Parliament's legislative authority under Henry's imperial crown.[145] Yet this was for the future. By October 1530, Henry had come to see that Thomas Cromwell was a most resourceful and astute politician, and he admitted him without delay to the Council. After which Cromwell, with a toe-hold fixed on the greasy pole, began the long haul of winning over the duke of Norfolk, while at Court, Anne Boleyn angered Henry by insolently demanding immediate adoption of a radical solution to the divorce issue.

The second new initiative indicative of Cromwell's rise to influence was the Council's resolution to threaten the whole clergy of England with a *praemunire* charge. This truly momentous decision was taken by the third week of October 1530, within weeks of Henry's first reading *Collectanea satis copiosa*. [146] It marked a major revision of a plan formed the previous July, which aimed at indicting a few selected persons associated with Wolsey's papal legacy.[147] The initial manoeuvres had begun on 11 July when Christopher

---

143 *Ibid.*

144 Roper, 93.

145 The best discussion is in Nicholson's dissertation, 157–273. When published in due course, this will supersede all other accounts.

146 The standard article on these manoeuvres is by J. J. Scarisbrick, 'The Pardon of the Clergy, 1531', *Cambridge Historical Journal*, vol. xii (1956), 22–39; see also the same author's *Henry VIII*, 273–6. The interpretation offered here differs on some points of fact, based on new evidence.

147 Scarisbrick, 'Pardon', 25–9.

Hales, the attorney-general, filed indictments against fourteen clerics in King's Bench.[148] Those named were the bishops of Coventry and Lichfield, Norwich, St Asaph, Bangor, Ely, Rochester (John Fisher), Bath and Chichester, the abbots of Westminster, Bury St Edmunds and Waltham Cross, the archdeacon of Wiltshire, the dean of Hereford and a subdean of Salisbury. All were charged with abetting Wolsey's legacy by having made an agreement whereby he received a percentage of their annual income of casualties.[149] The indictments, as such, were plainly malicious and we may agree with Chapuys that they had a tripartite purpose: to 'cause the greater number of those who hold with the Queen to lose their preferment', to net 'a large sum of money', and to frighten the clergy into approving Henry's divorce which 'he has always said should have the advice and authority of the English Church'.[150]

During the late summer, in contrast, the Council's objectives became confused, and this uncertainty of direction concealed an attempt from within to revise the whole thrust of the government's policy.[151] Examination of the King's Bench records reveals that two additional persons received writs of *praemunire facias* shortly after the close of Trinity term, one being Anthony Husye, a notary public, proctor in the court of Arches and sub-delegate in the court of Admiralty.[152] Why was Husye, a layman, indicted with the others? It is possible that the Council held that he had honoured Wolsey's legacy in 1525 by assisting Cromwell to dissolve the monasteries used to endow the cardinal's colleges,[153] but it is much more likely that he was included at the last moment as a lawyer concerned, *ex officio*, in the dispensation of the spiritual jurisdiction. If so, this is the first hint we receive of possible wider action against the clergy. A second clue comes from Chapuys, who had heard by 20 September that at least sixty bishops and abbots, and a hundred and fifty lesser clergy were under imminent threat of indictment in King's Bench.[154] The ambassador realized, too, that this step was a change from the original plan of 11 July: the substantial difference between fourteen (later sixteen) indictments and some two hundred and ten indicated that someone in or close to the Council was

148 KB 9/513/14 (endorsement).
149 KB 9/513/1–14.
150 *CSPS, 1529–1530*, 396.
151 Scarisbrick, 'Pardon', 29–30.
152 KB 27/1077, *ro.* 27 (*Rex*). For Husye's background, see HCA 3/2, *passim*. The other person indicted was Adam Travers, archdeacon of Exeter.
153 *LP* iv. 1137.
154 *CSPS, 1529–1530*, 433.

pressing for the prosecution of the entire clerical estate. Who that someone was became clearer in October. Of those originally indicted, Bishop Nix of Norwich and Abbot Melford of Bury had to appear in King's Bench on 17 October, while the rest were not due there until the 31st.[155] Nix and Melford apparently arrived on schedule,[156] but then all the cases begun by indictment were hastily abandoned. Cromwell wrote cryptically to Wolsey on the 21st, 'the prelates shall not appear in the praemunire. There is another way devised in place thereof'.[157] Cromwell was now in the Council's secrets. He knew that the remaining clerics and Anthony Husye would not appear in court ten days later.[158] He knew of the 'other way', the decision to level the threat of a *praemunire* charge against the whole clergy in Convocation,[159] and he did so because he was himself promoting that policy.[160] Cromwell had perceived the overriding importance of the jurisdictional issue during the 1529 session of Parliament. The autumn of 1530 saw the first intrusion on government policy of this central aspect of the Cromwellian reform scheme as it would finally be unveiled in 1532.

Cromwell's rise in 1530 soon led to overt rivalry between Queen Catherine's party and the spokesmen and promoters of *Collectanea satis copiosa*. The Queen's supporters crystallized into what is now called (for convenience alone) the Aragonese group: Thomas More, the earl of Shrewsbury, John Fisher, Cuthbert Tunstall, Bishop Nicholas West (of Ely), Bishop John Clerk (of Bath), Bishop Henry Standish (of St Asaph), William Peto, head of the Franciscan Observants of Greenwich, Richard Reynolds, a Bridgettine of Syon monastery (Isleworth), and Nicholas Wilson, archdeacon of Oxford.[161] These men quickly organized themselves as a cohesive faction, acting on leaks (from More?) of impending government moves, which were then countered in advance by public sermons and propagandist treatises.[162] More had to keep strictly quiet on the divorce issue itself, but believed himself free to speak out on other matters.[163] He steeled himself, therefore, to defend the church from

---

155 KB 9/513/1–14 (endorsements), and entries on KB 27/1077, *roti.* 27–28 (*Rex*).
156 No process for default issued against them.
157 R. B. Merriman, *Life and Letters of Thomas Cromwell* (Oxford, 1902), vol. i. 334.
158 KB 27/1077, *roti.* 27–28 (*Rex*).
159 See below, pp. 148–9.
160 Cf. Elton, *Reform and Reformation*, 140–4.
161 Cf. *ibid.*, 122.
162 See below, chs. 8–9.
163 Rogers, no. 199 (p. 496).

attack, at times even regardless of personal risk. Reporting the proposed policy change on *praemunire* in mid–September 1530, Chapuys warned the emperor that More had come within an ace of dismissal for his opposition tactics.[164] Much friction was also generated over a proclamation put out with a flourish of trumpets on 19 September 1530, which forbade the reception into England of papal bulls prejudicial to Henry's royal prerogative.[165] Designed in general terms to obstruct Catherine's conduct of her case and timed to greet the arrival of the papal nuncio, the document was even more contentious as a specific response to an attempt by Bishops Fisher, West and Clerk to appeal to Rome against the three anticlerical acts passed in the first session of the Reformation Parliament.[166] Eager to test on their part, too, the question of Parliament's legislative authority under Henry's imperial crown, Fisher and his supporters had actually invited the pope to annul the three controversial statutes as an infringement of ecclesiastical immunity from secular jurisdiction. Since Clement VII was unlikely to cross the Rubicon voluntarily, the proclamation now issued was, to a great extent, tilting at a shadow.[167] Nevertheless, the writing was on the wall in larger script than before. Meanwhile, Henry had again set back the new session of Parliament from 1 to 22 October, ostensibly to enable the pope to reply to his letter of late August concerning England's new-found 'privilege', but in reality to allow more time to resolve bitter clashes of opinion in the Council.[168]

Further conflict still, however, was unleashed by a meeting at Hampton Court in the second week of October 1530, when Henry openly sounded out his clergy and lawyers on the power of Parliament.[169] Following Cromwell's (and perhaps St German's?) advice in the light of *Collectanea satis copiosa*, the king wanted to know whether Parliament 'could and would enact' that his divorce might be granted by the archbishop of Canterbury despite papal inhibition.[170] But after deliberation, a majority verdict was returned that this was not possible. Henry at once lost his temper, proroguing

---

164 *CSPS, 1529–1530*, 433 (p. 727).
165 *Tudor Royal Proclamations*, ed. P.L. Hughes and J. F. Larkin, vol. i (New Haven, 1964), 197–8; Hall, *Henry the VIII*, vol. ii. 180; *CSPS, 1529–1530*, 433.
166 J. J. Scarisbrick, 'The Conservative Episcopate in England, 1529–35' (Ph.D., University of Cambridge, 1955), 107.
167 Cf. Elton, *Reform and Reformation*, 133.
168 *CSPS, 1529–1530*, 429, and 433 (p. 723). Parliament was due to reassemble on 1 October; Lehmberg, *Reformation Parliament*, 105.
169 *CSPS, 1529–1530*, 460.
170 *Ibid.*

Parliament again until January 1531. According to Chapuys, the king needed the extra time to coax the lawyers into changing their minds.[171] Was More, though, at the Hampton Court meeting? It is possible that he was, because he was afterwards in quite serious trouble with the king. Henry now complained (for the first time) that he had had to excuse his lord chancellor from signing the letter of 13 July 1530 to Clement VII.[172] He was also furious at finding out that the Queen's party in Council was leaking details of confidential debates to Chapuys, whom Henry believed (correctly) to be co-ordinating opposition on behalf of the Aragonese faction.[173]

The autumn of 1530 was thus a time of crisis for More. Had he spoken at Hampton Court, his opponents could have argued well enough that his pledge not to impede the divorce had been compromised. To Anne Boleyn and Wiltshire, opposition to a statute authorizing Warham to grant a divorce in England on the ground that such legislation was beyond Parliament's power was straightforward obstruction of the divorce itself. But whether More had pronounced on the power of statute or not, he had become locked into a struggle for influence in Council. His concern, too, was with adversaries far from transparent, as Suffolk had been in 1529. Sir Thomas wrestled now with Cranmer, Edward Foxe and Thomas Cromwell — men as capable and complex as himself, but less restricted by troublesome consciences. More later summarized the battle for power thus:

> Master Cromwell . . . you are now entered into the service of a most noble, wise and liberal prince. If you will follow my poor advice, you shall, in your counsel giving unto his grace, ever tell him what he ought to do, but never what he is able to do. So shall you show yourself a true faithful servant and a right worthy Councillor. For if a Lion knew his own strength, hard were it for any man to rule him.[174]

171 *Ibid.*
172 *Ibid.*
173 *Ibid.*
174 Roper, 56–7.

8

MORE, POLITICS AND HERESY

THE TWENTY months which followed the presentation of *Collectanea satis copiosa* to Henry VIII were among the most politically complex of the whole reign. Groupings and re-groupings of both men and ideas followed each other with infinite variety and within a baffling labyrinth of pleomorphic manoeuvres. A basic pattern is, however, discernible as an extended battle between rival individuals and factions to control Henry's policy — a battle which ended in May 1532 with More's resignation as lord chancellor.[1] The older interpretations of the reign which saw nothing worth mentioning between Wolsey's fall and the Act of Appeals may at last be discarded, being erected (as all invariably were) on the mistaken assumption that Henry's strategy at Rome mirrored the policy he projected at home.[2] In reality, Henry's ambassadors at Rome received instructions to stall throughout 1531, precisely because of incessant conflict between his domestic advisers, and should be given credit for skilfully freezing the king's case before the Rota until after Cromwell's victory over More.

The forces in collision by the end of 1530 were essentially three in number. First there was Thomas More, George, earl of Shrewsbury, Bishops Fisher, Tunstall, West, Clerk, Standish and the remainder of the Queen's supporters. Relatively homogenous, More's party was loyal to Catherine, united against heresy, and resolved to defend the English Church from attack. It was also aligned politically against such persons as Thomas Cranmer, Thomas Cromwell, Edward Foxe and Christopher St German, making its influence felt by daily argument within the Council chamber, by leaking news of impending government moves to Queen Catherine and Chapuys, and by a vigorous propaganda and sermon campaign co-ordinated by Fisher. Polemical treatises against heresy written by More were published by his nephew William Rastell, and against the divorce by Fisher were circulated in manuscript or smuggled abroad for foreign publication.[3] Sermons

---

1 This interpretation was first suggested to me by Professor Elton, who has summarized his latest views in *Reform and Reformation* (London, 1977), ch. 6.
2 E.g. G.R. Elton, *England Under the Tudors* (London, 1955), 122.
3 *LP* v. 460–1, 941; *St. Pap.*, vii. 489–90. J.K. McConica, *English Humanists and Reformation Politics* (Oxford, 1965), 125, 128–33. M. Macklem, *God Have Mercy: The Life of John Fisher of Rochester* (Ottawa, 1967), 181–2. For Fisher's statement in 1535 concerning earlier events, see *LP* viii. 859 (4).

were delivered by the Franciscan Observants of Greenwich, led by William Peto, John Forest and Henry Elstow, the Syon Bridgettines, notably Richard Reynolds, and Fisher himself.[4] Less active at first in Parliament than the Council, the Aragonese party soon found allies among the prelates in the House of Lords, and was assisted in the Commons by the Queen's Head group, an inchoate band of catholic members who dined and talked politics together at the Queen's Head Tavern. Among them were Sir George Throckmorton (a relation of Friar Peto),[5] Sir William Essex, Sir Marmaduke Constable, Sir William Barantyne and Sir John Gifford.[6] Throckmorton later confessed to engaging in Parliamentary opposition in 1532 at the behest of More and Fisher.[7] Sir Thomas had summoned him to a little room off the Parliament chamber. Interrupting a discussion with John Clerk, More called Throckmorton a good catholic, and added: 'if ye do continue in the same way that ye began and be not afraid to say your conscience, ye shall deserve great reward of God and thanks of the king's grace at length'.[8] More was too discreet to visit the Queen's Head himself, although Cromwell later alleged that he had attended other meetings to frame plans 'very different from what the peace and interest of the realm required' — whatever that means.[9] The Aragonese faction was also represented in the Lower House of Convocation by a hard-core group of conservatives: Peter Ligham (a friend of Fisher), Thomas Pelles, Robert Clyff, John Baker, Adam Travers and Rowland Philips — men all indicted for *praemunire* by Cromwell in June 1531.[10] More was in contact with Pelles and others about the assault on heresy in 1531 and 1532. But he was politically active, too, within the Aragonese framework, finally accepting (alongside Fisher and Nicholas Wilson) that conscience could rightly drive a man into distasteful activities if the cause was just, and if opposition was politically feasible.[11]

The men who strove to isolate and defeat the Aragonese party were those promoting radical ideas, namely Cranmer, Foxe and Cromwell. These three now began to coalesce into a unified

---

4 *LP* v. 879, 941. Macklem, 143–4. D. Knowles, *The Religious Orders in England: The Tudor Age* (Cambridge, 1971), chs. 17–18.
5 Knowles, 206 n. 2.
6 *LP* xii. II. 952–3.
7 SP 1/125, fos. 247–51 (*LP* xii. II. 952). See below, p. 161, and Appendix 2.
8 See Appendix 2. This document was discovered by Professor Elton.
9 G.R. Elton, *Studies in Tudor and Stuart Politics and Government* (Cambridge, 1974), vol. i. 165.
10 KB 145/10/23.
11 See below, pp. 158–61.

grouping, having found common ground by December 1530, and were soon joined by Thomas Audley (Speaker of the Commons), and Sir George Boleyn (Anne's brother).[12] They attempted in 1531 to persuade Henry to translate *Collectanea satis copiosa* into some form of immediate action, and all agreed that the 'privilege' of England demanded trial of Henry's marriage by English judges — by the archbishop of York or English Church in Convocation failing Warham's co-operation.[13] Cromwell believed, too, that Parliament was the right body to declare that this could be done despite papal anathema. However, Henry wavered on the marriage question for a further two years. Remorselessly driven by Anne Boleyn, he inclined to a radical policy insofar as it offered a final solution to the divorce crisis. He also felt an intense desire to assume the caesaropapism he had found in the *Collectanea*. On the other hand, Henry VIII was catholic by temperament, and Cromwell's proposals were truly drastic and possibly dangerous.

While Henry thus mused upon his doubts, Cromwell aimed to strengthen his position by destroying the English Church's legislative independence. No one could then dispute the power of an act of Parliament to bind all Henry's subjects, and the logical outcome could be a domestic solution of the divorce issue, followed by acts of appeals, supremacy, succession and treasons. Cromwell was steadily convincing himself that statute provided an effective means both to govern the realm and to impose a measure of religious reform which appealed to national unity on a basis of moderation, avoiding both popery and sacramentarianism.[14] How far these beliefs, which later became matters of principle for Cromwell, were original in 1531 is unclear. They may have owed much to the widely-held (and wholly responsible) convictions of moderate common lawyers like St German, whose tract *New Additions* (published before 25 March 1532) and *Treatise Concerning the Division between the Spiritualty and Temporalty* (before 25 March 1533) now became the premier justifications of Parliament's legislative supremacy in the interests of national unity and reconciliation between clergy and laity.[15] Nevertheless, Cromwell's views gained expres-

12 Audley and Sir George (now viscount Rochford) both assisted Cromwell in the assault on Convocation in February 1531.
13 C[alendar of] S[tate] P[apers] S[panish], *1529–1530* (London, 1879), 429, 433, 460.
14 Elton, *Studies*, vol. ii. 215–35.
15 *A Little Treatise Called New Additions*, in *Doctor and Student*, ed. T.F.T. Plucknett and J.L. Barton (Selden Society, London, 1974). *A Treatise Concernynge the Division Betwene the Spirytualtie and Temporaltie*, in *The Complete Works of St Thomas More*, vol. ix, *The Apology*, ed. J.B. Trapp (New Haven, 1979).

sion through the medium of political opportunism. A year after the Pardon of the Clergy, Cromwell would bring into play the Commons' own grievances, working up anticlerical feeling and xenophobia in Parliament in order to create an emotionally-charged consensus by which the clergy and Aragonese faction might be destroyed politically.[16] He would declare a personal war on chapter one of Magna Carta, and would ensure in his triumph his arrival as Henry VIII's chief minister. In other words, Cromwell aimed to tame the clergy as the means to dictate future royal policy, and his one trump card in an outrageous political gamble was that Henry needed a divorce.

Unlike the Aragonese faction, Cromwell and his confederates had to work through Parliament rather than the Council. Cranmer and Foxe were not even in the Council proper in 1531, so that the radicals were weak there until they gained Henry's undivided support. Cromwell would defeat More in May 1532 by means of the Supplication against the Ordinaries, although in order to win he had ultimately to rely on direct royal intervention rather than a Parliamentary statute. That fact alone tells us something about Cromwell's rise to power. Henry's egoistic attraction to caesaropapism was undoubtedly a hindrance rather than a help to true political revolution. If Cromwell had once aimed to declare the English 'privilege' and national sovereignty by act of Parliament, making human positive law the foundation of a radical exercise in statecraft, it was singularly unfortunate that Henry VIII had opted so firmly and so soon for Byzantine supremacy over the church. It was also a sign of weakness that Cromwell's Act of Appeals in 1533 was obliged to define Henry's sovereignty in terms of 'divers sundry old authentic histories and chronicles'.[17] Henry VIII became *rex imperator*; England became an empire. But a political revolution was unnecessarily made to rest on an ideological presumption which could not be made good by an agreed definition of an imperial constitution.[18] It was at worst a political fiasco, at best an anomaly which took Cromwell untold effort to rectify.[19]

The third and most powerful political grouping during 1531 comprised the dukes of Norfolk and Suffolk, the earls of Wiltshire and Sussex, Stephen Gardiner (promoted bishop of Winchester in

16 See below, ch. 9.
17 24 Hen. VIII, c. 12.
18 Cf. R. Koebner, 'The Imperial Crown of this Realm', *Bulletin of the Institute of Historical Research*, vol. xxvi (1953), 30.
19 Elton, *Reform and Reformation*, ch. 8.

October 1531),[20] lord Darcy, and other former members of the inner ring of early 1530.[21] With the exception of Gardiner, these men were neither first-rate nor principled, but were a reshaped version of the aristocratic reaction against Wolsey. Gardiner was the exception in terms of ability. Elected Master of Trinity Hall in 1525 while still under thirty, he was (as Cranmer put it) a man of 'fine wit' and 'crafty cavillation'. Formerly Wolsey's protégé and secretary, he became Henry's secretary in July 1529, in which role he became noted for unusual secrecy and intrigue behind the scenes.[22] Younger than Cromwell, he was equally ambitious and did much to impede Cromwell's rise to power — convincing Cromwell that the principal secretary's office was now the key to political ascendancy. Treacherous to Wolsey in 1529, Gardiner had also played a part in ensuring the cardinal's failure to make a comeback in 1530.[23] He was plainly allied with Norfolk in 1531 to further his own advancement.

But Cromwell, too, was allowed to work his passage with Norfolk's group, both as a Parliamentary draftsman and executive in government. As a councillor, Cromwell was an asset to Norfolk's regime by virtue of sheer slog and efficiency, and the duke used him constantly on government business during 1531 and 1532.[24] However, Norfolk accepted few of Cromwell's political opinions until the summer of 1532, when it became clear that Henry would at last adopt a radical policy on the divorce. It was this lack of heavyweight support which obliged Cromwell to outfoot the Aragonese faction in Parliament rather than the Council, since Norfolk sprang back from schism now as surely as he had in 1529. On learning the true nature of *Collectanea satis copiosa* in September 1530, the duke hastened to assure the papal nuncio that he was himself devoted to Rome and 'had always stood and would in future stand by the clergy'.[25] He would give ground only insofar as the king 'distinctly declared his will more for one thing than for the other' — a classic statement of Norfolk's political alphabet.[26] All the same, this position had real validity for the duke, since he and his supporters knew that Henry was of their persuasion, too, when away from Anne Boleyn. They also still believed that a way could

20 *LP* v. 484.
21 See above, p. 128.
22 A.J. Slavin, *Politics and Profit* (Cambridge, 1966), 22.
23 *LP* iv. 6112, 6204.
24 S.E. Lehmberg, *The Reformation Parliament* (Cambridge, 1970), 132.
25 *CSPS, 1529—1530*, 429.
26 *Ibid.*

be found to bully Clement VII into referring Henry's divorce suit back for English judgment. Thus Norfolk, Wiltshire and Suffolk had been eager to announce the 'privilege' of England to the nuncio in September 1530,[27] while their considered attitude to Cromwell's concurrent wish to destroy the clergy's independent jurisdiction by *praemunire* proceedings would take shape as the Pardon of the Clergy in February and March 1531.

Nevertheless, Norfolk's aristocratic group was not particularly homogenous. Loyal to the king and anxious to solve the divorce crisis, the conservative nobility lacked (as ever) an agreed prog-ramme of its own making. Gardiner, its one claim to creativity, would soon revolt against Cromwell's attack on ecclesiastical lib-erty, and risked (and gained) Henry's wrath by defecting to More's camp in March 1532.[28] Similarly, Norfolk and Wiltshire were uneasy bedfellows. The duke had temporarily split the Boleyns in his own interest, imbuing Wiltshire with a healthy respect for conservatism since the latter's ennoblement, while Anne and Sir George Boleyn looked to Cromwell by 1531. But it could only be a matter of time before the overriding need for the Boleyns to dis-place Catherine as Queen caused the lines to be redrawn. Norfolk was himself poised for flight from Wiltshire. He wished to confirm his standing as chief councillor against the earl and his now insolent daughter,[29] a tactic made possible for the duke by the death of Wolsey.[30] He wished also to rally the forces of traditional nobility against an anticipated alliance between the reunited Boleyns and Cromwell. Norfolk thus began a remarkable campaign for influ-ence against his niece, the strategies of which were played out entirely at Court although interactions no doubt occurred in the Council. Whereas Anne had attempted to persuade Henry that her young cousin should marry Princess Mary, she thus now argued the exact opposite, insinuating dangerously that Norfolk had dynastic ambition.[31] The duke accordingly killed the suspicion by contracting his son to Frances Vere, daughter of the earl of Oxford.[32] In May 1531 Norfolk expressed open sympathy for the Queen, informing the marquis of Exeter that her courage was 'supernatural', and that 'it was the Devil . . . who was the inventor

27 *CSPS, 1529–1530*, 445; *LP* v. 45.
28 *LP* v. 1013, 1019. See below, p. 194.
29 *LP* v. 216.
30 On 29 November 1530.
31 *CSPS, 1529–1530*, 373.
32 *LP* v. 941.

of this accursed dispute'.[33] Norfolk's duchess had meanwhile become fully reconciled to Catherine, and was dismissed from Court for a time at Anne's instigation 'because she spoke too freely . . . for the Queen'.[34] By early June, Norfolk and Suffolk were known to have agreed that 'now the time was come when all the world should strive to dismount the King from his folly'.[35] Chapuys was naturally elated by these developments, but Norfolk was not to live up to the ambassador's hopes despite continuation of his pension from Charles V. The duke's effort against a Boleyn ascendancy would be thwarted, as was inevitable, by his failure to end the divorce crisis.[36] In the face of Cromwell's bid for power in 1532,[37] Norfolk could only assist Wiltshire in a futile attempt to bludgeon Archbishop Warham into pronouncing immediate sentence of annulment for Henry according to the 'privilege' of England,[38] and, failing this, to realign as best he could with the Boleyns and (ultimately) Cromwell. In a gesture of astounding hypocrisy, then, Norfolk instructed Benet to assure the pope that he had discharged his conscience in this matter 'like a true catholic man'.[39]

The conflict in Council after October 1530 ensured that no immediate government business was placed before Parliament when it reassembled on 16 January 1531.[40] Attention was instead focussed on Southern Convocation which had gathered four days before.[41] The *praemunire* indictments filed the previous July against the fifteen clerics and Anthony Husye had been left pending in King's Bench until 20 January, when in theory those persons who had not already done so were due to enter their postponed appearances.[42] No further indictments had been filed in connection with Cromwell's revised proposal of the autumn: since the clergy did not form a legal entity, it is more probable that from the first he planned to deal with them in Parliament and Convocation.[43] What actually happened in the first three months of 1531 reflected Henry VIII's implementation of a short-term policy thrashed out in Council. The Aragonese party, opposed to any action against the clergy,

33 *LP* v. 238.
34 *Ibid.*
35 *LP* v. 287.
36 See below, ch. 9.
37 Begun in mid-February.
38 *LP* v. 805.
39 *St. Pap.*, vii. 349; *LP* v. 831.
40 Lehmberg, *Reformation Parliament*, 118.
41 *Ibid.*, 109–10.
42 KB 27/1077, *roti.* 27–28 (*Rex*).
43 Lehmberg, *Reformation Parliament*, 108 n.5.

were overruled by the aristocratic and radical groups. Norfolk would not consent to the reduction of the clergy's independent jurisdiction, but he and Cromwell were united on the need to assert over Convocation the 'privilege' of England and Henry's imperial status. Agreement had been reached by 13 January, when Norfolk and Gardiner treated Chapuys to a garbled precis of some Cromwellian research on English imperial history.[44] The duke began by referring to the statutes of provisors and *praemunire*, and drew attention to the resolute will of the English people to oppose any papal attempt 'to usurp authority'. Henry 'had a right of empire in his kingdom, and recognised no superior'. There had been 'an Englishman who had conquered Rome, to wit, Brennus; that Constantine reigned here, and the mother of Constantine was English'. Norfolk argued that the pope, in claiming jurisdiction over Henry's divorce, was trespassing on the preserves of the archbishop of Canterbury. He produced an inscription copied on parchment relating to King Arthur: *Patricius Arthurus, Britanniae, Galliae, Germaniae, Daciae Imperator*. Chapuys, in a riposte worthy of More, answered, 'I was sorry he was not also called Emperor of Asia'![45] The conversation left him mystified, but it had manifestly been arranged in the hope that Charles V would be persuaded by incipient events to allow Clement to refer the divorce case back for English judgment. Henry had attempted meanwhile to induce Warham to disobey the papal prohibition on hearing the suit, but had totally failed.[46] Plans for measures and pressures were therefore finalized as the logical next step against both archbishop and Convocation directly, and pope and emperor vicariously. Such devices were usually financial in Tudor England, and Henry and the aristocratic group gave high priority to obtaining a large cash composition from the whole clergy in Convocation, a motive Chapuys had believed lay behind the earlier indictments.[47] The Aragonese party was greatly alarmed by these developments,[48] but the radical group continued to support Norfolk, having done well enough in the circumstances.

Very early in the session, Convocation learned of Henry's demand for a substantial sum of money.[49] This was ingeniously presented: it was declared 'what great charges the king had wrong-

44 *LP* v. 45.
45 *Ibid.*
46 *Ibid.*
47 *CSPS, 1529–1530*, 396.
48 *LP* v. 105, 112.
49 Lehmberg, *Reformation Parliament*, 110.

fully been at . . . about the matter of divorce in suit to the Court of Rome, and obtaining of sundry instruments of foreign universities'. Henry's expenses amounted to £100,000, the 'only cause whereof' was the dissimulation of the clergy. He therefore required reimbursement.[50] Despite Fisher's protests, the clergy realized that they would have to compound quickly for fear of revived *praemunire* proceedings against the entire clerical estate. At first they hoped to settle for £40,000, but Henry refused to haggle and on 24 January they agreed to £100,000. The money was to be payable over five years, supposedly in appreciation of Henry's past services to the church. In return, Convocation begged 'most humbly prostrate' that the king would 'grant to all and singular the prelates and clergy of the province of Canterbury, and to all the registers and scribes' a general pardon for their offences in *praemunire*.[51] Shortly afterwards, the clergy also petitioned Henry to guarantee their ancient liberties and privileges, and to declare the precise meaning of *praemunire* that they might not again incur its penalties.[52]

After some sparring, the majority in Council replied by issuing the texts of five articles it wished to be added to the subsidy prologue.[53] These were introduced into Convocation by Warham on 7 February.[54] The first article added to Henry's style the title of protector and supreme head of the English Church (*ecclesiae et cleri Anglicani cuius protector et supremum caput is solus est*); the second demanded that the clergy should speak of the 'cure of souls' having been committed to the king; the third that the liberties the clergy had petitioned Henry to defend were to be defined as those which 'do not detract from his regal power and the laws of the realm'; the fourth that the clerics should seek pardon more humbly; finally, they were to acknowledge that the laity were likewise guilty of *praemunire*.[55] As so composed, the first three articles seemed to represent a compromise between the views of Henry VIII and the aristocratic and radical groups. As a majority statement, this was no doubt exactly what they were. A critical week followed. Despite the arguments of Audley, Cromwell and other councillors who

---

50 *Ibid.* Henry wanted a repeat of the clerical subsidy of 1523.

51 SP 1/56, fos. 84–88 (*LP* iv. 6047 [3]). This document was, in fact, drawn in the King's Council, being in the hand of Thomas Eden, clerk of the Council in Star Chamber.

52 J.J. Scarisbrick, 'The Pardon of the Clergy, 1531', *Cambridge Historical Journal*, vol. xii (1956), 32–4.

53 *Ibid.*

54 *Ibid.*

55 *Ibid.*

were present as negotiators in Convocation from the 7th to the 10th, the supremacy article encountered stiff resistance.[56] Eventually, the words 'as far as the law of Christ allows' (*quantum per Christi legem licet*) were added as a saving clause.[57] Often credited to Fisher, this limitation was more likely, and ironically, the work of Cromwell or Audley.[58] The second article the clergy rejected outright. By the deft alteration of a case-ending, the king's claim to the cure of souls was obliterated and the doctrine of the two swords preserved intact.[59] This the Council accepted in exchange for the concession of Henry's new style. Nobody except Henry VIII seriously believed that the king had the cure of his subjects' souls. Henry had probably himself insisted on the article against Norfolk's better judgment after re-reading *Collectanea satis copiosa*.[60] The Council's remaining articles were either made innocuous or deleted.[61] But a failure for Convocation was marked by the clergy's inability to secure confirmation for the future of their ancient liberties and privileges. In the face of the contentious and indefinite grant offered by article three, the clergy preferred to substitute an entirely new article which prayed that Henry would continue to defend the church with his customary zeal against heretics 'et alios oppugnatores'.[62]

Convocation's certificate of the subsidy, engrossed on parchment and incorporating all the changes, was presented to Henry on 8 March by Warham, John Stokesley and John Vesey.[63] By the end of the month, both Lords and Commons had passed a bill for the Pardon of the Clergy, with the proviso that the benefits of the act should be denied to the clergy of the Northern Province unless they agreed to pay a sum equal to two years' revenues from their offices.[64] All other clerics, their judges, registrars, scribes and other officials were pardoned, and the various persons indicted the previous July could plead the benefit of the statute and secure their discharge. A bill was next introduced for the pardon of the king's temporal subjects. The Commons had expressed concern early in the session that all men 'which had anything to do with the Cardinal

56 Lehmberg, *Reformation Parliament,* 113–14.
57 Scarisbrick, 'Pardon', 34.
58 Lehmberg, *Reformation Parliament,* 114.
59 Scarisbrick, 'Pardon', 34–5.
60 Henry's target at this stage was still, however, the pope rather than the English clergy.
61 Scarisbrick, 'Pardon', 34.
62 *Ibid.*
63 Lehmberg, *Reformation Parliament,* 116.
64 22 Hen. VIII, c. 15.

were in the same case' as the clergy.[65] At length, Henry conceded the point, and the act as passed granted to all laymen a free pardon for all offences against the statutes of provisors and *praemunire* committed before 30 March.[66] These statutes were the only important business concluded by Parliament during the session of 1531, though other matters occupied Lords and Commons notably socio-economic problems and complaints against the clergy.[67] It is, however, almost impossible to discover who was promoting these other measures, mainly because of the conflict over policy in the Council itself. Whereas it was likely in 1529 that More would have approved as chancellor any government legislation, this assumption may not be applied in 1531. Government bills could have progressed through Parliament in 1531 with the sponsorship of the aristocratic group alone. More, as we shall see, was to make an important speech to both Houses on 30 March, but nothing can otherwise be discovered about his Parliamentary activities.

A remarkable document is, however, extant from the session of 1531, and it demands attention despite lack of concrete evidence that it was discussed formally in Parliament.[68] Extant now among Cromwell's papers, it is an undated collection of proposals for Parliamentary legislation, the first article of which concerned the call for a vernacular Bible. As a whole, the document is an incomplete but composite fair copy of earlier drafts (now lost), and had been written out fair in order to be checked, amended and further improved. Some of its ideas are thus well developed and cast as draft bills; others are no more than outline proposals. Some pages are blank, whole chunks have been cut out, and a few items are represented by headings only. Visually, it looks like an official document, but one with a great deal of work still to be done on it. But most interesting of all, the document proclaims the political involvement of Christopher St German. It is not, as was formerly thought, the masterpiece of Thomas Cromwell.[69] Not only is St German's quite unmistakable and distinctive hand (which also writes the famous St Germanism 'some say') one of two which compiled the document — the other hand belongs to an unknown clerk. St German's is the only hand which corrected it, and added all the afterthoughts and revisions. In other words, St German had full

65 Edward Hall, *The Triumphant Reigne of Kyng Henry the VIII,* ed. C. Whibley (London, 1904), vol. ii. 184.

66 22 Hen. VIII, c. 16.

67 Lehmberg, *Reformation Parliament*, 119–20, 122–6.

68 SP 6/7, art. 14 (*LP* v. 50).

69 G.R. Elton, *Reform and Renewal* (Cambridge, 1973), 71–7.

editorial control over his copy, and must thus be cast in the role of policy maker. As to the document's date, its contents show that we are reading a piece first begun, if not wholly completed, in 1530, which was worked up afresh for the 1531 session of Parliament.[70] Why the document ended up among Cromwell's papers is a question to which we shall return.

The document is important enough to be singled out, because it is a strikingly comprehensive, creative and non-partisan programme for the nation's religious and socio-economic reform in the context of 1530 and 1531. Arguably, it is the most comprehensive reform manifesto devised in the entire reign of Henry VIII. One half of it is concerned with the clergy, especially the familiar problem of relations between church and state. A proposed act of Parliament begins by remarking that the 'laws, uses and customs' of the spiritual jurisdiction as administered in the church courts seem so partial to the clergy that they have caused much lay resentment. Hence it is suggested that Parliament shall authorize a 'great standing council' of bishops and laity to review the problem, and determine which aspects of clerical jurisdiction should be avoided or reformed. Specific provisions included the following: the great standing council was to judge whether desire for an English New Testament sprang from 'meekness and charity'. If it did, the king would allow the council to 'have such part thereof translated into the mother tongue as shall be thought convenient'. The standing council was then to enquire into the spread of heresy, assuming control of all initial investigations. The council would reason with those detected or delated, in order to assess the level of seriousness and involvement, and would then hand over hard cases alone to the bishops for trial in the spiritual courts. Next, the council was to evaluate canon law and custom, reforming by Parliamentary statute those areas within Parliament's jurisdiction, and reporting the rest to Henry VIII, who would then negotiate direct with the clergy. Other detailed measures were designed to increase 'love, amity and good agreement' between churchmen and laymen, and to enforce on the parish clergy a rigorous observation of traditional liturgical practices. Particular abuses were also marked down for abolition or reform. For example, burial services and masses for the dead were to be said without fees. Pilgrimage centres and shrines were to be regulated by Parliament to avoid clerical rackets. Nobody having a financial interest in a shrine should have a monopoly of selling candles to pilgrims, or resell to the public candles already paid for

70 J.J. Scarisbrick, 'Thomas More: the King's Good Servant', *Thought: Fordham University Quarterly*, vol. lii (1977), 259–65.

by previous visitors. Similarly, a confessor should not supplement his income by requiring penitents to visit a shrine in which he had bought shares as an investment.

The second half of St German's document dealt with the perennial Tudor problems of poverty and unemployment, and is even more interesting. St German here proposed quite astonishing legislation for large-scale help for the poor, and has a clear claim to be named in consequence the father of Tudor paternalism. The great standing council was to organise a national programme of state works on the highways to create new employment, raising the necessary finance by levying a new tax on every household, church, abbey and college. Common chests were to be established in every town, city and county for this purpose, and funds were to be provided, too, for relief of the impotent poor. Henry VIII had himself, we are told, already promised £3,000 in cash for the fund, and had offered half the income from penal statutes. In short, England was to emulate a growing number of Continental cities, accepting the need for outdoor relief and public works, although with a note of harshness typical of Tudor paternalism, St German made it a felony to refuse wilfully employment offered and to persist in begging.

But the truly advanced feature of St German's programme was that, as well as tackling symptoms, it also attempted to penetrate the economic cause of poverty (as it was thought), namely inflation. The great standing council had the power to call merchants, clothiers, food suppliers and craftsmen before it, to see how prices, notably those of food and essential goods, could be controlled. The council would then review wages, enquire into enclosures, investigate rural depopulation, and reverse decay of cottages 'that were wont to nourish' husbandry. Finally, it would set up a pay research board to see whether existing wages in craft industries were sufficient to support basic subsistence at a time of rising living costs. In this connection, too, St German floated the idea of establishing a basic minimum wage for a fair day's work.

All this represents a most enlightened and Utopian scheme, and the obvious question is, did it involve Thomas More? Beyond reasonable doubt, it did not. More may have approved the call for an English New Testament, because he had argued in his *Dialogue Concerning Heresies* (1529) that the 'whole commodity' should not be withheld 'from any holy people because of harm that by their own folly and fault may come to some part'.[71] Some persons would

71 *The English Works of Sir Thomas More*, ed. W.E. Campbell (London, 1931), vol. ii. 243–4.

abuse a vernacular Bible, but More would permit individuals to enjoy this privilege under strict episcopal licence. He might have supported, too, St German's plan for a council to investigate heresy — though the council would supersede the bishops' investigatory functions — inasmuch as he was engaged in police work against heretics as lord chancellor. However, Sir Thomas would have objected to both tone and substance of those proposals which required the standing council to revise the law of the church, removing pro-clerical bias, and would have jibbed strongly at one of St German's detailed measures which attacked the spiritual courts by barring them from infringing 'royal' jurisdiction over lay property. Neither More nor his party could have accepted, either, an injunction forbidding criticism of certain acts of Parliament, notably that touching tithe on timber called 'silva cedua' (45 Edw. III, c. 3), and the three anticlerical statutes enacted in 1529. Above all, though, More could not have stomached the whole underlying premise behind St German's document, which was that Parliament had the power to correct clerical abuses and prune canon law in the interests of national unity. This was a theory identical to that worked out in St German's *New Additions* and *Treatise Concerning the Division between Spiritualty and Temporalty,* books which More unreservedly abominated.[72] *New Additions*, which aimed to discover Parliament's power with regard to the spiritual jurisdiction, had concluded that the human positive law of the realm might revise what the clergy conceived by prescription to be the liberty of the church, provided such law was consonant with conscience.[73] Even worse, St German had unashamedly implied that the ultimate test was pragmatic. Who living in Henrician England would argue in the last resort that Parliament would ever do anything it had not power to do?[74] Furthermore, the Cromwellian route to the Submission of the Clergy and the Act of Appeals was plainly signposted by *New Additions*; signposted, too, by St German's document of 1530/31, because the standing council was to prune canon law with Parliament's authority behind it, and restrict the activities of the church courts in England.

Similarly, the *Treatise Concerning Division* prompted vitriolic condemnation from More, who raised doubts in his *Apology* about St German's sincerity and professed purpose. Since St German

---

72 Cf. *The Complete Works of St Thomas More*, vol. ix, *The Apology*, ed. J.B. Trapp (New Haven, 1979), xxxvii–lxxxv.
73 Appendix to *Doctor and Student*, ed. Plucknett and Barton, 317–40.
74 *Ibid.*, 317–19.

wished to heal the division and 'grudge' between clergy and laity, Sir Thomas sarcastically dubbed his mild opponent 'the Pacifier'.[75] St German still wanted in the *Division* (1532) both restraint of *ex officio* investigations of suspected heretics and removal of pro-clerical bias from the ecclesiastical courts, and these suggestions continued to arouse More's bitter antipathy. St German re-stated in the *Division* the arguments of educated lay pietists and moderate common lawyers. However, More's position on the jurisdictional issue was entrenched. His *Apology* (1533), he declared, was 'a defence of the very good, old, and long-approved laws both of this realm and of the whole corps of Christendom, which laws this Pacifier in his "Book of Division", to the encouraging of heretics and peril of the Catholic faith, with warm words and cold reasons oppugneth'.[76] But St German was a most difficult adversary, because he was doctrinally non-partisan, and remained an orthodox catholic until the Act of Supremacy.[77] When More launched his diatribes, St German could not be branded a heretic himself. Sir Thomas thus had to settle for the (specious and untrue) argument that the *Division*'s author was deluded by 'some other subtle shrew that is of his counsel'.[78] Faced likewise with the clerical abuses which St German drew from John Gerson, More was obliged to fall weakly back on the argument that it was one thing to draw attention to clerical abuses in Latin, but quite another to lay them before the public in English.[79] The whole controversy continued (now somewhat tediously) with St German's *Salem and Bizance* and More's *Debellation* (both 1533).

It is probable that the antagonism between More and St German first arose when the latter devised his Parliamentary draft of 1530/31. But was St German, a man well over seventy in 1530, working for anyone other than himself and the public weal at this time? The question cannot yet be answered, although the sources may still be cajoled into yielding further secrets.[80] With his opinions as expressed in his draft, *New Additions* and the *Division*, it is hardly possible that St German was working for the Aragonese faction. Proof that he was an impossible associate of More's as early as 1530

---

75 *The Apologye of Syr Thomas More, Knyght*, ed. A. I. Taft (Early English Text Society, London, 1930), 60, 63. Since this book was written, the Yale edition of *The Apology* has appeared (n. 72 *supra*).
76 *Apologye of Syr Thomas More*, xli–ii.
77 After the act, St German wrote *An Answer to a Letter* (1535).
78 *Apologye of Syr Thomas More*, 67.
79 *Ibid.*, 66.
80 I am working on St German.

is surely supplied by the last chapter of the Second Dialogue of *Doctor and Student*, which enquired whether clerical privileges were any more immune from secular repeal than those of the laity unless justified explicitly by divine law.[81] On the other hand, there is not a scrap of evidence to connect St German with either the aristocratic or radical groups between 1530 and 1532. Was he, therefore, working directly for Henry VIII? The suggestion is not improbable. St German may well have been noticed during the abortive meeting of clergy and lawyers at Hampton Court in October 1530. It was then that Henry required to know about the legislative competence of Parliament,[82] and St German may have previewed the opinions he later presented in *New Additions*. Both *New Additions* and the *Division*, too, were published by Thomas Berthelet, the king's printer, during the official propaganda campaign to whip up support for a solution to the divorce crisis.[83] Assuredly, the otherwise obscure Middle Temple lawyer momentarily gained influence in the situation of 1530 and 1531 — a channel of communication to authority which enabled him to promote on a second flank the socioeconomic reforms set out in his Parliamentary draft. His was a classic case of the intellectual called from the Inns of Court (or wherever) to public service by a government short on workable ideas. Moreover, 'called' does seem to be the right word, because St German had seen Henry VIII at least once. That is apparent from the fact that the king had already promised in 1531 to put £3,000 into St German's poor box. As to why St German's reform plan eventually turned up among Thomas Cromwell's archives, the explanation is that Cromwell knew good ideas when he saw them. Henry VIII's second minister had long made a habit of filing away other people's papers for future use, as is best proved by the history of the Commons' Supplication against the Ordinaries.[84] The same can now be said about the 'Cromwellian' Poor Law of 1536.[85]

Before the end of the 1531 session of Parliament, it was decided to silence rumour and bolster the king's case by delivering to both Houses of Parliament those opinions (now printed by Berthelet) in favour of the divorce which Cranmer and others had gathered from the universities of Europe, together with a printed abridgement (annexed to the opinions, and still in Latin) of *Collectanea satis*

81 *Doctor and Student*, ed. Plucknett and Barton, 300–14.
82 *CSPS, 1529–1530*, 460.
83 B.L. C. 54. aa. 13; C. 142. dd. 14.
84 Elton, *Studies*, vol. ii. 107–36.
85 Elton, *Studies*, vol. ii. 137–54.

copiosa.[86] This was done on 30 March 1531, and the lord chancellor was made responsible. More discharged the duty with evident discomfort, and Roper implied that he had agreed to appear only at Henry's own request.[87] He began with a speech in the Lords, explaining that he was instructed to refute those who said that Henry pursued a divorce 'out of love for some lady', and not for genuine scruples of conscience.[88] The king's conscience was much troubled by his present marriage. More then asked the clerk to read the opinions. When he had finished, Bishops Stokesley and Long-land began to support the divorce, but Bishops Standish and Clerk protested that insufficient time remained to do justice to the Queen's position. The duke of Norfolk hastily intervened to the effect that the king had sent the documents to Parliament for information not debate. Nevertheless, someone was quick enough to ask More for his opinion, 'on which he said that he had many times already declared it to the king; and he said no more'.[89] The earl of Shrewsbury also declined to make a statement on the subject. In the afternoon, More next led a deputation of peers and bishops to the Commons, where his speech was noted by Hall.

> You of this worshipful House, I am sure, be not so ignorant but you know well that the king our sovereign lord hath married his brother's wife, for she was both wedded and bedded with his brother Prince Arthur, and therefore you may surely say that he hath married his brother's wife. If this marriage be good or no, many clerks do doubt. Wherefore the king, like a virtuous prince, willing to be satisfied in his conscience, and also for the surety of his realm hath with great deliberation consulted with great clerks, and hath sent my lord of London here present to the chief Universities of all Christendom to know their opinion and judgment in that behalf.[90]

More then asked the clerk to read the selected opinions again, after which he concluded:

> Now you of this Common House may report . . . what you have seen and heard, and then all men shall openly perceive that the

---

86 *Gravissimae atque Exactissimae Illustrissimarum totius Italiae et Galliae Academiarum Censurae*, dated 1530 (i.e. before 25 March 1531). B.L. C. 37. f.2; G. 1251.
87 Roper, 51.
88 *LP* v. 171.
89 *Ibid*.
90 Hall, *Henry the VIII*, vol. ii. 185.

king hath not attempted this matter of will or pleasure, as some strangers report, but only for the discharge of his conscience and surety of the succession of his realm.[91]

Hall thought the opinions convincing; Chapuys, in contrast, heard that Stokesley and Longland spoke in the king's defence, but were received by the Commons in silence.[92] The next day More ended the session in the Lords. Speaking for Henry (who also attended), he expressed the king's satisfaction with Parliament, which was prorogued until 13 October.[93]

More must indeed have done all this 'at the king's request', but Roper was perhaps right, too, that the duty was embarrassing enough to persuade him to solicit Norfolk for help in resigning on grounds of poor health.[94] There was nothing wrong with More's health: he would later endure the rigours of extended imprisonment in the Tower with few ill effects. Sir Thomas was concerned, rather, 'lest further attempts after should follow, which, contrary to his conscience, he was likely to be put unto'.[95] His position had become intolerable. Although excused by Henry in 1530 from active involvement in the campaign for the divorce, More was obliged by virtue of his office to preside a year later over a Parliamentary charade on that issue. This was inevitable and More knew it. Roper was also right in saying that the chancellor did not show his own mind in Parliament.[96] But this was not to More's credit: silence implied consent (*qui tacet consentire videtur*),[97] and he had not offered a word to suggest either that the opinions read out were not the truth or that they had been selected in the king's favour.[98] On the contrary, his assertion before the Commons that Catherine 'was both wedded and bedded' with Prince Arthur, by which 'you may surely say' that Henry had married his brother's wife was highly damaging to the Queen, whose whole case rested on her conviction that her first marriage had remained unconsummated. Only the subtlest among More's audience could hope to probe the meaning of 'you may surely say'. The chancellor had been obliged to associ-

---

91 *Ibid.*, ii. 195.
92 *LP* v. 171.
93 Lehmberg, *Reformation Parliament,* 130.
94 Roper, 51.
95 *Ibid.*
96 *Ibid.*
97 As Warham observed when Henry's new title was approved in Convocation on 11 February 1531.
98 Only opinions in Henry's favour were, of course, laid before Parliament.

ate himself unquestionably with the king's policy. As a minister of state, he could not escape the greatest issue on the current political scene: 'no gracious concession, sincere or not, to his conscience could insulate him against the contagion'.[99] No wonder that rumours gained currency that he would resign. These had been heard as early as 21 February 1531, based at that time on the known mortification of the Aragonese faction at the débâcle in Convocation over the king's new title.[100]

Why then did More not resign? The answer lies in his convinced belief that the battle in Council could still be won; the Aragonese faction was not conceding defeat in the spring of 1531. With Anne Boleyn's insolence growing, the duchess of Norfolk reconciled to Catherine, Norfolk and Suffolk hovering in the same direction and the aristocratic group in potential disarray, there was a chance that the Aragonese party might yet obliterate the thrust of the radical group. For a moment in April, even Henry VIII seemed to doubt his Anne: he complained to Norfolk that he was abused daily by her in a way Catherine had never contemplated.[101] The duke sympathized, sent words of comfort to the Queen and began some serious thinking. Similarly, the Pardon of the Clergy had proved a limited success for Cromwell and a major setback for the Aragonese faction, but Cromwell remained dependent on Norfolk throughout 1531, and it is to be doubted whether the duke had grasped the full significance of the concessions the Council had obtained from Convocation in February. More was certainly fighting to regain lost ground in February and March: he was described by Chapuys as 'the true father and protector' of the Aragonese interest, helping the ambassador's business forward in Council and at Court.[102] In recognition of his services, Charles V sent via Chapuys a friendly letter of thanks to More.[103] This was written in Brussels on 11 March and had arrived in England by the 22nd.[104] In the last week of March, however, Sir Thomas showed even greater preoccupation than usual with the need to appear loyal to Henry. He began avoiding Chapuys, a sure sign that the battle in Council had resumed. Shortly after More laid the universities' opinions before Parliament, Chapuys sent him word of the emperor's letter

99 Elton, *Studies,* vol. i. 163.

100 *LP* v. 112.

101 *LP* v. 216, 287 (p. 138).

102 *LP* v. 120.

103 Printed by H. Schulte Herbrüggen, *Sir Thomas More: Neue Briefe* (Münster, 1966), 97.

104 *LP* v. 148.

and requested leave to visit his house.[105] The ambassador reported
Sir Thomas's response in a despatch to Charles; always careful,
More was now obsessed by the need for discretion.

> He begged me for the honour of God to forbear, for although he
> had given already sufficient proof of his loyalty that he ought to
> incur no suspicion, whoever came to visit him, yet, considering
> the time, he ought to abstain from everything which might
> provoke suspicion; and if there were no other reason, such a
> visitation might deprive him of the liberty which he had always
> used in speaking boldly in those matters which concerned your
> Majesty and the Queen. He said he would not hold them in less
> regard than his life, not only out of the respect which is due to
> your Majesty and the Queen, but also for the welfare, honour,
> and conscience of his master, and the repose of his kingdom.
> With regard to the letter he begged me earnestly that I would
> keep it as it is till some other time, for if he received it he must
> communicate it, and he hoped a more propitious time would
> come for its acceptance, begging me to assure you of his most
> affectionate service.[106]

This was one of More's most important statements. It confirms that
the chancellor was acting as a principal spokesman for the Aragonese faction in Council; that this faction was engaged in opposition to
an extent that would ruin More if it could be proved that he had
liaised with Charles V; and that More was anxious not to lose such
influence as he had over policy, itself an admission that he did have
influence still. Sir Thomas had hoped to come to terms with his
tortuous position in 1531. He had engaged in compromising activities
— in Parliament on the king's behalf, with Chapuys against the
king's divorce. A point of particular note is that More now avoided
Chapuys and refused Charles's letter in order to 'incur no suspicion'. He wished to escape the dismissal and disgrace that would
come should his part in the organized opposition be discovered,
say, by Anne Boleyn. Nowhere does More state that he was
unhappy at the prospect of losing his integrity *vis-à-vis* the king, his
sovereign lord. On the other hand, he had exerted himself at
Henry's request to the extent of embarrassing his conscience. The
'sufficient proof' he had 'already' given of his loyalty was most
recently his appearance in Parliament on 30 March, and this may
even have given the king renewed hope that he might eventually

105 *LP* v. 171.
106 *Ibid.*

win his chancellor round to supporting royal policy on the divorce.
More himself presumably saw the value of his Parliamentary performance in terms of increased influence over policy. His conscience could be appeased by reference to Henry VIII's own 'welfare,
honour, and conscience', and the 'repose' of England *in the long term*.
This was the exact argument More used when encouraging Sir
George Throckmorton to Parliamentary opposition in 1532. He
told Sir George that by discharging his conscience in support of the
catholic cause he would 'deserve great reward of God' and 'thanks
of the king's grace at length'.[107] Apart from supplying additional
proof that More well knew that for the present Henry's attitude was
likely to be very different, that the existing policy was hostile to the
catholic cause, and that he himself was endeavouring to change that
policy,[108] the statement shows that More held some sort of implicit
trust that a day would dawn when Henry would lose his infatuation
for Anne and come to his senses. After all, More had witnessed
while at Court the demise of Henry's previous amatory adventures.
Free of Anne's influence, the orthodox king would then perceive
the true worth of subjects whose ultimate loyalty was to the whole
corps of Christendom. Throckmorton was enough of a political
innocent to accept this remarkable reasoning, to such good purpose
that he maintained opposition in the Commons for five Parliamentary sessions. Nevertheless, there was clearly a genuine conviction
on More's side that his chancellorship could be justified in part as an
effort to unburden Henry VIII's conscience as well as his own.

During May 1531, the clergy of the Northern Province secured
their pardon by granting the king £18,840 and adopting the same
addition to the royal style as had been conceded by the Southern
Province in February.[109] After his success in steering the Council's
demands through Southern Convocation, Cromwell was also
given the job of arranging matters in the North, his man on the spot
being Brian Higdon, the dean of York.[110] The demands were fully
met after prolonged discussion, but Henry's new style did not pass
without a strong protest from Cuthbert Tunstall. Presiding over
Convocation during the archiepiscopal vacancy created by
Wolsey's death, Tunstall ordered his protest to be entered in the *acta*

---

107 SP 1/125, fo. 250. See appendix 2.
108 As Elton argued in *Studies*, vol. i. 169.
109 D. Wilkins, *Concilia Magnae Britanniae et Hiberniae* (London, 1737), vol. iii.
    744.
110 *LP* v. 224, 237.

of Convocation and sent an explanatory letter to Henry.[111] His protest identified well the issues and confusions which dominated the politics of 1531. It was interesting, too, as a broadside from one who shared the alarm felt by More and Fisher. Tunstall expounded the several possible meanings of the king's new style, which he argued might seem inoffensive in itself were it not for the fact that certain persons lately prosecuted as suspected heretics had interpreted it in an ill sense. The royal 'supremacy' had misled heretics into questioning the jurisdiction of their ordinaries, and Tunstall believed that the clergy's concession should be couched in precise language to prevent such misconstruction. If it was meant that Henry was supreme head under Christ in his dominions, and in respect of the English clergy in temporal affairs, that was nothing more than all clerics were willing to acknowledge. The words *in temporalibus* should therefore be added to the new style. If, in contrast, it was meant that Henry was supreme head of the church both in spirituals and temporals, and that this supremacy was conferred upon him by the law of Christ — there were some 'malevolent' persons who had, apparently, so construed the proviso *quantum per Christi legem licet* — then this construction was repugnant to catholic doctrine and Tunstall must dissent from it. Even if the proviso was intended as a limitation (which it was by Southern Convocation), it was necessary to discharge all ambiguity since the concession still appeared to pertain in some way to spiritual matters. The king could not be supreme head of the church: royal supremacy was not allowed by the law of Christ. The visible unity of the church would otherwise be nullified.

Henry responded with a letter which he probably composed himself.[112] This would have confirmed Tunstall's worst fears. Long, learned and thoroughly specious, the document merged ideas culled from *Collectanea satis copiosa* and Marsiglio of Padua with Henry's own conception of his new Byzantinism.[113] The king argued that Tunstall's proposed addition of *in temporalibus* suggested that he needed to protect himself against claiming to be head of the Mystical Body of Christ. But a claim of such perversity was never intended. Obviously, the concession could only mean 'in temporal affairs'. As St Paul spoke both of the church and the

---

111 Tunstall's letter to Henry is lost, but can be reconstructed from the king's reply. The protest was transcribed from the *acta* of Convocation by Wilkins, *Concilia,* vol. iii. 745.
112 Wilkins, *Concilia,* vol. iii, 762–5.
113 Cf. P. Hughes, *The Reformation in England* (New York, 1951), vol. i. 230–2; J.J. Scarisbrick, *Henry VIII* (London, 1968), 278–80.

Church of Corinth, so Tunstall should speak of the church as a whole whose head is Christ, and of the Church of England whose head is the king. Moreover, in speaking of *ecclesia,* the phrase *et cleri Anglicani* restrained 'by way of interpretation' the word *ecclesiae* as used in the concession, and amounted to meaning 'the clergy of England'.[114] Yet Henry refused in his next paragraph to accept that it was a power over the church in temporal matters alone that Christ's law had left to princes, power in spirituals having been left to the clergy. Tunstall's alleged proofs had contained no scriptural evidence that spiritual things should be wholly excluded. Scripture did not prove that the clergy's office was so excellent that their persons, acts and deeds should not be under the power of their prince by God assigned 'whom they should acknowledge as their head'. The clergy's spiritual preserve was to preach and administer the sacraments, and emperors and princes obeyed them as Christ's ambassadors for that purpose. In all other respects, the clergy were subject to princes as their head. Did not Justinian make laws *De episcopis et clericis*? Would he have done so had he not been persuaded that he was charged with a God-given sovereignty? Over the persons of priests, their laws, their acts and order of living, then, Henry was indeed *supremum caput.* As to spiritual things 'meaning by them the sacraments', not being worldly 'they have no worldly nor temporal head, but only Christ that did institute them'. If, however, the bishops have corrected clerical misconduct in the administration of the sacraments to alleviate public scandal, such correction has in reality always been through authority 'derived from the prince': the prelates 'intromit' themselves in such matters 'by sufferance or privilege'. Tunstall's protest had thus revealed fundamental differences of opinion as to what constituted 'temporals' and 'spirituals'. 'Spirituals' had hitherto meant, and meant to Tunstall, the teaching, sacraments, jurisdiction and government of the church. As stated in Henry's reply, it was to mean only the preaching and administration of the sacraments. The exchange of views indicated just how far the king's mind had moved towards royal supremacy in 1531. His ideas were outpacing in radicalism those of the majority in his Council. Henry's Christendom, composed of a collection of national congregations under the supreme headship of princes, allowed as little room for the papacy as it permitted unity within the universal church.

114 The relevant passage of the clergy's concession ran: '. . . in perniciem ecclesiae et cleri Anglicani (cuius singularem protectorem, unicum et supremum dominum, et quantum per Christi legem licet, etiam supremum caput ipsius majestatem recognoscimus) . . .'.

Although Parliament had been prorogued until October 1531, it did not meet again until January 1532. The new session was first postponed until 6 November, and then to 15 January.[115] Henry was said to be awaiting last-minute news both from Rome and from Edward Foxe, who had been sent to re-open negotiations with the French.[116] The Council, meanwhile, was unable to agree on a Parliamentary programme, and word was put out that the air in London and Westminster was too 'insalubrious' for members to return.[117] When Parliament did reassemble, the Commons first discussed uses, and financial and commonwealth matters, but little was achieved and Chapuys reported on 14 February that nothing had passed except a bill regulating imports of French wine.[118] Later in February, however, the anticlerical grievances of 1529 obtained a new hearing, especially the 'cruelty of the ordinaries' in *ex officio* proceedings for heresy.[119] According to Edward Hall (who was present again), anticlerical feeling was as strong as in 1529, the difference being that debate now focussed on heresy trials and the church courts rather than mortuary and probate fees, non-residence and pluralism. It is likely that renewed anticlerical discussion was, in fact, engineered wholly or partly by Thomas Cromwell, but the specific issues seized on by the Commons plainly arose from the sudden rise in burnings for heresy which had occurred since the end of the previous session. During Wolsey's ascendancy, not a single heretic had been burned in England.[120] Only one was consigned to the flames in 1530, namely Thomas Hitton, burned at Maidstone on 23 February.[121] Between August 1531 and April 1532, though, five persons were tried and burned, four of these before the Commons returned in January 1532. Thomas Bilney, a Cambridge Lutheran leader, died in the Lollards' Pit at Norwich on 16 August 1531; Richard Bayfield, John Tewkesbury and James Bainham were burned in London on 4 and 20 December 1531, and 30 April 1532 respectively; and Thomas Benet died at Exeter on 10 January 1532.[122] While the Commons sat, too, Hugh Latimer was inves-

115 *LP* v. 559 (5).
116 *LP* v. 472.
117 *LP* v. 559 (5), 614.
118 *LP* v. 805.
119 See below, pp. 186–7; Hall, *Henry the VIII*, vol. ii. 202.
120 A.F. Pollard, *Wolsey* (London, 1929), 208.
121 *The Complete Works of St Thomas More*, vol. viii, *The Confutation of Tyndale's Answer*, ed. L.A. Schuster *et al.* (New Haven, 1973), Pt. 3, 1207 and n. 3.
122 *Ibid.*, Pt. 3, 1247; *LP* v. 372, 373. *Sermons and Remains of Hugh Latimer*, ed. G.E. Corrie (Parker Society, Cambridge, 1845), 221–4. Pollard, *Wolsey*, 351.

tigated for heresy in Convocation, and imprisoned by Warham at Lambeth.[123]

Hall knew that the main grievance of the Commons in 1532 was the method used to conduct heresy trials.[124] First, because accusers were neither named nor examined judicially. Secondly, because 'purgation' was not allowed — the canonical procedure whereby a suspect justified his innocence on oath, and brought his honest neighbours with him to swear that he spoke the truth.[125] Persons accused of heresy thus had either to abjure beliefs they might never have held in practice, or else be burned as heretics at the stake.[126] In other words, *ex officio* procedure, with its pro-clerical bias, had now become the principal matter in dispute between clergy and laity. However, the method was a cherished immunity of the spiritual arm, and to impeach it was to hack away a central pillar of episcopal discipline as traditionally constituted. This Thomas Cromwell realized, and it suited his purpose very well.[127] Accordingly, the issue of heresy trials became integral to the wider battle to destroy the church's independent jurisdiction and the Aragonese faction, and we must consider in detail how More and the bishops had earned themselves extensive public odium by February 1532, thanks to a policy aimed at exterminating heresy and heretics regardless of hostile lay opinion.[128]

We recall that extermination of heresy was official government policy as announced by More to Parliament on 3 November 1529. As the revival of burnings showed, the authorities were acting with renewed severity, though whether heresy was being contained thereby is another matter. The whole business is both complex and emotive, and concrete evidence of More's involvement alone will be considered here. Serious analysis precludes the repetition of protestant stories that Sir Thomas flogged heretics against a tree in his garden at Chelsea. It must exclude, too, the accusations of illegal imprisonment made against More by John Field and Thomas Phillips. Much vaunted by J.A. Froude, such charges are unsupported by independent proof.[129] More indeed answered them in his *Apology* with an emphatic denial.[130] None has been substantiated, and

123 Lehmberg, *Reformation Parliament*, 144.
124 Hall, *Henry the VIII*, vol. ii. 202.
125 *Ibid.*
126 *Ibid.*
127 Cf. Elton, *Reform and Reformation*, 150.
128 See also A. Ogle, *The Tragedy of the Lollards' Tower* (Oxford, 1949).
129 Cf. G.R. Elton, *Studies*, vol. i. 159–61, where the complaints are discussed.
130 *Apologye of Syr Thomas More*, 131–5, 142–4.

we may hope that they were all untrue.[131] However, other evidence does exist to explain the hostile attitude of the Commons and the reality of an anticlerical consensus in 1532, though in considering it we should realize that the factional boundaries as delineated for political interpretation cannot be applied unqualified. Opponents of heresy trials and *ex officio* proceedings obviously included genuine protestants as well as anticlerical common lawyers and political opportunists. Similarly, More acted against heresy alongside all the bishops and their staffs, working thus in London with John Stokesley (a hammer of heretics), despite Stokesley's role as a leading promoter of Henry VIII's divorce.

In close co-operation with Stokesley, More brought about the arrest for heresy and detention of George Constantine at Chelsea towards the end of 1531. Constantine was a dealer in protestant books, who gave away much information about his fellow reformers before escaping in early December. More had imprisoned him in the stocks — Sir Thomas kept a set in his Porter's lodge at home — but Constantine broke the frame, scaled More's garden wall, and fled to Antwerp.[132] Sir Thomas joked in his *Apology* that he must have fed Constantine properly for him to achieve this feat of strength.[133] Yet More's humour was sadly inappropriate. It was on information gleaned from Constantine that Richard Bayfield, a Benedictine monk and book pedlar, was seized, interrogated by Stokesley and burned at Smithfield.[134] John Tewkesbury, a leather seller, was held by More at Chelsea in the same month until tried by Stokesley. On sentence, he was handed back to the secular arm and likewise burned.[135] James Bainham, a common lawyer married to Simon Fish's widow, was also delated to More at the end of 1531. Examined by Stokesley at Chelsea, he was found to own books by Tyndale, Frith and Joye. At first Bainham abjured and performed his penance, but later reaffirmed his protestant faith. He was tried and burned at the stake in April 1532.[136] More's apologists cannot thus deny that he was personally involved in detecting three out of

---

131 There can be no ultimate certainty either way.
132 *Apologye of Syr Thomas More*, lxxviii–ix, 133–4, 315–16. *LP* v. 574. *The Confutation of Tyndale's Answer*, Pt. 3, 1247–48.
133 *Apologye of Syr Thomas More*, 133.
134 *Ibid.*, 298–9; *The Confutation of Tyndale's Answer*, Pt. 3, 1247.
135 *Apologye of Syr Thomas More*, 304–5; *The Confutation of Tyndale's Answer*, Pt. 3, 1247. *LP* v. 589.
136 *Apologye of Syr Thomas More*, 297–8; *The Confutation of Tyndale's Answer*, Pt. 3, 1251. *LP* v. 583. *Remains of Hugh Latimer*, 221–4.

the six cases of heresy which resulted in execution during his chancellorship.[137] Neither was he inactive in two of the remaining cases. He railed at Hitton (whom he had never met) in his *Confutation of Tyndale's Answer* as 'the devil's stinking martyr', who had 'taken his wretched soul with him straight from the short fire to the fire everlasting'.[138] He also launched a most irregular inquiry into the question of Thomas Bilney's supposed recantation at the stake in Norwich, an illuminating episode surprisingly neglected by More's biographers.

More claimed in the *Confutation* that eyewitnesses at Bilney's burning had heard him recant.[139] According to More, Bilney reaffirmed his belief in the catholic faith some days before his death, renounced his former heresies, and begged to be absolved from excommunication. Prior to his execution, he heard mass on his knees and received the eucharist, and at the stake read a bill of revocation. The question whether Bilney did or did not recant is, of course, contentious. Protestant apologists refuse to accept the story of a recantation;[140] catholics (like James Gairdner) tend to see the evidence in its favour as 'perfectly clear'.[141] Although not personally involved in Bilney's arrest, trial or execution, More had begun an inquiry into the matter in Star Chamber by early November 1531, the signed depositions of eyewitnesses examined by him on oath being now in the Public Record Office.[142] These statements make absorbing reading. Bilney had received absolution and the sacrament, and at the stake a bill of revocation was handed to him by Thomas Pelles, chancellor of Norwich diocese, by whom he had been sentenced. Bilney took the paper and read it through, but whether he did so 'softly' to himself or audibly to the crowd was contested. Either he read the bill aloud and nothing else, or he read it to himself and then made a different declaration to the people. After the execution, Pelles brought the paper to Edward Reed, mayor of Norwich, asking to have it exemplified under the civic seal. Reed summoned the aldermen, and the document was scrutinized; but all agreed at once (according to Reed) that it did not tally with Bilney's

---

137 Cf. R.W. Chambers, *Thomas More* (London, 1938), 278–80.
138 *The Confutation of Tyndale's Answer*, Pt. 3, 1208.
139 *Ibid.*, Pt. 1, 22–6.
140 *The Acts and Monuments of John Foxe*, rev. by J. Pratt, 4th ed. (London, 1887), iv. 619–56.
141 J. Gairdner, *The English Church in the Sixteenth Century from the Accession of Henry VIII to the death of Mary* (London, 1903), 129–30.
142 SP 1/68, fos. 45–52 (*LP* v. 522); SP 1/68, fos. 80–85 (*LP* v. 560); SP 1/68, fos. 86–89 (*LP* v. 569). Subsequent analysis is based on these documents.

declaration. Reed had himself taken notes of Bilney's words, notes which were pronounced a true record by a majority in Norwich. Alderman John Curatt even doubted whether the document shown by Pelles was the original bill of revocation at all — an opinion not to be discounted, since Curatt was a scribe to the archdeacon of Norfolk.[143] Against it, Curatt admittedly swore later before More that he had heard a recantation from Bilney — all (significantly?) but the end when his shoe needed re-lacing! — but Curatt (as he himself claimed) stood in terror of Richard Nix, bishop of Norwich.[144]

More asserted dogmatically in his *Confutation* that those of Curatt's party 'plainly proved' a recantation, Reed and his supporters having 'confessed' that Bilney looked upon a paper, but 'could not tell whether it were the bill of his revocation or not'.[145] Yet this evaluation ignored basic problems posed by evidence which we still possess. First, had Bilney read Pelles's paper aloud *as* his recantation or 'softly' *prior to* a different declaration? Secondly, was that document later tampered with to suggest a fuller recantation? Since More took the evidence and met the witnesses, the least controversial solution would be to give him the benefit of the doubt. But this will not quite do, and it should be said that More's opinion conflicts with that of another eyewitness at the stake, Matthew Parker — Elizabeth I's archbishop of Canterbury — who strenuously denied that Bilney had recanted.[146] Nevertheless, the episode's historical value is not its aspersion on More's elementary truthfulness, but its political importance. The undoubted reason for More's inquiry, which was assuredly not prompted by idle curiosity, was that Reed, as senior burgess for Norwich, intended to lay the whole question of Bilney's execution before the Commons at the next (i.e. 1532) session of Parliament. On 24 September 1531, he assembled the aldermen in the Council House and asked them to sign a 'true' statement of events. This document was then sealed by Reed with the civic seal, and held ready for the reassembly of the House of Commons. Reed thus had local support for voicing nationally questions raised by the proceedings against Bilney, no doubt (among others) from Alderman Thomas Necton, brother of Robert Necton, the Lutheran book pedlar whom Wolsey had caught in 1528 and handed over to Tunstall.[147] By coincidence, too, Alderman Curatt (which side was he really on?) had for years been in

143 *LP* iv. 5491–92, 5589, 6139.
144 SP 1/56, fo. 209 (*LP* iv. 6139).
145 *The Confutation of Tyndale's Answer,* Pt. 1, 23–4.
146 A.G. Dickens, *The English Reformation* (London, 1964), 80.
147 See above, p. 108.

close touch with Thomas Cromwell, a connection going back to the halcyon days of Wolsey's papal legacy.[148]

Why, then, was Bilney's end so controversial? From the layman's point of view, the affair was indeed disturbing, showing (in Professor Dickens's words) 'the rigid, merciless legalism of the system at its worst'.[149] Bilney was, above all, a conscientious Christian, who desired to die as he had lived. He sought absolution from excommunication, and was deemed fit to receive the sacrament by Pelles, his judge spiritual. These are agreed facts. Pelles made 'great sticking and difficulty' about allowing Bilney the sacrament, but could not ultimately refuse, seeing that Bilney was 'of a true, perfect faith'[150] — and there lies the heart of the matter. The commotion over Bilney's recantation was secondary to a wider argument in Norwich that this mild and scholarly 'heretic' had nothing to recant anyway.

At his first trial (before Wolsey and Tunstall in 1527), Bilney had been allowed a quite exceptional form of abjuration. This allowed him to abjure without acknowledgement of having held the heresies imputed to him, or of penitence for having done so.[151] There was no conclusive proof in 1527 that Bilney was heterodox. Tunstall acted accordingly, though his philosophic reaction provoked a diatribe from More, who argued in his *Dialogue Concerning Heresies* that the court's formula strained the law to breaking point in favour of the accused.[152] Then in 1531 Bilney openly breached an injunction barring him from preaching without express episcopal licence,[153] and was said to have supplied Tyndale's books to an anchoress in Norwich.[154] He was condemned as a relapsed heretic, sentence being automatic. But it was as difficult as before to work out Bilney's actual heresies, and Pelles was well enough aware of local prejudices in Norwich to know that this gave him a public relations problem *par excellence*. Local opinion favoured Bilney, not Bishop Nix or Pelles. Even worse, Bilney was one of those 'heretics' who — as Tunstall had noted in his protest — appealed at his trial from episcopal jurisdiction to Henry VIII as supreme head of the English Church, which had led to a splendidly rustic debate in which Reed (as mayor) asked Pelles (as a member of Convocation)

148 *LP* iv. 5491–92, 6139.
149 *The English Reformation*, 80.
150 *The Confutation of Tyndale's Answer*, Pt. 1, 24.
151 Ogle, *Lollards' Tower*, 266–75.
152 Quoted in *ibid.*, 269–71.
153 *The Confutation of Tyndale's Answer*, Pt. 1, 23.
154 *Ibid.*

to explain to the locals what *supremum caput* meant in the king's new title! After Bilney's condemnation, Pelles thus laboured to discover when and where the temporal arm proposed to carry out the spiritual sentence, with a view to staging an edifying end for his own propaganda purposes. Recantation by the 'heretic', Pelles reasoned, would appease public opinion; it would establish, too, that Bilney admitted his offence and accepted ecclesiastical jurisdiction. But nothing moved in Norwich without Reed's knowledge, and the mayor got wind of Pelles's game. As to his motive, the mayor was not merely in sympathy with the victim. He was genuinely afraid that he had erred by not reporting Bilney's appeal to Henry VIII, according to the terms of the Pardon of the Clergy, and wished now to see that nothing irregular took place at the stake.

On the day of his execution, Bilney was interviewed in the prison chapel after mass by Pelles and another. The three talked 'secretly' by the altar, and Bilney handed to Pelles two books he had written in gaol. Reed then arrived, demanding the books on the ground that Bilney wrote them after his surrender to the lay power. Pelles next bragged to Curatt that he had just persuaded the 'heretic' to read a bill of revocation that he (Pelles) had devised. At the stake, the events occurred as already described, and Pelles then came to Reed to obtain civic exemplification of Bilney's recantation. Only then did he learn that he was outfooted by the mayor, who had taken a synopsis of Bilney's actual declaration. Later he learned, too, that Reed was preparing a dossier for Parliament. By the end of October 1531, Pelles was out of his depth. We have already seen that he was linked to the Aragonese faction in the Lower House of Convocation,[155] and by early November he was in touch with Thomas More, who quickly began a Star Chamber inquiry. Meanwhile, Reed had sent Bilney's prison writings to the duke of Norfolk, enclosing his synopsis of the condemned man's speech at the stake. If this last document is to be believed, Bilney admitted his failings with regret, but made no substantive recantation on the subjects of the saints, their shrines, and the merits of pilgrimages — the matters alleged against him. He also denied specifically that he had taught heresy to the Norwich anchoress.[156]

The Bilney affair provides both an instance of public opinion hostile to More's extermination campaign against heresy, and also a concrete example of his willingness to initiate proceedings to justify clerical actions. His inquiry was, furthermore, most irregular, since

155 See above, p. 142.
156 SP 1/66, fos. 296–317 (*LP* v. 372).

More himself now acted *ex officio*, using his Star Chamber powers inquisitorially without bill of complaint or information filed in proper form, and thus contrary to Star Chamber's due process.[157] His eventual verdict was very satisfying to catholics. But the significant facts were that Reed and his friends intended to speak against Pelles nationally, and that many in Norwich believed that a man had been burned for nothing. If Reed indeed spoke in the Parliamentary session of 1532, episcopal jurisdiction would have suffered bitter attack. Interestingly, too, More did not deem it necessary to put Pelles on oath during his inquiry, although all the other (lay) eyewitnesses summoned to Star Chamber were sworn to their statements. Under normal circumstances, the omission might have been acceptable. But in view of Curatt's suggestion that Pelles had faked a new bill of revocation after Bilney's burning, such a self-denying ordinance was truly remarkable. Pelles wanted Bilney's recantation publicly exemplified for propaganda purposes. His conduct should therefore have been as suspect as Reed's in the eyes of a judge as good as Sir Thomas More.

More's campaign against heresy was further defined by two proclamations against heretical books.[158] The first of these was issued on 22 June 1530, being wholly concerned with the need for censorship.[159] Promulgated on the advice of More and Fisher, it was designed (as William Rastell knew) 'to repress the heresies and new opinions' encouraged by protestant printed literature.[160] As such, it implemented the findings of a conference on heretical books which Henry VIII had organized the previous month.[161] Specific titles by William Tyndale, Simon Fish and John Frith were now formally proscribed, and it was laid down that no other vernacular books printed outside England on any subject at all should in future be imported into the realm, the same titles being forbidden also in French or Dutch translations.[162] All banned books were to be handed to the bishops within fifteen days, and the authorities were urged to identify persons subsequently possessing proscribed books, presenting all suspects before the King's Council at West-

---

157 Cf. J.A. Guy, *The Cardinal's Court: the Impact of Thomas Wolsey in Star Chamber* (Harvester, Hassocks, 1977), ch. 4.
158 *Tudor Royal Proclamations*, ed. P.L. Hughes and J.F. Larkin, vol. i (New Haven, 1964), 181–6, 193–7.
159 *Ibid.*, 193–7.
160 Harpsfield, 223.
161 Wilkins, *Concilia*, vol. iii. 728–35.
162 *Tudor Royal Proclamations*, vol. i. 194–5. The listed titles were those protestant books printed between 1526 and 1529.

minster — a remarkable innovation. For the future, no new Scriptural books or Bible translations were to be printed in England unless 'examined and approved' by a bishop, and books approved and printed were to include the name of both examiner and printer. The view of Henry's conference, which More had attended, was then repeated that the Bible in English was 'not necessary'. Sir Thomas, since writing his *Dialogue Concerning Heresies*, had capitulated to the bishops on this point — to both Henry VIII's and St German's disgust. The reason given for this change of heart was 'the malignity of this present time, with the inclination of people to erroneous opinions'.[163] Scripture was, instead, to be expounded in sermons. Nevertheless, More announced that if the people abandoned all heresies, the king would go ahead, after all, with an official English Bible, an expectative grace which was Henry's personal contribution to this proclamation. Lastly, More ordered all existing English, French or Dutch Bibles in print or manuscript to be surrendered to the bishops within fifteen days, unless retained by episcopal licence.

Later in 1530, a second proclamation was issued 'for resisting and withstanding' heresy.[164] Essentially a law and order measure, its rationale was (in Harpsfield's phrase) that no bigger threat faced a community than 'wretched and desperate heretics'.[165] It began by denouncing Lutheranism as sedition, and warned that heresy was afflicting England through 'blasphemous books lately made and privately sent into this realm' by Luther's disciples and other heretics. It then summarized the existing heresy laws at length, commanding all officers from peers to village constables to execute them and wipe out heterodox teaching and preaching. Sermons and books against catholic doctrine were forbidden, all unlicensed preaching was banned, and heretical books were again to be handed in within fifteen days to the bishops. The proclamation next

163 *Tudor Royal Proclamations,* vol. i. 196.
164 *Ibid.,* 181–6. This proclamation could not have been issued in 1529, as Larkin states, because several books proscribed by it were not published until 1530. These include Tyndale's *Practice of Prelates* and *Book of Moses Called Genesis,* the anonymous *Hortulus Animae: the Garden of the Soul* and (Constantine's?) *Examination of William Thorp.* See A. Hume, in *The Complete Works of St Thomas More,* vol. viii, Pt. 2, 1065–91. It is, however, probable that More revised and re-issued in 1530 a proclamation originally published in 1529. The evidence for this is More's own statement in *The Confutation of Tyndale's Answer,* Pt. 1, 28. I have suggested that this proclamation came after that of 22 June, rather than before, because it condemned books published later than those banned in June.
165 Harpsfield, 207.

threatened the penalties of existing (medieval) heresy legislation for offences against it.[166] Finally, fifteen books by William Roy, Heinrich Bullinger, Tyndale and others were listed and banned, and those persons owning copies were to be delated to the bishops.

These proclamations codified More's policy of catholic repression. They stood in line with the policies of such rulers as Charles V in the Netherlands and Francis I in France, but a material difference was the intensity of More's devotion to press censorship. Fundamental to his scheme, too, was the rule announced by the June proclamation that offenders were to be brought before the King's Council rather than their bishops. It was as if More despaired of the bishops' stamina against literate heretics.[167] Plainly, he now intended to attack protestant literature by prerogative methods. He had erected an *Index Librorum Prohibitorum*, and had empowered himself to enforce it in Star Chamber by virtue of the Council's inherent (but hitherto seldom used) powers to punish breaches of proclamations.[168] It was, in fact, the beginning of Star Chamber's censorship jurisdiction — later infamous — and that More meant what he said is shown by three Star Chamber cases brought on the June proclamation. On 25 October 1530, John Porseck, one Seymour and their associates were sent by More from Star Chamber to the Tower 'for having books against the king's proclamation'.[169] In addition, they had to perform public penance, wearing humiliating papers while led through London's streets on horseback but facing back-to-front. After this, they had to burn their protestant books on a bonfire in Cheapside.[170] About the same time, John Tyndale (William's brother), Thomas Patmer (a London merchant) and another were delated to More by Bishop Stokesley as distributors of Tyndale's New Testament. Sir Thomas had them arrested and hauled into Star Chamber. They confessed, and were imprisoned by More in the Counter. The next market day, they, too, performed public penance on horseback, being pelted with rotten fruit while wearing coats 'pinned thick' with the proscribed books. After another bonfire at Cheapside, the men were gaoled pending More's assessment of their fine.[171] The third case brought on the June

---

166 Namely, 2 Hen. IV, c. 15; 2 Hen. V, st. 1, c. 7.
167 Cf. G.R. Elton, *Policy and Police* (Cambridge, 1972), 219–20.
168 Only two cases were heard on proclamations in Star Chamber under Wolsey; Guy, *The Cardinal's Court*, 70. These were both for engrossing grain.
169 Ellesmere MS. 2652, fo. 15. A different reading of the same case is Ellesmere MS. 436, where 'Borseck' is given.
170 Ellesmere MS. 2652, fo. 15.
171 B.L. Harleian MS. 425, fo. 15.

proclamation was heard as late as 14 October 1531.[172] John Cook was on that day convicted in Star Chamber of owning an English New Testament, his Bible being confiscated and he himself imprisoned in the Fleet by More.

Patmer's case, interestingly, had a sequel.[173] He was imprisoned again in 1531, this time by Stokesley. His servant John Stanton tried to raise the matter in the 1532 session of Parliament, but More (he alleged) intervened to attack him as a favourer of heresy, sending him to the Fleet as a frivolous suitor.[174] Stanton next complained to Henry VIII, but Patmer remained in prison until 1533.[175]

More, then, used his office of lord chancellor to defend the catholic faith. The extermination of heresy had been his second objective when he accepted promotion in October 1529.[176] It was a policy, too, which was in accord with majority opinion in the Council during More's thousand days in office. Although intense to an unprecedented degree (for a layman), More's zeal was thus objectionable only insofar as it resulted in hysterical polemic (as in Hitton's case),[177] and obscured his regard for the truth (as in his inquiry into Bilney's recantation). In other words, the anticlerical House of Commons could not fault More in 1532, and proved as anxious as ever to justify their orthodoxy.[178] But because heresy trials and *ex officio* proceedings were now the sensitive issues between church and state, More and the bishops became politically vulnerable in Parliament. Sir Thomas had collected essential evidence against three protestant martyrs; he had defended the rigour of episcopal jurisdiction in his *Dialogue Concerning Heresies*. He stood impassively, but hardly impartially, for the procedures and immunities of spiritual jurisdiction in the session of 1532. His political credit and that of Queen Catherine's supporters had become inextricably linked to that of the bishops. When the Aragonese and radical groups thus resumed political warfare in February 1532, Thomas Cromwell could calculate that the Commons offered the consensus and collective advocacy needed to launch a political *coup*.

172 Ellesmere MS. 2652, fo. 15.
173 Elton, *Studies,* vol. i. 159.
174 SP 1/70, fos. 2–3 (*LP* v. 982).
175 *Ibid.*; *Remains of Hugh Latimer*, 321 (*LP* vi. 573).
176 See above, ch. 6.
177 See above, p. 167.
178 See below, p. 186.

9

THE EVENTS OF 1532

WITH the shift in the centre of political gravity from the King's Council and Court to Parliament in 1532, the story of More's public career merges with that of the Henrician Reformation. A premier figure on the national stage who resigned in defiance of Henry VIII's adherence to a policy which he believed to be unconscionable, Thomas More's final days as lord chancellor were consumed in the overt battle for power fought out in the dramatic third session of the Reformation Parliament. For the historian, More's role in the struggle of January–May 1532 is inseparable from national events until the second week in May, when the Aragonese leaders at last broke out to oppose Henry VIII directly. Prior to May, a lack of closer personal perspective arises mainly from More's relentless vigil of discretion: he would have been even more careful to cover his tracks in 1532 than he was with Chapuys in March and April 1531. However, the nature of the struggle itself in 1532 is also responsible for the blurred pattern. The Aragonese faction waged a defensive campaign throughout the session, drawing strength from the fact that it was up to Cromwell and the radicals to make the running. More knew well enough that Cromwell, as it seemed until too late, would have to gain majority support for his revolutionary proposals from *both* Houses of Parliament in order to win control, a level of acceptance unimaginable in 1532. Arguably, More's fatal miscalculation was his probable assumption that Cromwell could achieve his ambition by Parliamentary statute alone, following the precedent of the Pardon of the Clergy.

In retrospect, the Pardon of the Clergy itself appeared a relatively healthy omen to the Aragonese party. The English Church had shown creditable resistance to Cromwell's designs on its freedom in 1531, and the agreed compromise by which Henry's royal supremacy was subjected to Christ's law quickly backfired on the radical group.[1] Not only had Tunstall's protest begun a potentially endless debate, but the Aragonese group in the Lower House of Convocation fought back further by organizing and sending a signed declaration of the supremacy's 'true' meaning to Rome. Couched almost as a manifesto, this document argued that Henry's title was not intended to weaken the laws of the church, or to threaten

---

1 G. R. Elton, *Reform and Reformation* (London, 1977), 144–5.

ecclesiastical liberty, the unity of Christendom, or the authority of the Apostolic See. The words *supremum caput* had conceded nothing new to the king, and anything granted to him in future in derogation of canon law, the church's integrity or papal primacy would reflect the intervention of Satan or human frailty.[2] This statement naturally drew the government's fire, which took the form of new *praemunire* indictments against six Aragonese opponents of Henry's title from the Lower House of Convocation — a counterattack neatly executed by Cromwell, who had already excluded the six from the clergy's Act of Pardon.[3] In quick succession, Peter Ligham, Adam Travers and Rowland Philips were indicted in King's Bench on 27 June 1531, followed three days later by Thomas Pelles, Robert Clyff and John Baker.[4] Yet all except Ligham (who fought back) succeeded in buying Henry's pardon in November 1531.[5] Furthermore, Cromwell failed to change a government decision to base the indictments on the old canard of Wolsey's papal legacy, the new charges being that the six had variously appealed to Wolsey from the vice-chancellor of Cambridge, had acted as advocates in the legatine court, had contributed to the procuracies of a visitation by legatine commission, and had granted pensions to Wolsey to enable him to maintain his legatine authority more 'decently'.[6] The indictments were thus another step in the extension of *praemunire*, the matters alleged being wholly spiritual, whereas previous convictions had been for matters partly spiritual and partly temporal, but they were a signal reversal (from Cromwell's viewpoint) on the earlier Act of Pardon, which had included a last-minute definition of *praemunire* in terms of the clergy's independent jurisdiction exercised through church courts.

Cromwell had also failed in 1531 to impress on Henry's teeming brain the merits of the 'radical' solution to the divorce issue as underpinned by *Collectanea satis copiosa*. He had gained much indirect influence during the year as Norfolk's Parliamentary manager, and a Venetian observer placed him seventh on a list of premier councillors in November 1531.[7] His high executive position was illustrated by many requests addressed to him for permission to be

2 J. J. Scarisbrick, *Henry VIII* (London, 1968), 277–8.
3 KB 145/10/23; 22 Hen. VIII, c. 15; Scarisbrick, *Henry VIII*, 278.
4 KB 145/10/23 (the original indictments).
5 *LP* v. 559 (22), and (33)—(37); 1139 (10).
6 KB 145/10/23; *The Reports of Sir John Spelman*, ed. J. H. Baker, vol. ii (Selden Society, London, 1978), *69*.
7 S. E. Lehmberg, *The Reformation Parliament* (Cambridge, 1970), 132.

absent from the Parliamentary session of 1532.[8] But purely administrative influence was not enough, as memoranda of Cromwell's official duties during the summer vacation of 1531 make plain.[9] Arranging matters like transport of grain supplies, exchange of manors, customs and import controls, and the pursuit of royal debtors through the courts was the workload of third-rate civil servants not omnicompetent ministers. Similarly, the official bills Cromwell drafted in expectation of Parliament's reassembly concerned, with two exceptions, subjects such as export of kerseys, import of wines, uses (less mundane), sewers and apparel. The exceptions did have some potential: one was a 'bill of Augmentation of Treasons', the other that beneficed clergy resident abroad without royal licence should forfeit their incomes. But both measures were dropped in 1532 — the former after much pre-sessional labour by Cromwell and Audley[10] — and neither, in any case, had true political value, being directed, rather, towards intensifying the king's campaign against the pope. The problems tackled by these two bills indeed offer the key to government thinking and Henry's mind in late 1531, namely unlicensed departure from the realm and sending into it foreign (i.e. papal) documents to the prejudice of the king's case. Henry VIII had himself assumed command of his policy in advance of the 1532 session of Parliament, and his conservatism was ascendant. For instance, Cromwell's task was not to extend the treason laws in favour of either royal supremacy or Henry's imperial crown, as these regal powers were worked out in *Collectanea satis copiosa*. His various drafts had instead to profess ignorance of the twin pillars of the ultimate revolution. The projected new treasons thus covered, in addition to unlicensed departures and foreign documents, such offences as holding the king's castles against him, transferring allegiance to a foreign ruler, fleeing the realm after a proclamation had ordered a man to appear before the king, and impeding the king's ambassadors abroad — the last offence arising from a case of alleged interference with the diplomatic mail reported by Richard Croke.[11] Everything goes to suggest, in brief, that Cromwell gained invaluable experience as the linkman between Henry and official policy during 1531, but that he exercised no personal influence in face of Henry's renewed desire to resume the bullying diplomacy at Rome and fruitless parley with

8 *Ibid.*
9 *St. Pap.*, i. 380–3.
10 G. R. Elton, *Policy and Police* (Cambridge, 1972), 267–74.
11 *Ibid.*

the French which had characterized earlier stages of the divorce crisis.[12]

Cranmer and Edward Foxe had meanwhile lost ground, too, after Henry had himself decided to offer the vacant archbishopric of York to Reginald Pole. A distinguished scholar educated at Oxford and Padua, Pole was Henry's close kinsman, his father being Henry VII's cousin and his mother a Plantagenet. Reginald could hardly have been expected to connive in the divorce project, as his mother was Queen Catherine's friend and Princess Mary's governess.[13] Nevertheless, he played a reluctant part alongside Foxe in obtaining a favourable opinion on the divorce from the University of Paris in 1530,[14] and Henry — still the supreme egoist — thus believed he could be manipulated into promoting the royal cause. Within days of Wolsey's death, Pole had been offered the archbishopric, Henry's voice being transmitted by the duke of Norfolk.[15] But there was a condition. Reginald had to give his true opinion of the divorce before accepting, since Henry, as Norfolk observed, 'did not wish to confer such a high honour on an adversary'.[16] Pole hesitated. He attempted to compromise: 'I remember', he wrote later, 'saying to Doctor Foxe that I trusted I had found a way to satisfy his Grace'.[17] Henry, however, would not budge, and there was a row. Pole next presented a treatise to the king, justifying his views — a shrewd and temperate statement of the conservative position, which Henry found difficult to refute.[18] Cranmer, who got to see it, frankly admitted that if leaked to the common people, 'I suppose it were not possible to persuade them to the contrary'.[19] This was because Pole had brilliantly interwoven dynastic, economic and diplomatic arguments into mainstream questions of theology, papal authority and Henry's conscience. What discord would ensue within the realm 'by diversity of titles', should the king remarry? Could Charles V wreck England simply by 'forbidding the course of merchandise into Flanders and Spain'? Would the divorce make England a diplomatic shuttlecock and prey of a catholic alliance

---

12 Cf. Elton, *Reform and Reformation*, 144–6.

13 W. Schenk, *Reginald Pole, Cardinal of England* (London, 1950), 23.

14 *Ibid.*, 24–5.

15 *Ibid.*, 25–6.

16 *Ibid.*, 25.

17 *Ibid.*, 25–6.

18 The treatise is lost, but its contents are known from Cranmer's report to Wiltshire, dated 13 June 1531; *Records of the Reformation*, ed. N. Pocock (Oxford, 1870), vol ii. 130–4.

19 Pocock, vol. ii. 130.

between France and Spain? Pole's document was shown to Henry in May or June 1531, and in January 1532 its author was allowed to leave England for Avignon, after hints that he would speak against the divorce in Parliament.[20] Yet much time had been wasted, and Foxe and Cranmer had not gained an opportunity to refute Pole's treatise before the king. Even worse, Edward Lee was finally promoted archbishop of York, a setback because he was a religious conservative despite his presence among Foxe's research team after 1529. The new archbishop accepted the drift of Henry's policy and the dogma of royal supremacy, but was never regarded by Cranmer and Cromwell as either radical or reliable.[21]

But the radicals had snatched a few crumbs of comfort during 1531, which helped them set the pace in 1532. The notable advance was that Queen Catherine was sent away from Court in mid-July, never to meet Henry again, and Anne Boleyn thereafter hunted openly with the king, who allowed her to keep public state as his betrothed.[22] Catherine's dismissal followed shortly upon a failed attempt by a delegation led by Norfolk, Suffolk and Wiltshire to persuade her to withdraw her suit from Rome in favour of 'independent' arbitration in England.[23] The Queen met this request with composure and dignity, and her serene resolution in adversity annoyed Henry more than ever. He thus made Anne his constant companion out of spite as much as anything else; but the change raised radical morale, since Anne reiterated demands for Cranmer's proposed solution of the divorce issue in the belief that it would make her queen within four months.[24] Above all others, Anne Boleyn kept the radical thrust alive in 1531. She patronized at Court the interests of Cromwell, Foxe and Cranmer, while vigorously attacking the conservative peers, accusing Norfolk of dynastic ambition, Suffolk of incest, and the marquis of Dorset of plotting rebellion in Cornwall.[25] She likewise stirred the must of royal supremacy, which still fermented at the back of Henry's mind, and taunted him with the painful ineffectiveness of his present style of government. The radicals also drew comfort from the value to their cause of a piece of propaganda in 1531. As Cranmer told Wiltshire with reference to Pole's treatise, 'goodly eloquence both of words

20 Schenk, 29–30.
21 Cf. Elton's comment, *Reform and Reformation*, 146.
22 *LP* v. 340.
23 *LP* v. 287.
24 *LP* v. 340.
25 *LP* v. 287, 340, 941.

and sentence . . . were like to persuade many',[26] and to prove his point, he translated into English the document previously laid before Parliament in Latin — the opinions of the universities with an abridgement of *Collectanea satis copiosa* appended.[27] Henry's approval was secured, and the work was published by Berthelet on 7 November 1531 under the title *The Determinations of the most famous and excellent Universities of Italy and France, that it is so unlawful for a man to marry his brother's wife and the pope hath no power to dispense therewith.*[28] The tract was, in fact, tedious in comparison with such later Henrician productions as, for example, the pithy *Glass of the Truth* (1532) or *A Little Treatise against the mutterings of some papists in corners* (1534).[29] Cranmer's translation required 154 printed folios, and was enlivened only by a salacious discourse on the sinfulness of forbidden copulation. Nevertheless, Cranmer's style was usually direct and disarming, and the book offered much on which to sharpen wits either in universities or village alehouses. More important, it was the complete ideological justification for the Henrician Reformation, and was widely enough read to justify reprinting. The genius of Cranmer's move, though, was its timing. He had put an English version of *Collectanea satis copiosa* on sale to the public immediately before Parliament's reassembly, fixing a date of issue which was just too late for the Aragonese faction to get out their reply in time for the session. In the event, indeed, the Aragonese *Invicta Veritas*, written by Thomas Abel, one of Catherine's chaplains, was not available until May 1532, by which time Cromwell's *coup* had already succeeded.[30]

When the third session of the Reformation Parliament eventually got under way, bad feeling was at once engendered over money. The Commons were reluctant to concede Henry's latest demand for a sizeable lay subsidy, and rejected outright his haggling attempt to pass a bill of uses which increased the royal share of the cake above that agreed with the Lords in 1529.[31] Even so, secret new moves to obtain Henry's divorce proved even more controversial. Norfolk and Wiltshire mustered their forces in early February 1532, and barefacedly asked the aged William Warham, archbishop of

26 Pocock, vol. ii. 130.
27 See above, p. 156.
28 B.L., 228. c. 38 (1); C. 21. b. 43. The identification was made by Dr Graham Nicholson, and the relationship between the *Collectanea* and Henrician propaganda is discussed in his dissertation, esp. ch. 3.
29 Elton, *Policy and Police*, 175–86.
30 B.L., G. 12. 36.
31 Lehmberg, *Reformation Parliament*, 133–4.

Canterbury, to pronounce Henry's divorce by unilateral action in England.[32] Warned in advance by a leak, Warham had already decided to resist both this request and subsequent pressure.[33] Norfolk thus assembled all his supporters a few days later and reminded them of the 'privilege' of England, adding news of a sudden discovery by Henry's canon lawyers that matrimonial causes 'belong to the temporal jurisdiction, not the spiritual'.[34] The response was one of intense hostility, and this incident, above all others, precipitated the break-up of the aristocratic grouping, lord Darcy and others now objecting testily that marriage matters were spiritual and that the Council 'knew what had to be done' without resorting to blackmail and subornation.[35] Faced with this threatening rebuff, Norfolk puzzled over the mechanics of unilateral action. Having finally accepted the necessity of adopting some version of Cranmer's original suggestion of 1529, the new element in the situation seemed to be Warham's intransigence. Norfolk accordingly took counsel, and two bills were drafted which throw into profile the confused strategies under review in February 1532. The first (in Audley's handwriting) outfooted Warham by authorizing (in effect) Edward Lee to investigate 'finally and summarily' whether Henry was married or not.[36] The second bill (mostly Cromwell's work) assumed that a divorce would soon be pronounced in Convocation[37] — less realistically, unless a rumour was true that abolition of archiepiscopal jurisdiction and its transfer to the king was also under discussion.[38]

Audley's draft began on a note of deceptive innocence. It reported that the validity of Henry's marriage was doubtful because the pope could not dispense the Levitical law, on which the universities of Christendom and 'sage and learned men' were all agreed.[39] As a result, the king was much afflicted by remorse and conscience. He had begged the pope to execute divine and canon law, but papal action had also to respect Henry's 'imperial estate'. Clement had usurped royal privileges by not remitting the king's suit back for English judgment. He had wilfully delayed the case, too, in disregard of Henry's good intentions, his imperial crown and the safety

32 *LP* v. 805.
33 *Ibid.*
34 *Ibid.*
35 *Ibid.*
36 SP 2/N, fos. 155–62 (*LP* vi. 311 [4]).
37 SP 2/N, fos. 163–64 (*LP* vi. 311 [5]).
38 *LP* v. 850.
39 SP 2/N, fo. 155.

of the realm. This situation could not be tolerated, not least because 'sundry histories' showed how fate punished princes who offended against God's law. If the pope would not comply, then, by authority of Parliament, all the evidence submitted to Wolsey's legatine court in 1529 should be re-examined by a committee consisting of one archbishop and other convenient persons. Written answers would be given to six questions: (1) Whether Catherine was wedded to Prince Arthur, (2) Whether Arthur was Henry VIII's brother, (3) Arthur's age on his wedding day, (4) The duration of the marriage, (5) How often Arthur slept with Catherine, (6) Whether intercourse took place. After the answers were published, the archbishop in charge of the committee had 'full power and authority' to assemble as many bishops as would come to pronounce in solemn form whether Henry's marriage was valid or not, a judgment which was to be 'firm, stable, constant and perpetual'. Assuming the marriage was indeed invalid, Henry would be free to marry 'at his pleasure'; Catherine (if she complied) would retain her property for life; and Princess Mary would succeed to the throne if Henry died without male heirs, her legitimacy being restored to her automatically on that contingency. If the pope objected, his process would not be heeded, and English religion would not be interrupted, on authority of Parliament, by any form of papal anathema. In particular, a possible papal interdict would be ignored.

Cromwell's draft tackled the question of enforcement.[40] Audley had said nothing of this beyond a sentence making resistance punishable by outlawry, imprisonment and loss of property — the existing penalties of the Statute of Provisors (16 Ric. II, c. 5) — and something stronger was needed. Cromwell was, in fact, working on the basis of an annulment pronounced by Convocation, promptly followed by a statutory announcement that Catherine had become princess dowager and that the succession was now vested in the king's heirs by his second marriage. The draft proper then proclaimed that actual deeds against Henry's divorce, second marriage or the new succession were high treason, for which principals and abettors would suffer equally. The measure was necessary, Cromwell argued, to put fear and dread into persons who would otherwise malign and divide the realm over Henry's private affairs. Secondly, attempts to encourage papal interference in England in derogation of 'the Imperial Crown of this realm' became subject to the penalties of provisors. Thirdly, Cromwell advised the nation that efforts to involve the pope in English affairs were, in any

40 SP 2/N, fos. 163–4.

case, irrelevant, since papal process could never be received into England unless it was consistent with Henry's policy as declared by Parliament. Once again, king and realm would continue to enjoy the benefits of Christianity regardless of papal interdict — as in Audley's draft.

Such bills could not, however, be laid before Parliament. Tortuous and impractical, their principal weakness, other defects apart, was a lack of finality, since Catherine would at once appeal to Rome from the sentence of archbishop or Convocation. In the circumstances, her appeal would bring Parliament itself into disrepute as the upholder of injustice, even assuming the bills could ever have been got through both Houses. Catherine's appeal, Norfolk and Henry now realized, was the insuperable obstacle to a domestic solution of the divorce issue along moderate lines. Her right of appeal had blocked Cranmer's original proposal of 1529; it remained the insurmountable problem in 1532. To his credit, the king had grasped this from the beginning. With the diplomatic door locked fast against him by Charles V, he knew, when honest with himself, that his ultimate dilemma was his own inability to break with Rome. Unilateral action in England was impossible as long as Henry VIII could not face the inevitability of schism. By February 1532, however, the king had exhausted the entire multiplicity of moderate possibilities in a vain struggle to obtain his divorce while preserving his orthodoxy. All roads now led either back to Rome or on towards revolution.

Unknown to Henry, the clarion call to revolution had already been sounded. While the Commons were generating heat over royal financial demands, the Lords were debating a proposed attack on annates.[41] Annates (or first fruits) were the payments exacted by the pope from each new appointee to a benefice on admission to his living, and amounted to a national contribution to Rome of about £4,500 per annum.[42] A bill had been introduced in the Lords to stop this drain abroad of English cash before the end of January 1532, and this bill was derived from a paper, probably not itself used, which purported to be an original Commons' petition on the subject.[43] Historically, the paper on annates is more important than the bill, because it is demonstrably not a Commons' petition at all, but a fabrication directly linked to the manuscript of *Collectanea satis*

41 Lehmberg, *Reformation Parliament*, 135–8.
42 Elton, *Reform and Reformation*, 148–50.
43 B.L. Cotton MS. Cleopatra E. vi, fos. 274–5.

copiosa.[44] As such, its revolutionary import lay not in its assault on papal revenues, but in a suggestion, rather, that Henry should greet any papal countermoves on annates with a Parliamentary renunciation of papal jurisdiction. The actual bill of annates (now lost) was probably less extreme: annates were, in the words of the statute finally enacted, 'impoverishing' the realm, and should cease.[45] Clergy could pay up to five per cent of their first year's income to cover administrative charges in obtaining their bulls of appointment, but nothing more. If the pope retaliated by refusing bulls to future English bishops, they would be consecrated by their archbishops. If an archbishop was refused, he would be consecrated by two bishops named by the king. Furthermore, papal process designed 'unreasonably' to vex the realm in form of excommunication or interdict would be ignored, and English religion would continue as usual, the clergy administering the sacraments 'without any scruples of conscience'.

This remarkable bill which so claimed power over clerical consciences marked the turning-point in Henry's policy. For the king and Norfolk, the objective had not gone beyond the need to bully the pope more effectively than in 1531. The English clerics, Norfolk wrote on 28 February 1532, had 'many wringers at their high authorities, yet nothing hurtful shall be done, unless the fault be in Him [Clement VII] in proceeding wrongfully and ungrately[46] against the King'.[47] For Cromwell and Audley, in contrast, the bill of annates was the first to ask Parliament's opinion of the argument that papal authority could be repudiated by statutory enactment. As such, Parliament's answer was one of strenuous opposition — a sure sign that some people were alert to the true situation.[48] Cromwell himself soon remarked of the bill, 'for what end or effect it will succeed surely I know not'.[49] Resistance in the Lords was indeed so great that Henry had to concede a clause suspending the act's effect until it was confirmed by royal letters patent, an attempt to emphasize the threat while playing down the fact. But the concession availed him little. He had to attend the Upper House in person several times to get his way,[50] and even then it was a close finish,

44 This crucial discovery was made by Dr Nicholson, and is discussed in his dissertation, 139–44.
45 23 Hen. VIII, c. 20.
46 Unacceptably.
47 *St. Pap.*, vii. 349.
48 Elton, *Reform and Reformation*, 149.
49 R. B. Merriman, *Life and Letters of Thomas Cromwell* (Oxford, 1902), vol. i. 343.
50 *LP* v. 879.

since the bishops unanimously opposed the final reading on 19 March.[51] The Commons, too, were hostile, and Henry had to arrange a division on the question, a rare thing before 1550 in that House.[52] Nevertheless, the Act in Conditional Restraint of Annates had passed both Houses by 26 March 1532.[53]

On the likely assumption that Thomas Cromwell regarded the bill of annates as a litmus test of Parliament's attitude to its own legislative power, the result was another defeat for political radicalism.[54] Here was certain proof that the two bills already drafted on divorce and succession, with their necessary repudiation of papal sanctions against England, were absolute lame ducks. Yet Henry's policy was excessively complex, and Cromwell was as resourceful and buoyant as ever. Although working as the king's link-man and Norfolk's Parliamentary manager throughout the session of 1532, Cromwell was also busily forging alliances behind the scenes for the benefit of himself and the radical group. He was in close touch with Anne Boleyn and Wiltshire, and the object was to destroy both the English Church's legislative independence and the Aragonese faction. No one could then dispute the power of an act of Parliament to bind Henry's subjects in all aspects of life, and the result would be a speedy royal divorce coupled with Cromwell's appointment as Henry's chief minister. But the question remained, how might Cromwell win the necessary consensus? He still needed to cement a firm power-base for the radical cause within existing political institutions. Cromwell thus transferred the scene of action in 1532 to the House of Commons, and was mobilizing opinion there during the second half of February.[55] By the end of that month, Norfolk was tetchily bemoaning 'the infinite clamours of the temporalty here in Parliament against the misusing of the spiritual jurisdiction'.[56] By 6 March, Wiltshire had proposed in public that neither pope nor clergy should enjoy privileges or immunity in future.[57] The Aragonese faction quickly rallied to its colours, and the decisive manoeuvres culminating in the Submission of the Clergy and Thomas More's resignation as lord chancellor now commenced.

---

51 *Ibid.*
52 *LP* v. 898.
53 *Ibid.*
54 Cf. Elton's remarks in *Reform and Reformation*, 150.
55 This statement rests on my interpretation of the Supplication, for which see below, pp. 186–8.
56 *St. Pap.*, vii. 349.
57 *LP* v. 850.

It is well known that the Submission was made possible by the adroit use of a document known as the Commons' Supplication against the Ordinaries, but the immediate circumstances of the Supplication's genesis raise unusual problems of evidence and argument.[58] Two accounts of its history are plausible, and both must be considered as the prelude to More's political demise. One alternative is that the Commons debated spontaneously the issue of church courts and *ex officio* proceedings from the start of the 1532 session, emotional agitation being sparked off solely by the recent spate of heresy trials and burnings.[59] We recall that Hall knew that it was the inquisitorial method and pro-clerical bias of spiritual process which most offended the Lower House. Persons accused of heresy had either to abjure beliefs they perhaps had never held, or else face a martyr's death at the stake.[60] Stirred by these unfairnesses, members of the Commons, like Edward Reed of Norwich,[61] refurbished drafts of anticlerical petitions formerly drawn by their committees in 1529 (and perhaps also in 1531), and new committees then worked these up to incorporate the latest grievances on heresy trials. But the Lower House was as sensitive as ever to smears against its orthodoxy, and to safeguard itself from attack by the bishops put on its new committees those M.P.s most familiar with the king's latest opinions. Cromwell, as Henry's link-man, and Audley, despite being normally excluded from committees as Speaker, thus, the argument goes, played a leading role in producing a polished version of the Supplication. The completed document was then presented to Henry VIII, who exploited it opportunistically. In doing so, he used Cromwell and Edward Foxe as agents between himself and Convocation, and in the process Cromwell gained executive control of a rejuvenated royal policy aimed at reducing the clergy to impotent obedience.

The second interpretation is that the renewed anticlerical debate in the Lower House began a month after Parliament's reassembly, and was engineered almost entirely by Cromwell, who orches-

---

58 G. R. Elton, *Studies in Tudor and Stuart Politics and Government* (Cambridge, 1974), vol. ii. 107–36; Elton, *Reform and Reformation*, 150–6; J. P. Cooper, 'The Supplication against the Ordinaries Reconsidered', *English Historical Review*, lxxii (1957), 616–41; M. Kelly, 'The Submission of the Clergy', *Transactions of the Royal Historical Society*, 5th Series, xv (1965), 97–119; Lehmberg, *Reformation Parliament*, 138–42, 145–53; Scarisbrick, *Henry VIII*, 297–300.

59 This possibility was suggested by Mr Cooper.

60 *The Triumphant Reigne of Kyng Henry the VIII*, ed. C. Whibley (London, 1904), vol. ii. 202–3.

61 See above, pp. 168–71.

trated the grievances described by Hall into organized debates in order to gain the consensus needed to implement a pre-planned strategy leading to the Submission of the Clergy.[62] Well before the opening of the new session, Cromwell had retrieved from his archives copies of anticlerical drafts prepared by Commons' committees in 1529 and 1531, and these were welded together by himself and Audley to make the completed Supplication, the final text of which was in Cromwell's pocket (alongside the fabricated petition on annates) before the Commons returned in 1532.[63] But although the Supplication was prepared in advance, there is no doubt about the genuine nature and far-reaching extent of the Commons' sympathy for lay victims of clerical investigations and *ex officio* proceedings. The point is that debate could not begin spontaneously upon a subject so likely to anger an orthodox king, until it was believed (wrongly) that Henry supported manoeuvres which were being steered through the House by his councillor Cromwell. This was Cromwell's trick. Circumstantial evidence that anticlerical debates did not begin spontaneously in January 1532 is provided by the fact that Chapuys, always well informed by More and Fisher, knew nothing of the Supplication until after 14 February 1532.[64]

Of course, Henry VIII was in reality not encouraging anticlerical debate in 1532 at all. He was intent instead on getting a lay subsidy and approval of his bill of uses from a reluctant Commons; intent, too, on threatening the pope with a bill of annates which he and Norfolk interpreted strictly in a non-revolutionary sense, remaining ignorant of the petition on annates which the radical group had not dared to place before king or Parliament. The government's moves on annates, however, misled the Commons into thinking that Henry also wanted action on the Supplication — which is why they miscalculated that Henry would dissolve Parliament as soon as they laid its final version before him on 18 March 1532.[65] In other words, Cromwell was lending Henry's royal authority to his own Parliamentary manoeuvres, and this audacious (and confusing) strategy has given historians many sleepless nights. Yet the genius of Cromwell's plan was exactly that Henry should not connive in the Supplication, and thus learn of its extended

---

62 This case was argued by Professor Elton, whose latest views are found in *Reform and Reformation*, 150–6.
63 Elton, *Reform and Reformation*, 151.
64 *LP* v. 805 contains a report on Parliamentary business, but does not mention the Supplication.
65 Hall, *Henry the VIII*, vol. ii. 203.

revolutionary thrust, until after such time as its momentum had become irreversible. Only in that way could the trick succeed, because, as we recall, Henry VIII remained orthodox in February and March 1532. The king could not have approved the Supplication in advance of its presentation without already having decided to break with Rome, and this he had conspicuously failed to do. The anticlerical agitation of the Commons — genuine but not spontaneous — thus had to *appear* spontaneous, its apparent spontaneity providing Cromwell with the political camouflage essential to launching a premeditated *coup*.

External evidence strongly supports the view that Henry was not personally behind the Supplication. First, he showed little interest when it was placed before him on 18 March.[66] Secondly, he used neither it nor the resultant Submission of the Clergy as part of his campaign against the pope — in marked contrast to his exploitation of his title of 1531 and the bill of annates.[67] Thirdly, the Supplication was answered by Stephen Gardiner on 15 April 1532 in a style sufficiently abrasive to suggest that Henry's adopted stand as an impartial adjudicator between clergy and laity carried conviction even among his most intimate councillors.[68] As to attributing the Supplication to Cromwell's pre-sessional planning, and thus vindicating the second of the two possible interpretations, the external evidence is again strong. First, those who argue in favour of spontaneous anticlerical debates beginning in January 1532 have not satisfactorily explained why it then took as long as two months to get a petition before Henry VIII.[69] Secondly, the later versions of the Supplication were demonstrably drafted in Cromwell's office, and the final text was corrected by Audley.[70] As Speaker, Audley would not have acted as drafting clerk to a Commons' committee, but he regularly assisted Cromwell in pre-sessional work.[71] Thirdly, Hall himself remarked that the Supplication was drawn up 'by great advice' — namely, by those royal councillors who sat in the Lower House and guided its affairs.[72] Fourthly, the advance

---

66 *Ibid.*
67 Kelly, 'The Submission of the Clergy', 104.
68 *Ibid.*, p. 105; Elton, *Reform and Reformation*, 153.
69 Elton, *Reform and Reformation*, 151 n. 28.
70 SP 6/7, arts. 21–22 (*LP* v. 1016 [4]); SP 2/L, fos. 193–202 (*LP* v. 1016 [2]); SP 6/1, art. 22 (*LP* v. 1016 [1]).
71 Elton, *Reform and Reformation*, 151. An earlier statement of this argument was challenged by Mr Cooper, 'The Supplication against the Ordinaries Reconsidered', 630 n. 1.
72 Elton, *Studies*, vol. ii. 128.

preparation of a fabricated Commons' petition on a controversial subject was the identical ploy attempted by the radicals in the case of the paper on annates. Fifthly, Cromwell had already planned a flank attack on clerical jurisdiction in King's Bench, timed to begin in February 1532. The attorney-general filed *quo warranto* informations there on 8 February against twenty-two persons enjoying private jurisdictions, which was hardly routine since those challenged included Archbishop Warham, Bishop Skeffington of Bangor (who compounded in May 1532 for 500 marks),[73] Richard Pace (dean of St Paul's), six premier abbots, the wardens of All Souls College Oxford and St Mary's College Winchester, and the president of Queens' College Cambridge.[74] Sixteen of the informations were devised to test an opinion increasingly shared by common lawyers that similar cases should not be treated differently by spiritual and temporal courts, and that privileges granted to ecclesiastical jurisdictions by temporal law and custom were given on trust.[75] If that trust were subsequently abused, it was now argued, then the royal justices or even Parliament were bound to provide appropriate remedy.[76] From Cromwell's position, *quo warranto* proceedings, in which he had become versed as Wolsey's counsellor, thus seemed likely to form a better base for attacking spiritual immunity than trumped-up *praemunire* charges. This was because almost all aspects of ecclesiastical jurisdiction had temporal overtones in practice, upon which the legal doctrine of abuse could be trained as a machine-gun until the clergy either withdrew or capitulated. It is difficult to believe that this flank attack was not co-ordinated with the birth of the Supplication, working, as it was, towards an identical goal, although the King's Bench proceedings would soon become insignificant in the shadow of the Supplication's (unexpected?) success.

The Supplication was presented to the king on 18 March 1532 by a Commons' delegation led by Audley, when it consisted of a dozen anticlerical charges prefaced by a preamble.[77] The preamble was more moderate in tone than that of earlier drafts, deploring simply the bad relations, 'discord, variance and debate' between clergy and

---

73 *LP* v. 1052.
74 KB 9/518, fos. 1–20.
75 For this opinion, *The Reports of Sir John Spelman*, ed. J. H. Baker, vol. ii (Selden Society, London, 1978), *64–66*.
76 This theme was developed in St German's *Treatise Concerning Constitutions Provincial and Legatine* (London, 1535).
77 SP 6/1, art. 22. Printed by A. Ogle, *The Tragedy of the Lollards' Tower* (Oxford, 1949), 324–30.

laity 'in most uncharitable manner to the great inquietation and breach of your peace within this your most Catholic Realm'.[78] Specific complaints then followed against the independent legislative power of Convocation, the blatant unfairnesses of existing *ex officio* proceedings for heresy, the nuisance caused by long-distance ecclesiastical citations, the excessive level of ecclesiastical fees, the preferment to benefices of episcopal siblings, the abuse of holy days for purposes of vicious amusement, and the continued exercise of secular offices by clergy.[79] All these matters, the Commons prayed in a now-genuine petitionary peroration, might receive redress in Parliament with royal approval, both to 'declare and establish not only those things which to your Jurisdiction and prerogative Royal justly appertaineth, but also [to] reconcile and bring into perpetual unity your said subjects spiritual and temporal'.[80] Henry VIII, however, was not impressed by the Commons' arguments, which he regarded as *ex parte* and biased.[81] Receiving their delegation at Westminster, he deftly turned the discussion about in order to emphasize his own desire for prompt action on the controversial bill of uses, convincingly adopting the role of arbitrator between clergy and laity as a mere secondary issue and as an act of grace.[82] He passed the Supplication to Warham for answer, but no more was heard about it before 28 March, when Parliament adjourned for Easter.[83]

When Convocation reassembled on 12 April, two days after Parliament, it at last began to consider its response, but even then an answer, based on Gardiner's draft, was not submitted to Henry until the 27th.[84] The matter seemed not to be urgent, and there was no sign of clerical panic or desire to appease the laity. On the contrary, Gardiner and Warham had resolved to concede nothing, an attitude fortified by Convocation's success in 1531. The Answer of the Ordinaries accordingly began by assuring the king that 'no such discord, debate, variance or breach of peace' existed on the clergy's part against the layfolk, as the Commons falsely alleged.[85] Ecclesiastical jurisdiction had simply been exercised 'with all charity' against 'evil-disposed persons infected and utterly corrupt with

78 Ogle, 324.
79 Ogle, 325–9.
80 Ogle, 330.
81 Hall, *Henry the VIII*, vol. ii. 203.
82 *Ibid.*
83 Lehmberg, *Reformation Parliament*, 141–5.
84 Kelly, 'The Submission of the Clergy', 109–11.
85 SP 6/7, art. 24 (*LP* v. 1016[5]). Printed by H. Gee and W. J. Hardy, *Documents Illustrative of English Church History* (London, 1910), 154–76.

the pestilent poison of heresy'. For the clergy to be at peace with heretics was obviously impossible, being contrary to Scripture. Next the Answer refuted individually the Commons' specific charges. Convocation's legislative authority was defended as grounded upon Scripture and ecclesiastical tradition, 'which must also be a rule and square to try the justice and righteousness of all laws, as well spiritual as temporal'. *Ex officio* proceedings were similarly justified as necessary and valid, being founded either upon Scripture or the universal law of Christendom, which 'hath universally done good'. Any defects in the system were the result of particular errors, not 'the whole order of the clergy, nor of the laws wholesomely by them made'. Pro-clerical procedural advantages in heresy trials were neither unfair nor unreasonable, given the clergy's thankless task of maintaining religious orthodoxy. All things considered, no better arrangements could be devised for the church than the existing ones, and any administrative mistakes would be corrected if proved to have occurred.

On the question of citations and fees, the Answer denied that parties cited by spiritual courts were often required to travel long distances, and Warham now personally inserted a reply to the charge of excessive fees. The question, he reminded Henry politely, had been tackled by his recent reforms enacted in Convocation,[86] something he bitingly presumed was 'not unknown unto your grace's Commons'.[87] Far less temperately, he next repeated an earlier protest against the Citations Act, a new anticlerical measure which had probably reached the statute book since the Easter adjournment, and which had especially offended him.[88] Passed like the Annates Act despite total opposition from the prelates, the reform, which strictly limited ecclesiastical citations and thus impeded spiritual justice, was 'directly against the liberty and privileges of the churches of Canterbury and York, lawfully prescribed'.[89] Not even the pope could justly invade these rights, claimed Warham — as if that argument might mollify a king whom Warham had roused in February 1532 by formally dissociating himself from all anticlerical laws made or yet to be made in Parliament since 1529.[90] Concerning the remaining replies of the clergy to

86 Lehmberg, *Reformation Parliament*, 116–17, 142–3; Kelly, 'The Submission of the Clergy', 98–102.
87 Gee and Hardy, 166.
88 23 Hen. VIII, c. 9.
89 Gee and Hardy, 168.
90 D. Wilkins, *Concilia Magnae Britanniae et Hiberniae* (London, 1737), vol. iii. 746.

the Commons' accusations, the presentation of infants to benefices was declared allowable if the stipend was used for educational purposes; the abuse of holy days was deemed regrettable, but did not justify their abolition; and the employment of beneficed men as stewards and receivers to bishops was held to be lawful.[91]

But to Warham's and Gardiner's stunned astonishment and dismay, the Answer of the Ordinaries unexpectedly enraged Henry VIII. For reasons now to be explained, the king hardened his heart against his clergy as soon as he had read their document, a momentous change of direction which gave birth to immediate political consequences. Signs of imminent royal action were given on 30 April, when Henry himself took the initiative in summoning the Speaker and some of the Commons to an audience.[92] He handed Audley the Answer, adding the famous words: 'We think their answer will smally please you, for it seemeth to us very slender. You be a great sort of wisemen. I doubt not but you will look circumspectly on the matter, and we will be indifferent between you'.[93] Three separate questions arising since the Easter adjournment had conspired to irritate Henry's tenderest nerves, matters which simultaneously served to incur his wrath, offend his principles and arouse his secret suspicions — a lethal combination. First, William Peto, head of the Observant Friars, chaplain to Princess Mary and a leader of the Aragonese group, had brought to a head the increasingly intolerable problem of the Aragonese sermon and propaganda campaign organized by Bishop Fisher.[94] On Easter Day 1532, Peto had preached a fiery sermon before the king at Greenwich, condemning the divorce project and exposing the royal advisers as liars and deceivers. He told Henry that it was the affliction of princes to be abused daily by flatterers, and warned him that if the divorce went ahead the dogs would lick his blood as they had done Ahab's. Interviewed by the king in the garden after the sermon, Peto dared to observe that canon law prevented Henry from marrying Anne Boleyn irrespective of the divorce issue, since it was public knowledge that he had 'meddled with the mother and the sister'.[95] The following Sunday, Richard Curwen, a royal chaplain, was sent to Greenwich to refute Peto's arguments, and was heckled in Peto's absence by Henry Elstow, warden of the Green-

91 Gee and Hardy, 171–3.
92 Hall, *Henry the VIII*, vol. ii. 209.
93 *Ibid.*
94 See above, p. 141.
95 *LP* v. 941. See Appendix 2.

wich community.[96] The king was now so choleric that Peto and
Elstow were arrested and placed in the custody of Bishop Standish.[97] But Standish remained a Queen's supporter, and the two
friars, with his connivance, succeeded in appearing in Convocation
on 19 April to accuse Curwen of preaching at their convent without
permission.[98] Peto had thus become a considerable thorn in Henry's
side, quite apart from suspicions that he had been responsible for
smuggling abroad at least two of Fisher's seven treatises against the
divorce in manuscript, including *De Causa Matrimonii* published in
1530 at Alcalá.[99] Peto consequently remained in custody at Lambeth
throughout the remaining manoeuvres antecedent to the Submission of the Clergy,[100] and Henry went as far as to apply to Rome for
a commission to try him and Elstow, a request which Chapuys and
Queen Catherine earnestly opposed through their own diplomatic
channels.[101] Meanwhile, Cromwell was not slow to seize an opportunity, and before May 1532 was in close touch with a malcontent
priest from Greenwich, John Lawrence, whose services he accepted
as an agent and informer.[102] Lawrence, who complained of persecution within his convent for his defence of the king and willingness
to preach in favour of the divorce, subsequently delated his
superiors and brethren to Cromwell and Henry without scruple,
and later still introduced Cromwell to Richard Lyst, a neurotic lay
brother, who had been Wolsey's former servant and Anne Boleyn's
client.[103] Lawrence was, in fact, too restless and disaffected to be
much use, but the episode shows Cromwell alert to techniques of
undoubted political sophistication.

The second question which had arisen since the Easter adjournment to the detriment of Henry VIII's position linked the divorce
with the equally sensitive area of taxation. On 16 April 1532, More
himself came down to the Commons, accompanied by the dukes of
Norfolk, Suffolk and other premier peers, to announce a policy of
improving national fortifications along the Scottish border and
elsewhere, for which the government required 'some reasonable

96 *Ibid*.
97 Lehmberg, *Reformation Parliament*, 146 n. 1.
98 *Ibid*.
99 *LP* v. 941; M. Macklem, *God Have Mercy: the Life of John Fisher of Rochester*
   (Ottawa, 1967), 155; J. K. McConica, *English Humanists and Reformation Politics*
   (Oxford, 1965), 125.
100 *LP* v. 989.
101 *Ibid*.
102 For the date, D. Knowles, *The Religious Orders in England: The Tudor Age*
    (Cambridge, 1971), 208.
103 *LP* v. 1259, 1312 (ii), 1371, 1525; Knowles, 208–9.

aid'.[104] The request for supply, cast in this new (and unconvincing) guise, generated hefty opposition, and Chapuys learned that the Commons' debates turned towards the international implications of the divorce.[105] Two quick-witted Aragonese M.P.s then took the chance to move that the king be petitioned to take back Catherine in the interests of Anglo–Habsburg relations and national economic security, one probably being Thomas Temse, burgess for Westbury in Wiltshire.[106] According to Hall, Temse expatiated on the 'great mischiefs' the divorce would bring, 'as in bastardizing the Lady Mary . . . and divers other inconveniences', a daring speech which so incensed the king that he rebuked the Commons for discussing matters which 'touched his soul' at the same time as he handed Audley the Answer of the Ordinaries.[107]

The third and most novel element in the situation of April and May 1532 — perhaps also the most potent in view of Henry's dedication to self-ordained principle — stemmed from a fundamental misjudgment by Stephen Gardiner. Formerly a leading luminary and policymaker of Norfolk's political group, the new bishop of Winchester reacted to the imminent collapse of the duke's regime after the defection of Darcy and other traditionalists[108] by himself shifting his weight, prudently as he thought, to More's camp in defence of the English Church. Gardiner was now counting on Henry's innate conservatism, a quality perceived by no one better than a principal secretary, and assumed the new posture immediately on return from a two-month embassy to France on 6 March 1532.[109] As an ex-pupil later observed, Gardiner 'would go with the king's highness, and as far as he, but he would never go before, nor enter into any dangerous matters'.[110] But the bishop made the biggest blunder of his career in couching his defence of Convocation's independent legislative authority in the Answer of the Ordinaries in terms not only of divine prescription, but a divine prescription which could not be penetrated as a matter of principle by Henry's kingly power.[111] Ecclesiastical canons were divinely

---

104 Hall, *Henry the VIII*, vol. ii. 204–5; *LP* v. 941.
105 *LP* v. 989.
106 *Ibid.*; Elton, *Studies*, vol. i. 164; Hall, *Henry the VIII*, vol. ii. 210.
107 Hall, *Henry the VIII*, vol. ii. 209–10.
108 See above, p. 181.
109 *LP* v. 850. The shift was perhaps presaged as early as June 1531, *LP* v. 287 (p. 137).
110 This was Thomas Thirlby, another Trinity Hall man. C. Crawley, *Trinity Hall* (Cambridge, 1976), 47, 54.
111 Gee and Hardy, 157–8. This case was first argued by Kelly, 'The Submission of the Clergy', 111–12.

ordained, and were applied by the clergy 'in the feeding and ruling of Christ's people', he wrote; they might, as such, not even be *submitted* to the king for his royal assent as the Commons had demanded in the Supplication, although Henry's wise opinion was naturally solicited. With hindsight, one wonders how a man close to Henry VIII could have been so incautious as to gloss so dogmatically the medieval view of spiritual immunity. The incident has to reflect the king's apparent orthodoxy in April 1532 and reveal just how unexpected the Supplication's impending success was. At any rate, Gardiner had completely mistaken the residual impact of *Collectanea satis copiosa* on Henry's conception of his regal power, and had forgotten the gist of the king's reply to Tunstall's protest in 1531.[112] Learning the true extent of his error, Gardiner beat a hasty retreat from Court on the pretext of gout, and wrote Henry an obsequious letter in which he expressed utter disbelief that the king's reaction could be so severe.[113] He then attempted to justify his part in the Answer by reference to Henry's own *Assertio Septem Sacramentorum* and Cranmer's translation of the *Collectanea*. Gardiner's mistake, which almost certainly lost him the succession at Canterbury,[114] was thus a classic instance of an academic missing the point.[115]

During the first week in May 1532, the prelates remained in a state of shock.[116] Their leaders were confused and hesitant, and on 8 May the initiative was seized by Convocation's Lower House once again.[117] Members successfully petitioned for the dispatch to Court of a clerical delegation to plead with Henry for the safe preservation

---

112 See above, pp. 162–3.
113 *The Letters of Stephen Gardiner*, ed. J.A. Muller (Cambridge, 1933), 48–9; *LP* v. 1025; Kelly, 'The Submission of the Clergy', 111.
114 Kelly, 'The Submission of the Clergy', 111.
115 Gardiner's dogmatic exclusion of regal power from the clergy's legislative function was the more untimely in that it coincided with a burst of ecclesiastical statute-making in Convocation on a scale unseen since Archbishop Peacham's Lambeth constitutions of 1281 or Stratford's canons of 1342. Widespread canonical reform was inevitably recognized as a marked departure from recent clerical policy in 1532, and the new legislation boomeranged on its inventors — ironically, because canonical reform had been in good measure forced upon the clergy by the intensity of lay criticism and their narrow escape from royal supremacy in 1531. Kelly, 'The Submission of the Clergy', 101–2.
116 Kelly, 'The Submission of the Clergy', 112. The draft of a second Answer to the Supplication may belong to the first or second weeks in May, but there is no evidence that it was ever presented to Henry. B.L. Cotton MS. Cleopatra F. i, fos. 101–3 (*LP* v. 1018 [1]).
117 Kelly, 'The Submission of the Clergy', 112.

of the liberties of the English Church, and six royal favourites agreed to go, namely John Longland, John Stokesley, the abbots of Westminster and Burton, Richard Sampson, and a fifth-columnist Edward Foxe.[118] However, this group achieved nothing. Indeed their intervention was disastrous,[119] since Henry, who plainly recalled the technique used a year before when the Council had forced the clergy along a pre-arranged route by direct pressure, took his opportunity to clarify the boundaries of his regal function.[120] The difference from 1531 was, though, that the clergy could no longer presume on the moderating influence of an aristocratic group united under Norfolk as a means to offset Henry's more radical or eccentric opinions. For the first time since Cromwell's rise to influence, the clergy and Aragonese faction were politically isolated in Council and at Court. Gardiner was neutralized, and Warham paralysed with fear or old age. Bishop Fisher was also absent from the scene of action, having returned sick to Rochester soon after the opening of the 1532 session of Parliament.[121] Convocation and the House of Lords thus remained the only institutions where the prelates and Aragonese faction retained a majority.

On 10 May in Convocation, Edward Foxe exhibited three articles of Submission sent to the clergy by Henry VIII.[122] No new canons were to be enacted or executed without royal assent; existing ones deemed prejudicial to Henry's prerogative or onerous to subjects were to be annulled on the judgment of a royal commission of clergy and laity — a proposal perhaps inspired by St German's document of 1530/31, which had also required a committee of clergy and laity to prune canon law;[123] and existing canons held consonant with God's and the king's laws could stand subject to royal assent. Foxe's statement of these demands was greeted with near panic, and a mission was hastily sent to gain Fisher's counsel from Rochester.[124] But Henry kept up the pressure, sending next day for Audley and twelve other M.P.s and announcing that the clergy were 'but half our subjects, yea, and scarce our subjects'.

For all the Prelates at their consecration make an oath to the Pope, clean contrary to the oath that they make to us, so that they seem

118 *Ibid*.
119 Suggested by Lehmberg, *Reformation Parliament*, 149.
120 Elton makes the same case in *Reform and Reformation*, 154.
121 Lehmberg, *Reformation Parliament*, 132.
122 Kelly, 'The Submission of the Clergy', 112–13.
123 See above, p. 152.
124 Kelly, 'The Submission of the Clergy', 113.

to be his subjects, and not ours. The copy of both the oaths I deliver here to you, requiring you to invent some order, that we be not thus deluded of our Spiritual subjects.[125]

The remark that the clergy were but half Henry's subjects was, in fact, one of Thomas Cromwell's favourite phrases, and transcripts of the conflicting oaths had probably been among his papers since 1530.[126] Events were now moving fast towards the dénouement Cromwell had mooted prior to the Pardon of the Clergy, although Henry's precipitate intervention after the Answer of the Ordinaries was an unexpected windfall. Equally welcome to the radical group was the king's choice of Foxe and Audley, two of its leaders, as his agents to concert developments in Convocation and the House of Commons respectively. That choice offered the opportunity for careful liaison between the radicals during the period 8–15 May, something assuredly more important now than anything formerly planned in advance by Cromwell. For although the Supplication had exploited the anticlericalism of the Commons sufficiently to launch an attempted Cromwellian *coup*, what mattered after 8 May was the mechanics of the chain reaction by which Henry's intervention led to the Submission of the Clergy. Pre-determined aims necessarily had to give way to nuts and bolts. This was because the king, listening behind the scenes to Cromwell and Foxe but as volatile as ever, had personally to provide the direct political coercion without which both Submission and *coup*, though planned in advance, would nevertheless have failed as surely as in 1531. But fortunately for Cromwell, Henry was blinded throughout the May manoeuvres by the issue of his regality. In stripping Convocation of its legislative independence and wiping chapter one of Magna Carta off the statute book, Henry was asserting his personal theology, not playing out a revolution. The king could act without stopping to think, not least because he did not see the Submission as a weapon in his main battle, which was the divorce.[127]

The oaths of the prelates were duly read before the assembled Commons on Audley's return to the House,[128] and a bill for 'the resumption of the liberties, etc. of the prelates' was perhaps introduced next, as is suggested by the juxtaposition of the two items in the list of failed bills 'depending in the Common House' at the end

---

125 Hall, *Henry the VIII*, vol. ii. 210.
126 *LP* vi. 299 (pp. 137, 139); Elton, *Reform and Reformation*, 154.
127 Cf. Elton's remark in *Reform and Reformation*, 155.
128 Hall, *Henry the VIII*, vol. ii. 210–12.

of the 1532 session.[129] Since a bill answering the list's description survives among Cromwell's papers,[130] it would appear that his original plan had aimed at a Parliamentary rather than a personal *coup*, no doubt to circumvent Henry VIII's proclivities towards caesaropapism. Cromwell's draft announced in an extravagant preamble that England was a sovereign national state, composed of three estates (the clergy, the nobility and the commons) — 'one body politic living under the allegiance, obedience, tuition and defence of the king's royal majesty being their one supreme imperial head and sovereign'.[131] Within this system, legislative power resided in the king alone — curiously, Cromwell here deleted all reference to the assistance of Parliament — 'which authority and jurisdiction royal is so united and knit by the high providence of God to the imperial crown of this realm that the same is not under the obedience or appellation of any worldly foreign prince'. Cromwell then stripped the clergy of their legislative privileges, ordering that no enactment made by them contrary to English law or royal authority was valid unless endorsed by Parliament.

Further evidence that Cromwell aimed at a statutory *coup*, and that he encountered concerted resistance from Thomas More and the Aragonese faction in Parliament, is perhaps given by the confession of Sir George Throckmorton.[132] Written in October 1537, Throckmorton's document appears at first sight to be subject to the same sort of chronological confusion which mars Roper's *Lyfe of Sir Thomas Moore*. Sir George confessed that More, 'then being chancellor', sent for him 'after the beginning' of the Reformation Parliament, but shortly after he 'had reasoned to the bill of Appeals'. When he arrived at Westminster, More received him 'in a little chamber within the Parliament chamber where, as I do remember me, stood an altar or a thing like unto an altar whereupon he did lean'. As previously mentioned, Sir Thomas interrupted his conversation with John Clerk to tell Throckmorton, 'I am very glad to hear the good report that goeth of you and that ye be so good a catholic man as ye be; and if ye do continue in the same way that ye began and be not afraid to say your conscience, ye shall deserve great reward of God and thanks of the king's grace at length and

---

129 SP 1/74, fos. 146–47 (*LP* vi. 120). This important reference was noted first by Mr Cooper, 'The Supplication against the Ordinaries Reconsidered', 634.
130 Two versions of this bill are extant. SP 2/L, fos. 78–80 (*LP* v. 721[1]) is a draft corrected by Cromwell. SP 2/P, fos. 17–19 (*LP* vii. 57 [2]) is a fair copy incorporating the changes of the draft.
131 SP 2/L, fo. 78 v.
132 See Appendix 2.

much worship to yourself'. The Act of Appeals was not passed until 1533, a year after More's resignation as lord chancellor. But those writers who have found this apparent chronological muddle too puzzling to give full credence to Throckmorton's story have failed to notice two things. First, Throckmorton was opposing a *bill* of Appeals at the time More urged him to keep up the good work. Secondly, Sir George also stated categorically that his interview with More was during that meeting of Parliament which *immediately followed* Friar Peto's fiery sermon before the king at Greenwich. He remembered this, because Peto, too, had summoned him to his tower of confinement at Lambeth to explain the implications of Henry's divorce policy, and to exhort him to stick to the catholic cause 'as I would have my soul saved'. Peto's sermon was delivered on 31 March 1532, and Parliament reassembled on 10 April after its Easter adjournment. If Throckmorton was in retrospect confused over the wider chronology of the Reformation Parliament, he would not have mistaken the occasion when Peto threatened him with hellfire. In other words, it is entirely possible that the 'bill of Appeals' to which Throckmorton referred in the context of April and May 1532 was in fact Cromwell's extant bill for a Parliamentary Submission of the Clergy. With hindsight, the Cromwellian bill of 1532 and the later Act of Appeals could have appeared as brother and sister to a rank and file M.P. looking back from the vantage point of 1537. In all probability, they looked this way to Thomas More. The substance of each measure was addressed to aspects of the same international problem, the legislative and judicial authority of Rome and the clergy, while the preambles of both documents loudly proclaimed the Cromwellian theory of national sovereignty under Henry VIII's imperial crown.

In any event, a Parliamentary Submission was never a serious possibility in the climate of 1532, and Cromwell had to wait two years to achieve this ambition (by 25 Hen. VIII, c. 19). On the contrary, Henry and Cromwell predictably lost control of the Lords on 12 or 13 May, either over Cromwell's bill for Submission, or another to prevent the bishops making arrests for heresy.[133] Whatever happened exactly, Parliament was abruptly prorogued on 14 May, a move which effectively forestalled the coalescence outside Convocation of an opposition to Henry's demands there.[134] As such, the prorogation came not a moment too soon. By 13 May,

---

133 *LP* v. 1013; Cooper, 'The Supplication against the Ordinaries Reconsidered', 633–4.
134 Kelly, 'The Submission of the Clergy', 118.

the Aragonese faction had broken its cover, opposing Henry's policy publicly and led from the front, as it seems, by Thomas More. In the absence of a Parliamentary archive, we do not know precisely what More said or did in the second week of May 1532, but Chapuys knew for certain on the 13th that Henry had been thwarted head-on by More, with whom he was as angry as he had been with Gardiner over the Answer of the Ordinaries.[135] To have offended to this extent, More must plainly have spoken his mind for once. Fisher, too, was an opponent in May 1532. Although confined to Rochester, he had been receiving news from Chapuys in cypher since January, and was writing a learned justification of clerical immunity.[136] No retributive action was taken against him in 1532, but Cromwell took the precaution of obtaining a copy of the offending treatise.[137]

On 13 May, Convocation began to waver under the threat of the king's demands. Despite Aragonese opposition, a compromise was attempted by which the clergy surrendered their right to enact any more legislation in Henry VIII's reign, and agreed to submit existing ecclesiastical law to the king's 'examination and judgment'.[138] Henry's response was, however, to raise the stakes no less than three times, once on 13 May and twice on the 15th.[139] The major reprisal came on the 15th, when Convocation was told that it 'always hath been and must be' assembled only by royal writ.[140] This idea came straight out of Cromwell's draft bill for a Parliamentary Submission, and its last-minute addition to Henry's own programme suggests that the radicals were gaining hold daily over the royal mind. Meanwhile, a writ was issued proroguing Convocation, which was Henry's way of commanding instant action, and this peremptory call for Submission was reinforced by the irregular appearance in Convocation of Norfolk, Wiltshire, Exeter, Sandes, Oxford and Rochford.[141] Some tortuous soundings next occurred between Convocation's two Houses, after which Warham, whose war-cry was consistently *Ira principis mors est*,[142] asked the prelates for their approval of the Submission.[143] Bishops Stokesley, Long-

---

135 *LP* v. 1013.
136 *LP* v. 737; Macklem, *Life of John Fisher*, 238 n. 24. Fragments of the tract are SP 6/1, art. 7; SP 6/11, arts. 15–17.
137 SP 6/1, art. 7 (*LP* v. 1020).
138 Kelly, 'The Submission of the Clergy', 114.
139 *Ibid*.
140 *Ibid*.
141 Kelly, 'The Submission of the Clergy', 115.
142 *LP* v. 287 (p. 137).
143 Kelly, 'The Submission of the Clergy', 115.

land and Standish (now an Aragonese defector) reluctantly consen-
ted; John Clerk was totally opposed.[144] Only three other bishops —
Warham, West and Vesey — perhaps acknowledged the Submission unequivocally, along with a suspiciously vague number of
monastic prelates.[145] The schedule was then presented to the Lower
House, but Warham at once announced the royal prorogation in
order to disperse the inferior clergy without effective opposition.[146]
In other words, the Submission of the Clergy was (in Dr Kelly's
phrase) 'enacted by a rump Convocation'.[147]

On Thursday 16 May, the archbishop, Longland, Standish and
four abbots duly subscribed the articles of Submission in a ceremony at Westminster before commissioners who included Cromwell.[148] Within hours of that ceremony, Thomas More resigned as
lord chancellor. At 3 p.m. in the garden at York Place, Westminster,
More came into the royal presence and, watched by the duke of
Norfolk, handed back the white leather bag containing the great
seal to Henry VIII.[149] It was the final, most awkward and most
poignant moment of his public career. It was an admission of
political defeat, but it was also an act of public defiance. The ironical
inflexion of More's voice, the piercing gaze of his eyes, and the
nobility of his composure all gave the lie to his excuse that he was
'not equal to the work'.[150] The clergy's Submission and More's
resignation were lineally connected: the one succeeded the other as
night day. Directed by Cromwell, the radical group had won the
factional battle for control both of the clergy and Henry VIII's
policy.[151] At a stroke, the Aragonese party was irrevocably discredited, Norfolk's regime irretrievably overbalanced, and England's course set fair towards the Henrician Reformation. More had
played his part, and lost; discharged his duty, and could quit the
arena in good conscience, vindicated by the knowledge that
Cromwell's victory of 15 May was 'narrow, blundering and legally
suspect'.[152] More's gaze in the garden told Henry so, and the king
averted his eyes. Henry and More could no longer communicate.
On the king's own former advice, Thomas More had finally earned
his epitaph 'the king's good servant, but God's first'.

144 *Ibid.*, 116–17.
145 *Ibid.*, 116–17.
146 *Ibid.*, 115.
147 *Ibid.*, 117.
148 *LP* v. 1023 (1).
149 *LP* v. 1075.
150 *LP* v. 1046.
151 Cf. Elton's comments in *Reform and Reformation*, 155–6.
152 Kelly, 'The Submission of the Clergy', 119.

CONCLUSION

WITHIN thirteen months of More's resignation, Thomas Cromwell had inscribed the Act of Appeals on the statute book and gained sway as Henry VIII's chief minister, Audley was lord chancellor, Cranmer was archbishop of Canterbury, the king had obtained his divorce, and Anne Boleyn was Queen of England. Although More's departure had, in fact, come as a shock to some people, these facts confirm his realization of the extent of his political defeat in May 1532. His decision to resign is also explicable, in the obvious absence of comment from More himself, in terms of what Sir George Throckmorton was told by Bishop Fisher and Nicholas Wilson after his confidential interview with Sir Thomas in the room next to the Parliament chamber.[1] Contrary to the advice of Father Reynolds of Syon, who warned Throckmorton that failure to play out his conscience in Parliament would result in his damnation in hell, leaving political suicide as his one hope of eternal salvation, Fisher and Wilson instead opined 'that if I did think in my conscience that my speaking could do no good, that then I might hold my peace and not offend'.[2] Was not this More's opinion too? With the Aragonese faction frustrated and future events seemingly inevitable in May 1532, More could see with immense relief the moral validity of total withdrawal from public life, conceiving his remaining years as a personal struggle in which he would seek strength to protect his conscience against the greater trials he knew must come. Resignation was not only More's acknowledgement of Cromwell's political victory; it was his statement of recognition that the 'indirect approach' had failed. 'Practical philosophy' was no use any more. More could no longer 'seek . . . to handle matters tactfully', making bad better, even though bad could not be made wholly good. In the metaphor of *Utopia*, More's ship had sunk with all hands.[3] Both Erasmus and Hythlodaeus had been right. 'Practical philosophy' might have helped during the years of Wolsey's ascendancy, but it was impotent amid a cut-throat world of true political crisis, where corruption, vice and evil counsels were

1 See above, p. 198.
2 See Appendix 2.
3 *The Complete Works of St Thomas More*, vol. iv, *Utopia*, ed. E. Surtz and J. H. Hexter (New Haven, 1965), 99–101. See above, pp. 10–11.

measured only by the standard of success. More's public career was over, and the time had come to devote himself to God alone and not to meddle in affairs again, 'but that my whole study should be upon the passion of Christ and mine own passage out of this world'.[4]

The ultimate tragedy was, however, that More's alternative position was equally untenable. As he was informed by Cromwell in 1535, 'though I was prisoner and condemned to perpetual prison, yet I was not thereby discharged of mine obedience and allegiance unto the King's Highness'.[5] Failing his political conversion, More's continued presence in Henrician England undermined the forces of social constraint which buttressed the revolutionary morality of blameless conformity and obedience to royal and Parliamentary authority. Armed with both humanist technique and secure faith, More combined a clear vision and direct insight to truth with a prominent public reputation. As such, he was an intolerable threat to the new regime, irrespective of Thomas Cromwell's genuine affection and respect for his former opponent. As expressed in his *Dialogue of Comfort against Tribulation*, written during the fifteen months of his imprisonment in the Tower, More aspired to an ideal of spiritual manhood which would transcend the accepted bounds of human capacity. He stood for moral crusade, and Henry VIII was adroitly cast in this work as the Great Turk.[6] More's brilliant career in law and politics, in particular his active role in the events of 1529–32, meanwhile ensured that his morality would soon become his executioner. Yet by suffering torment for the truth he had discovered, More gave posterity an assurance that it was not an illusion. When the axe finally fell on 6 July 1535, 'the king's good servant' also earned his place among the very few who have enlarged the horizon of the human spirit.

4 Rogers, no. 214.
5 *Ibid*.
6 *The Complete Works of St Thomas More*, vol. xii, *A Dialogue of Comfort against Tribulation*, ed. L. L. Martz and F. Manley (New Haven, 1976).

APPENDIX 1

MORE'S SUITS IN STAR CHAMBER

References to 167 suits in the Star Chamber Proceedings, Henry
VIII (STAC 2) at the Public Record Office, London.[1]

STAC 2/1/136, 141–47, 175A, 176–78
STAC 2/2/39, 159–60, 171–73, 221, 228–29, 244–62
STAC 2/3/43–48B, 120–22, 192–97, 198, 206–7, 219, 244–46,
 249–53, 278, 279, 312
STAC 2/4/119–23, 185, 194–95
STAC 2/5/32, 57–57A, 130–34
STAC 2/6/34–45, 126–28, 204–8, 217, 251–54, 282–92, 294
STAC 2/7/107–8, 166, 167, 181, 187, 214
STAC 2/8/4–6, 66–67, 68, 73–75, 103, 184, 223, 226–27, 229–32,
 275
STAC 2/9/205–8, 231–40
STAC 2/10/8–9, 10, 11–13A, 60, 67, 130, 150–51, 263–64, 269,
 294–99
STAC 2/11/63–73, 91–100
STAC 2/12/46–65, 106, 145–48, 150, 153, 154, 158–59, 160–61,
 236, 249
STAC 2/13/30–46, 64–68
STAC 2/14/60–86, 164–66
STAC 2/15/66, 93
STAC 2/16/4, 67–68, 181–82, 335–38, 402
STAC 2/17/5, 26, 59, 68, 83, 133, 145, 160, 251, 257, 287, 290, 339,
 349, 380, 386, 395, 396, 401, 403, 405, 407
STAC 2/18/49, 129, 131, 147, 177, 178, 223, 242, 249, 325, 330,
 331
STAC 2/19/51, 56, 57, 78, 91, 100, 133, 146, 156, 173, 178, 180,
 181, 205, 239, 258, 272, 286, 288, 300, 304, 317, 320, 332, 336,
 345, 363, 370, 373, 375, 392
STAC 2/20/44, 45, 76, 80, 88, 91, 139, 141, 142, 223, 330, 335, 340,
 349, 367, 400
STAC 2/21/108, 117, 134, 136, 149, 167, 180, 182, 210, 231

---

1 See above, pp. 50–1. These references should be used in conjunction with Public
 Record Office, *List of Proceedings in the Court of Star Chamber*, vol. i (New York,
 1963). A number of suits have references scattered through several bundles.

STAC 2/22/20, 46, 70, 71, 78, 82, 145, 151, 204, 205, 215, 264, 266, 281, 284, 315, 349, 367

STAC 2/23/11, 145, 171, 216, 246, 247, 261, 275, 282, 289, 296, 297

STAC 2/24/27, 42, 48, 52, 97, 105, 117, 126, 139, 145, 155, 158, 162, 208, 223, 248, 327, 359

STAC 2/25/8, 18, 21, 64, 176, 249, 326

STAC 2/26/7, 102, 105, 178, 204, 209, 219, 221, 235, 250, 256, 319, 347, 361, 362, 368, 378, 383, 421, 443

STAC 2/27/6, 96, 116

STAC 2/28/12, 17, 19, 32, 36, 52, 65, 71, 94, 136

STAC 2/29/19, 53, 60, 64, 84, 86, 88, 146, 149, 157, 158, 186

STAC 2/30/11, 56, 64, 138

STAC 2/31/50, 55, 61, 79, 118, 153, 164

STAC 2/32/3, 75, 126, 130

STAC 2/33/20, 67

STAC 2/34/2, 12, 14, 34, 48, 52

APPENDIX 2

DOCUMENTS

A. 1 July 1529, Darcy's 'memorandum' (SP 1: 54, fo. 240v.)[1]

MEMORANDUM, PARLIAMENT MATTERS

First to approbate and affirm every captain slain in the king's service by sea or land, h . . . for that one time next suing to . . . ward, but freely to enter to [his] lands, and semblable to have his . . .

Item that no nobleman ne gentleman be outlawed ne condemned without specialty of his band,[2] sealed and signed and delivered for his deed afore witness therein.

Item that from Trent north ordinary, the terms and laws to be kept as is at Westminster, treasons etc., urgent causes reserved.

Item that both offenders in the spiritual law against God in the decrees openly, and open and presumptuous offenders against the king's laws, for usury, simony etc., for false clothes making, and in many other crimes be more roundly, from time to time, sore punished, or else etc.

Item that all knights' fees, baronies and earldoms be viewed, and how many of them be in spiritual hands.

Item to view what of all temporal lands the spiritual men hath, and by what titles, and for what purposes and whether it be followed or no.

Item better and much more merit, honour and virtue is it for the king's grace to proceed and determine all reformations of spiritual and temporal [matters] within this realm, so that . . .

Item that never legate nor cardinal be in England.

Item their legacies and faculties clearly annulled and made frustrate.

Item that sure search and inquiries be made what hath been levied thereby.

Item that it be tried whether the putting down of all the abbeys be lawful and good or no, for great things hang thereupon.

Item for that etc., good it is to see all the surmises of the cardinal for obtaining of his authorities and totcotts, both for him and others,

1 Mutilated sections in the manuscript are indicated by three dots.
2 Bond.

and to see how they stand with the decrees and laws divine.

Item some straiter[3] laws for punishments of usurers, pollers, extortioners and bribers, and colourers of authorities or otherwise.

Item exactions and such used by spiritual men.

Item for probations of testaments after the old rate.

Item against letters of administration, and what great injuries and wrongs daily grows [sic] of these besides, death is well broken thereby.

Item some provisions for repairings and fortifying of the marches and frontiers.

Item for services in the wars and maintaining the king's . . . of the church and religion . . . the parishes, frank archers etc. in ordinary, peaces [sic] and wars, both a surety and a common wealth, with taxes etc.

B. October 1537, confession of Sir George Throckmorton to Henry VIII, implicating Thomas More and others (SP 1: 125, fos. 247–56)

In my most humble manner to your highness remembered, pleaseth the same to be advertised about six or seven years past, as I do remember, I met with Sir Thomas Dingley at St John's,[4] and he and I walked into the garden till the dinner was ready, and he fell in communication with me of the Parliament matters, marvelling greatly that such acts as the Appeals and other should pass so lightly as they did, or words much like to these. And I said it was no marvel for that the common house was much advertised by my lord privy seal,[5] and that few men there would displease him. And the said Sir Thomas said, 'I hear say ye have spoken much in divers matters'. And I said, 'true it is, I have spoken some thing in the act of Appeals, whereupon the king's grace did send for me and spake with me in divers matters, so that I perceive his grace's conscience is troubled for that he hath married his brother's wife, and he thinketh God is not pleased therewith'. And I said to him that I told your grace I feared if ye did marry Queen Anne, your conscience would be more troubled at length, for that it is thought ye have meddled with the mother and the sister. And his grace said, 'never with the mother',

3 More rigorous.
4 St John's Priory, Clerkenwell.
5 Thomas Cromwell.

and my lord privy seal standing by said, 'nor never with the sister neither, and therefore put that out of your mind'. And this is all that I said to him or he to me, or words much like to the same effect to my remembrance, as God shall judge me at my most need. And if he have spoken these words or any like upon my mouth to your grace's displeasure, it is without my knowledge or consent. For I will take it on my soul when so ever it shall please our Lord to take me to his mercy, I thought no harm to your grace in the speaking of them. For that I ever spake these words to him, or to any other man, was to lament what I thought would follow of the marriage to your grace, and to your realm in time to come. And to declare the very intent whereupon I spake it, I think in my conscience upon a proud and a vainglorious mind, as who saith[6] they that I did tell it to should note me to be a man that durst speak for the common wealth and never for untruth in thought, word or deed. And if ever it can be otherwise proved in this matter or in any other, I utterly refuse your gracious pardon and that I may have the shamefullest death that ever had man to the utter rebuke and infamy of me and all mine. And if, good and gracious lord, it was of negligence and arrogance spoken and not of no untruth, I humbly beseech your highness of pardon. And forasmuch [as] my lord privy seal willed me to write with whom I had any communication in this matter besides Dingley, as also what other communication I have had at the Queen's Head or in any other place concerning your grace, which is very hard for me to do and in manner impossible. Notwithstanding, as much as I can call to my remembrance I will declare hereafter following. These words afore rehearsed to Sir Thomas Dingley incontinent[7] after I came from your grace, I showed the same words to Sir Thomas Englefield in the Sergeants' Inn in his chamber. And as I think in my conscience, I spake them to Sir William Essex. And whether I spake them to Sir William Barantyne or no I doubt, but I think rather yea than nay. And these be all that I can remember that ever I spake it to, never for ill intent as I take God to record. Also Sir William Essex, Sir William Barantyne, Sir John Gifford, Sir Marmaduke Constable with divers others and I myself did much use the Queen's Head at dinner and supper, and there we have had many communications concerning the Parliament matters. As they were in ure,[8] so we did commune of them, and every man showed his mind, and divers other of the Parliament house would come thither to dinner and

6 In order that.
7 Immediately.
8 As they arose.

supper and commune with us in like manner. And lightly[9] when we did commune, we would bid the servants of the house go out, and in like manner our own servants because we thought it not convenient that they should hear us speak of such matters. But to say that ever we met there by any appointment or for ill intent, or ever had any suspicious communication whereby it may appear that any of us thought evil, let us be punished in the example of all other. For if we had meant any ill, as God knoweth we did not, I think there is few men would think that place to be meet for such a purpose. In consideration whereof, I most humbly beseech your highness to have mercy and pity on me, my wife and poor children for the service that I and all my blood hath done to you and your progenitors in time past, and not for these lewd and indiscreet words spoken upon a proud and vainglorious mind not intending any harm as God shall judge me. And in especial seeing how good and gracious lord ye were to me at Grafton to pardon and forgive me all things past concerning the Parliament, as all other speaking and lewd demeanour misused to your highness in time past. And seeing these words were spoken so long ago and to no ill intent, as I shall be saved at the day of Doom. And that it will please your highness to accept me into your favour and mercy, without the which I do not desire to live. Written with the most sorrowful heart and by the most unhappy man that ever I think did live in this world.

And further, because your highness should conceive nothing against me concerning my unthrifty and unnatural brother,[10] [I now confess] what I have heard of him or spoken of him to any man since his departure. About midsummer term last past, I was at St John's at dinner where, as I do remember, I met with Sir Thomas Dingley and with a young man that I suppose should dwell with Richard Fermor. The one of them said these words following: 'your brother Michael is in good health, for I saw him of late in Antwerp in a chapel at mass'. And I said, 'if it were the will of God, I would he had never been born'. And this is all that ever I heard of him or from him since he departed. But to say precisely which of them did say these words I doubt, but I think Fermor's man. And also I heard say that he wrote Dr Wotton a letter since his departing. And since that time I wrote him a letter by my lord privy seal's mind, which I will surely follow both upon him and his master[11] and if it be to Rome['s] gates to die upon them both in that quarrel if your grace's

9 Commonly.
10 Michael Throckmorton, servant to Reginald Pole.
11 Reginald Pole.

pleasure be I shall so do. In consideration whereof, most dread sovereign lord, if ye have conceived any thing in your heart concerning me touching him, I most humbly beseech your highness to put it away. For I had liefer[12] end my life in perpetual prison than to live at large having your indignation. And this I am bold to require of your highness, knowing your gentle nature and pity to all men that will amend and ask mercy. For surely I [ac]knowledge myself I did very lewdly and naughtily to show these matters to any man, and much more offence to so light a man.[13]

But now, good and gracious lord, to open and declare unto you the inward part of my heart and what was the original cause and ground of all my proud, lewd and indiscreet handling of myself to you ward, and in all your affairs since the beginning of your Parliament in anno vicesimo primo or thereabouts.[14] It may like your highness to be advertised that a little before the beginning of that Parliament, Friar Peto, then being in a tower in Lambeth over the gate, sent for me to come and speak with him. And so I did go to him, where we had long communication together; and he showed me of two sermons that he and another friar had made before your grace a little before at Greenwich, and of a long communication that was between your grace and him in the garden after the sermon. And he showed me that he did tell you that in his conscience ye could never have other wife while the Princess Dowager[15] did live without ye could prove a carnal knowledge betwixt Prince Arthur and her, which he said in his conscience could never be well proved, for he said such[16] should best know it of any living creature, and that such had received the sacrament to the contrary. And such being so virtuous a woman, there ought to be more credence given to her than to all the other proofs. And as to all the other proofs, he said [these] were but upon presumptions save the saying of Prince Arthur that he had been in the middle of Spain, which he supposed was but a light word spoken of him. And further said that he did show your grace that ye could never marry Queen Anne for that it was said ye had meddled with the mother and the sister. And in conclusion he advised me if I were in the Parliament house to stick to that matter as I would have my soul saved. And shortly after the beginning of the Parliament, and after I had reasoned to the bill of

12 Rather.
13 I.e. to discuss the king's affairs with common persons.
14 Throckmorton gives the date as 1529, but his description fits best the session of 1532. See above, p. 199.
15 Catherine of Aragon.
16 I.e. Catherine.

Appeals,[17] Sir Thomas More then being chancellor sent say[18] for me
to come speak with him in the Parliament chamber. And when I
came to him, he was in a little chamber within the Parliament
chamber where, as I do remember me, stood an altar or a thing like
unto an altar whereupon he did lean. And as I do think the same
time the bishop of Bath[19] was talking with him. And then he said
this to me, 'I am very glad to hear the good report that goeth of you
and that ye be so good a catholic man as ye be; and if ye do continue
in the same way that ye began and be not afraid to say your
conscience, ye shall deserve great reward of God and thanks of the
king's grace at length and much worship to yourself', or words
much like to these. Whereupon I took so much pride of this that
shortly after I went to the bishop of Rochester,[20] with whom I was
divers times, and had much communication as well of the act of
Appeals as of that of Annates, and of the Supremacy and of the
authority that our Lord gave to Peter above the other disciples. And
at the last time I was with him, he gave me a book of his own device
to prove much of this matter to be true, which book I delivered my
lord privy seal in his house in the Austin Friars. Also my lord of
Rochester advised me to speak with Master Wilson and take his
advice in this matter. And so I did, and came home to his house
divers times to him to St Thomas the Apostle's,[21] and he was of the
same opinion that my lord of Rochester was, and showed me divers
books noted with his own hand to prove that he said to be true. And
after all this, I went to Syon to one Reynolds of whom I was
confessed,[22] and showed him my conscience in all these causes and
other as they came to my mind at that time, who was of the same
opinion that they were of, and advised me to stick to the same to the
death. And if I did not, I should be surely damned. And also if I did
speak or do any thing in the Parliament house contrary to my
conscience for fear of any earthly power or punishment, I should
stand in a very heavy case at the day of Judgment. And [Reynolds]
further advised me that I should not hold my peace if I thought my
speaking could not prevail, which opinion was contrary both to the
bishop of Rochester and Master Wilson; for their opinion was that if
I did think in my conscience that my speaking could do no good,
that then I might hold my peace and not offend. But he said, I did

17 This is a chronological confusion; see above, p. 199.
18 Sent word.
19 John Clerk.
20 John Fisher.
21 By Knightrider Street, Vintry Ward.
22 Richard Reynolds.

not know what comfort I should be to many men in the house to see me stick in the right way, which should cause many more to do the same. Which sayings and counsels afore rehearsed entered so in my heart with the long custom of old time used that hath caused me to be so blinded as I have been. In consideration whereof, I humbly beseech your grace of mercy and pity, seeing I have opened to you the secret part of my conscience, which was the ground of all my misdemeanours to you and in all your affairs since the beginning of the Parliament. And to confess the truth, my lord privy seal gave me oft and divers times warning to beware of their counsels, but I had not so much grace as to follow it. So that when I do remember what he hath said unto me, and considering the books I have lately read, I do very well perceive mine own blindness, for the which I humbly beseech your highness of pardon. And if ever it can be proved in this matter or in any other that ever in thought, word or deed I meant untruth to your grace or had any cankered heart, I utterly refuse your pardon, and to have the shamefullest death that ever had man. And since that I have read the New Testament and a book called *The Institution of a Christian Man*, I do well perceive the great blindness that I have been in. And seeing that I did at that time according to my conscience and not of untruth, I most humbly beseech your highness of pardon. And this I beseech our Lord send your highness and your little son Prince Edward long life and prosperous estate long to endure to the pleasure of God. For surely he [Prince Edward] is the greatest treasure that ever came to this realm.

> By me your most humble subject and servant
> George Throckmorton

Endorsed: Interrogatories to be ministered to Sir George Throckmorton. His letter under his hand, etc.

INDEX

Abel, Thomas, 180
Abingdon (Berks), 15
Admiralty, High Court of, 51, 137
Agostini, Agostino (Wolsey's
    physician), 126
All Souls College, Oxford, 189
Allesley (Warw), 52
Ammonio, Andrea, 7
Ampthill (Beds), 19
Answer of the Ordinaries, 190–2,
    194–5, 197, 200
Antwerp, 75, 166, 209
Ardern, Anne, 71–2, 77
Ardeson, George, 24
Ardleigh (Essex), 55
Arthur, king of Britain, 148
Arthur, prince (son of Henry VII),
    100–1, 129, 157–8, 182, 210
Assistance, writ of, 91
Assizes, 54, 62
Audley, Sir Thomas, 45, 55, 63, 74, 92,
    114, 118, 143, 149–50, 177, 181–4,
    186–9, 192, 194, 196–7, 202
Austin Friars, 211
Avignon, 179
Aylesford (Kent), 60

Bailey, John, 72
Bainham, James, 164, 166
Baker, John, 142, 176
Baldwyn, John, 41
Bangor, bishop of see Skeffington,
    Thomas
Barantyne, Sir William, 142, 208
Barnborough (Yorks), 25
Barnes, Robert, 104
Bath, bishop of see Clerk, John
Bayfield, Richard, 164, 166
Beene, William (abbot of Burton), 196
Benet, Thomas, 164
Benet, William (ambassador at Rome),
    111, 128, 147
Berners, lord see Bourchier, Sir John
Berthelet, Thomas (king's printer),
    156, 180
Beverley (Yorks), 26

Bilney, Thomas, 164, 167–71
Bishop's Burton (Yorks), 26
Blachus, Richard, 69–70
Blackfriars, 31, 106, 109, 113
Blackwell Hall (London), 13
Blake, Thomas, 56
Blount, William (lord Mountjoy), 9
Blyth, Geoffrey (bishop of Coventry
    and Lichfield), 137
Bocking, William, 56
Boleyn, Anne, 30, 97–8, 108, 110, 116,
    126, 134, 136, 140, 143, 145–7,
    159–61, 179, 185, 192, 202, 207,
    210
Boleyn, Sir George (viscount
    Rochford), 143, 146, 200
Boleyn, Sir Thomas (viscount
    Rochford to Dec. 1529, then earl
    of Wiltshire and Ormond), 77,
    97, 103, 108, 110, 114, 124–5,
    127–8, 131, 134, 140, 144, 146–7,
    179–80, 185, 200
Booth, Charles (bishop of Hereford),
    12
Bourchier, Sir John (lord Berners), 9
Boys, Richard, 72, 77
Brandon, Charles (duke of Suffolk), 15,
    29–33, 97–8, 106–10, 112,
    114–18, 124–6, 131, 140, 144,
    146–7, 159, 179, 193
Bridewell, 19
Brighouse (Yorks), 58
Bristol, 78, 107
Broke, Richard (chief baron of
    Exchequer), 40
Broke, Thomas (lord Cobham), 60–1
Brown, Humphrey, 40
Brudenell, Robert (C.J.C.P. from
    1520), 40
Bruges, 16
Brundley, William, 52–3
Brussels, 159
Bryan, Sir Francis, 17
Buckingham, duke of see Stafford,
    Henry
Budd, Alice, 62–3